SAS Publishing

D0598505

SAS® System for Elementary Statistical Analysis

SECOND EDITION

Sandra D. Schlotzhauer

Ramon C. Littell, Ph.D.

55172

Comments or Questions?

The authors assume complete responsibility for the technical accuracy of the content of this book. If you have any questions about the material in this book, please write to the authors at this address:

> SAS Institute Inc.
> Books by Users
> Attn: Sandra Schlotzhauer and Ramon C. Littell
> SAS Campus Drive
> Cary, NC 27513

If you prefer, you can send e-mail to sasbbu@sas.com with "comments for Sandra Schlotzhauer and Ramon C. Littell" as the subject line, or you can fax the Books by Users program at (919) 677-8166.

The correct bibliographic citation for this manual is as follows: Schlotzhauer, Sandra, and Ramon C. Littell. 1997. *SAS® System for Elementary Statistical Analysis, Second Edition.* Cary, NC: SAS Institute Inc.

SAS® System for Elementary Statistical Analysis, Second Edition

Copyright © 1997 by SAS Institute Inc., Cary, NC, USA.

ISBN 1-58025-018-1

All rights reserved. Printed in the United States of America. No part of this publication may be reproduced, stored in a retrieval system, or transmitted, in any form or by any means, electronic, mechanical, photocopying, or otherwise, without the prior written permission of the publisher, SAS Institute Inc.

U.S. Government Restricted Rights Notice: Use, duplication, or disclosure of this software and related documentation by the U.S. government is subject to the Agreement with SAS Institute and the restrictions set forth in FAR 52.227-19, Commercial Computer Software-Restricted Rights (June 1987).

SAS Institute Inc., SAS Campus Drive, Cary, North Carolina 27513.

1st printing, May 1999
2nd printing, December 2001

Note that text corrections may have been made at each printing.

SAS Publishing provides a complete selection of books and electronic products to help customers use SAS software to its fullest potential. For more information about our e-books, e-learning products, CDs, and hard-copy books, visit the SAS Publishing Web site at www.sas.com/pubs or call 1-800-727-3228.

SAS® and all other SAS Institute Inc. product or service names are registered trademarks or trademarks of SAS Institute Inc. in the USA and other countries. ® indicates USA registration.

IBM® and all other International Business Machines Corporation product or service names are registered trademarks or trademarks of International Business Machines Corporation in the USA and other countries.

Oracle® and all other Oracle Corporation product service names are registered trademarks of Oracle Corporation in the USA and other countries.

OS/2® and OS/390® are registered trademarks or trademarks of International Business Machines Corporation.

Other brand and product names are registered trademarks or trademarks of their respective companies.

Contents

viii

Acknowledgments

For the second edition, we would like to thank the many people who have given us feedback on the first edition over the years. The results of your comments at conferences and business meetings have found their way into this edition. We are grateful to the reviewers in industry and academia whose thoughtful suggestions improved the book: Dennis Fisher, Edith Flaster, Jay Harrison, Jenny Kendall, and Larry Winner. We are also thankful for the many SAS Institute reviewers, especially Annette Sanders and Jack Berry, who were an excellent source of the "latest and greatest" features in SAS.

The work of several people has influenced our writing. In particular, we would like to thank Ann Lehman, Victor Lowe, Phil Spector, and Dennis Wackerly.

We appreciate the staff at SAS Institute who worked on our book. We would especially like to thank David Baggett for encouraging us to write a second edition; Judy Whatley for handling all the editing issues; our copy-editor, Josephine Pope; production specialist, Nancy Mitchell; and designer, Ellen Hood. And, of course, the fact that SAS Institute continues to enhance the statistical features of the software made our work easier in that we could add new topics and harder because we wanted to keep the book to a reasonable size.

Also, we would like to thank the individuals and publishing companies who gave us permission to use their data in examples in the book.

Finally, we would like to thank our families, especially Galen and Sue, for their support and understanding.

Part 1 # The Basics

Chapter 1 **Introduction**

The *SAS System for Elementary Statistical Analysis* is designed to help you analyze your data using SAS software. This chapter covers

- the purpose of this book
- the audience for this book
- what this book is and isn't
- how this book is organized
- how to use this book
- what parts of SAS software you need.

Contents

Purpose

This book shows how to use SAS software to perform basic statistical analysis and explains the statistical methods used—when to use them, what the assumptions are, and how to interpret the results.

Audience

This book is for people who have minimal knowledge of SAS software or statistics or both. You may have extensive knowledge in your field as a manager, researcher, or analyst in industry. Or, you may be a student or professor in academia. The key is that you intend to use SAS software to analyze your data.

What This Book Is and Isn't

This book is a task-oriented tool that covers several basic types of data analysis. It integrates analysis methods with the SAS statements needed to perform the analysis and then explains the output in detail. Through the use of examples, it describes how the analysis leads to decisions about the data.

For those of you who know some statistical terms, the book covers descriptive summaries and graphs, two-way t-tests, analysis of variance, basic regression, and basic contingency table analyses. Examples of data analyses not discussed in this book are analysis of variance for designs other than a completely randomized design, multivariate analyses, time series methods, quality control, and operations research analyses.

This book shows how to use SAS software to perform the data analysis methods discussed. Because SAS software is a versatile and powerful language, often, an analysis can be performed another way with the software. This book does not cover all the ways SAS software can do a particular analysis.

This book concentrates on data analysis. However, some statistical background is needed in order for the discussions on analysis to make sense. Although you can perform analyses using only the information in this book, you may also want to refer to statistical texts for more background theory or detailed information about the methods. In addition, the book includes very few formulas. Formulas for the statistical methods that are included in this book are available in many texts, as well as in other documentation for SAS software.

This book does not include methods for designing a study. Several references for the practical aspects of study design are given in the "Further Reading" sections at the end of Chapters 3-11. Designing your study is as important as choosing the correct analysis. No amount of high-powered statistical analysis will "fix" a study by answering questions that the study wasn't designed to answer. If you are uncertain about how to design your study, you should consult a statistician or one of the references given in "Further Reading" before you begin. You should also think ahead about how you record your data. You can save yourself a lot of time by planning to record the data in a way that can be easily read into SAS.

This book is designed to:

- be task-oriented

- explain basic steps to create a SAS data set

- discuss several SAS tools for statistical analyses

- discuss SAS plots and graphs as appropriate.

This book is not designed to:

- replace SAS manuals or statistics texts

- explain all the ways to do a task in SAS

- discuss experimental design

- discuss advanced statistical analyses.

How This Book Is Organized

This book is divided into five parts.

Part 1: The Basics

The first part of the book shows you how to get your data into the computer. The second part of the book gives you a statistical foundation for the analyses discussed in Parts 3, 4, and 5. These other parts of the book show you how to perform various analyses. Chapters are as independent as possible—you don't need to absorb the contents of several chapters to perform only one type of analysis.

Using Part 1

Part 1 is essential for all readers who don't have experience with SAS software. Chapter 1 contains a brief introduction. Chapter 2 tells you what you need to know before you can use SAS software and gives an introduction to the SAS System. Chapter 3 describes how to create a SAS data set. Chapter 4 shows how to use SAS software to get descriptive statistics, frequency tables, bar charts, and some simple plots of the data. The output is explained in detail.

Starting with Chapter 2, there are three summaries and a reading list at the end of each chapter. The "Key Ideas" summary contains the main ideas of the chapter. The "Syntax" summary gives the general form for all SAS statements discussed in the chapter. (There is one exception: the SAS statements to create a SAS data set are summarized in Chapter 3 only.) The "Example" summary lists the SAS statements used to produce all the output that is shown in the chapter. The reading list contains a list of books that give more information about the topics discussed in the chapter.

Starting with Chapter 4, this second edition of the book shows how to summarize or analyze the data with SAS/INSIGHT, as appropriate. This interactive graphical tool is used more and more for data investigation. However, since it requires more than just the basic SAS package, we show the SAS/INSIGHT methods as an addition to other methods.

Using Part 2

Part 2 focuses on statistical concepts and provides a foundation for analyses presented in Parts 3, 4, and 5. Some of the ideas discussed include populations and samples, the normal distribution, the Empirical Rule, hypothesis testing, the effect of sample size and population variance on estimates of the mean, the Central Limit theorem, and confidence intervals for the mean. For learning SAS to perform statistical tasks, the chapters discuss the following:

Chapter	Statistical Tasks in SAS
5	Testing for normality
6	Calculating confidence intervals

Using Part 3

Part 3 shows how to compare groups of data. The list below gives examples of the types of problems you can analyze by using the methods presented in Part 3.

• Your new employees must take a proficiency test before they may operate a dangerous and expensive piece of equipment. Some of your new employees are experienced with this equipment and some are not. You want to find out if the average test scores for the two groups (experienced and inexperienced) are different.

• You measured the heart rate of students before and after mild exercise on a treadmill. You think the "before" heart rates are likely to be lower than the "after" heart rates. You want to know if the changes in heart rates are greater than could happen by chance.

• You conducted a study to compare the effects of five fertilizers on potted geraniums. At the end of six weeks, you measured the height of the geranium plants. Now, you want to compare the average heights for the plants that received the five different fertilizers.

• You recorded the number of defective items from an assembly line on the workdays Monday through Friday. You want to determine if there are differences in the number of defective items made on different days of the week.

For learning SAS to perform statistical tasks, the chapters discuss the following:

Chapter	Statistical Tasks in SAS
7	two-sample *t*-test
	paired difference *t*-test
	Wilcoxon Signed-rank test
	Wilcoxon Rank-sum test
8	Analysis of variance (*ANOVA*)
	Kruskal-Wallis test
	Multiple comparison procedures

In addition, both chapters discuss methods for summarizing and graphing data from two or more groups.

Using Part 4

Part 4 shows how to fit a line or curve to a set of data. Here are examples of problems you can analyze when using methods from Part 4.

• You want to determine the relationship between weight and age in children. You want to fit a line or curve to define the relationship. You also want to produce a plot showing the data and the fitted line or curve. Finally, you want to examine the data to find atypical points that are quite far from the fitted line.

• You have varied the temperature of an oven in a manufacturing process. You want to determine the amount of change in hardness of the product that is caused by a given amount of change in temperature. You also want to be able to predict hardness of future products made using a given temperature.

For learning SAS to perform statistical tasks, the chapters discuss the following:

Chapter	Statistical Tasks in SAS
9	Correlations
	Straight-line regression
	Multiple regression
	Prediction and confidence limits
10	Plotting residuals and predicted values
	Plotting residuals and independent variables
	Plotting residuals in time sequence

In addition, the chapters discuss investigation of outliers in a regression analysis.

Using Part 5

Part 5 consists of Chapter 11, which shows some basic methods for analyzing data in tables. The list below gives examples of problems you can solve using methods from this chapter.

- You have collected data on the colors of shampoo preferred by men and women. You want to know if the way color preferences are distributed is the same for men and women.

- You have conducted an opinion poll to evaluate how people in your town feel about the proposal for a new tax to build a sports arena. You want to find out if the people who live close to the site for the proposed arena feel differently about the arena than do the people who live farther away.

- Your company is conducting a test-market for a new product. You have conducted a survey in which you asked shoppers if they had bought the product. You also asked a series of questions designed to get opinions about the packaging of the product. You want to find out if these opinions are different between people who bought the new product and people who have not.

For learning SAS to perform statistical tasks, the chapter discusses the following:

Chapter	Statistical Tasks in SAS
11	Chi-square test for independence
	Measuring correlation

In addition, the chapter explains how to summarize data in tables.

Appendices, Summaries, and Other Helpful Information

Other helpful features are the appendices and the summaries. Appendix 1, "Display Manager Basics," gives a brief introduction to the SAS Display Manager. Appendix 2, "Troubleshooting," provides solutions to common problems in SAS programs. Appendix 3, "Additional Information," tells how to get publications and training catalogs from SAS Institute and describes some of the additional information and services available. Appendix 4, "Syntax Summary," contains the syntax summaries from the ends of Chapters 2-11. The "Quick Reference Table" on the inside front cover provides a place for you to write down some specifics about the computer system you use. A glossary and an index are at the end of the book.

Typographical Conventions

The typographic conventions that are used in this book are

roman   used for most text.

italics   used to define new terms, indicate items in SAS statements that you need to supply, and point to items in the output.

bold   used in the general form of SAS statements, bold type indicates that you **must use the exact spelling and punctuation shown.** In addition, headings and phrases and sentences of extreme importance are in bold type.

code   used to show examples of SAS statements.

How to Use This Book

If you have never used SAS software before, first read all of Part 1. These chapters present the basics of using the software to create and summarize a SAS data set. Then, if you aren't familiar with statistics, read Part 2. Otherwise, you can skip to other parts of the book. The descriptions in "How This Book Is Organized" should give you a good idea of the chapters that best fit your problem.

If you have used SAS software before but are not familiar with statistics, skim Part 1. Then read Part 2, which gives an explanation of several statistical concepts. Then skip to other parts of the book that best meet your needs.

If you have used SAS software before and are familiar with statistics but don't know how to handle your particular problem, first skim Part 1. Then go to the chapter that best meets your needs to learn how to use the software for your problem.

Do not use this book as a substitute for a statistical text. While the book shows how to use SAS software to perform certain analyses and describes the statistical methods, the SAS statements, and the SAS output, it does not attempt to replace statistical texts.

What SAS Software Do You Need?

To do most of the summaries and analyses in the book, you need base SAS software and SAS/STAT software. To do the graphs shown in the book, you need SAS/GRAPH software. If you don't have SAS/GRAPH, you can get low-resolution graphs using base SAS software.

Several chapters show how to perform tasks using base SAS and SAS/STAT and then include an optional PROC INSIGHT section. For these summaries and analyses, you need SAS/INSIGHT software.

Chapter 2 # Getting Started

This chapter tells you what you need to know before you start to use SAS software. The questions that you need to answer are summarized in the table on the inside front cover of the book. As you answer these questions, you may want to complete the table. This chapter also introduces you to SAS software and

- explains the different ways you can use SAS

- summarizes the structure of the SAS language

- explains spacing and syntax conventions

- explains the two types of output produced by SAS software

- discusses the different releases of the software

- shows how to find out what release you are using

- gives a simple example of a SAS program and output

- introduces a few SAS statements that you can use anywhere in a program.

The SAS statements introduced in this chapter are the

- TITLE statement, for adding titles to output

- FOOTNOTE statement, for adding footnotes to output

- RUN statement, for executing a group of SAS statements

- OPTIONS statement, for controlling line length, page length, and whether the date appears in the output

- ENDSAS statement, for ending your SAS session.

Contents

Knowing about Your Computer

To use this book, you need to know some basic information about your computer system. The first part of this chapter gives the information you need to know before you start to use SAS software. Each of the following sections presents a question that you need to answer. For your future reference, write down your answers to these questions on the inside front cover.

Most computer centers have a Help Desk that can provide you with answers to your questions. Also, at each site where SAS software is licensed, there is a SAS Software Consultant who should be able to help you. Finally, if you have never used a computer before, find out if your organization has a special course for new computer users.

What Type of Computer Are You Using?

SAS software is available for mainframes, minicomputers, and the desktop environment (PCs and UNIX workstations), but different releases of the software may be available for different types of computers.

If you use a mainframe or minicomputer, you access the computer with a terminal. You may be using a PC as a terminal for another computer, on a PC network, or as a stand-alone system. You need to know the basics of using your terminal or PC. The manuals for the terminal or PC are the best source of this information.

You also need to know a few things about how to use your computer's operating system to access SAS software. For example, if you plan to run a batch job on OS/390 (formerly known as MVS), you need to know the JCL to execute a SAS program. For more advanced uses, such as permanently saving a data set or a program, you need to know some file management techniques such as how to create files, list a directory of files, or delete files.

How Do You Communicate with the Computer?

If you use a terminal, you need to know how to communicate with the mainframe or minicomputer. Do you have full-screen capabilities, or not?

When used as terminals, most PCs use emulators, that is, software that enables the PC to act as if it is a terminal. Which terminal are you emulating? Does it have the ability to display graphs? Can it be used in full-screen mode? Can it display multiple colors? Are you using an X-server? If yes, are the settings appropriate for using SAS?

Each computer center has its own method for connecting to (or *logging on* to) the computer. Typically, you need to specify a user id (also called an *id*), a password, and an account number. You need to know how to log on at your site. Equally important to knowing how to get on the system is knowing how to get off or *log off* the system. While many systems use "logoff" as the command to log off, you need to find out what your system uses.

If you use a stand-alone PC, "communication" with the computer consists of knowing the basics of using your PC. This book assumes SAS software is already installed on a PC; if it is not, you'll need to install it by using the instructions that came with the SAS CD-ROM.

Do You Need to Know How to Use a Text Editor?

Text editors allow you to prepare a program and correct typing errors before you submit the program to the computer. Examples are EDIT under OS and EDT under VMS from the Digital Equipment Corporation. Examples of text editors on UNIX include EMACS and TeX. On a PC, you can use a word-processor, save the text as ASCII files, and then submit the program. Or, you can use the basic text editor available with the DOS EDIT command. You can also use WordPad under Windows 95.

Whatever system you are using, you can use SAS software without knowing how to use a text editor, but knowing how to use one can save time and effort. Deciding whether you need to know how to use a text editor depends somewhat on how you will use SAS software. As discussed later in this chapter, if you use the SAS Display Manager System, you probably don't need to know how to use a text editor.

How Do You Get Output, and Where Is It Printed?

If you use a PC, you may have a printer attached directly to your PC. If you use a terminal or a networked PC, you need to find out how to get a printed copy of your output. Many computer centers have several printers, and you need to learn which one to choose.

Knowing about SAS Software and Your Computer

The three questions in this section relate both to SAS software and to your computing environment. Again, you may want to write your answers to these questions on the inside front cover of this book.

Who Is Your SAS Software Consultant?

At every site where SAS software is licensed, someone is designated to be the SAS Software Consultant. This person is usually available to answer questions from other users. Find out who your SAS Software Consultant is before you begin using the software.

In addition, some locations have a Help Desk that answers questions about SAS software. You may know other people who are experienced SAS users and can answer questions if you run into problems. It's always handy to know who to call if you encounter some unexpected situation.

How Do You Start SAS Software?

For most mainframe, minicomputer, and UNIX sites, you just type the word "sas" to start SAS. For most PCs running Windows, Windows NT, or OS/2, you double-click on the SAS icon in your desktop. For most PCs running Windows 95, you select Programs and then "The SAS System" from the task bar; or use a previously-defined shortcut. You need to find out what convention your site uses for starting SAS. (Exiting from SAS is discussed later in this chapter.)

How Will You Use SAS Software?

You can use SAS software in four ways: batch mode, noninteractive mode, interactive line mode, or Display Manager mode. In each of these modes, you prepare a SAS program that creates a data set and performs analyses.

In *batch mode*, you submit a batch program by submitting a file that contains the batch program. To submit a file, you need to be familiar with your operating system, because this file contains the necessary statements to start SAS software, run the program, and route the output. As an example, on the OS/390 operating system, the file must contain the appropriate JCL statements to perform these tasks. The output prints at either a remote printer or on your terminal, depending on what you specify in the file submitted. Some systems, such as UNIX, refer to batch mode as *background processing*.

In *noninteractive mode*, you prepare a file that contains a SAS program but no operating-system specific statements (such as JCL statements). Then you run SAS software using the SYSIN option, which reads the SAS program in your file. Your SAS program runs and the operating system creates a file that contains the output. The examples below show how to use noninteractive mode for an OS/390 mainframe and a PC.

OS/390: `sas -sysin lowe.genprogs.text(anova)`

`PC: sas -sysin c:\programs\anova.sas`

Both examples use "sas" as the command to start SAS software. If this command differs at your site, simply substitute the appropriate command.

In *interactive line mode*, SAS software responds to statements as you enter them. You can enter your data, perform an analysis, look at the results, and perform another analysis without exiting from SAS. In this mode, you get a question mark (?) as a prompt to enter the next statement.

In *SAS Display Manager* mode, the software responds to statements as you enter them, but this requires a full-screen terminal or a PC. In display manager mode, a set of windows appears on your terminal or PC screen. This mode provides you with all the capabilities of interactive line mode as well as a built-in text editor. In this mode, you can select choices from the menu bar, or *pmenus*. Or, you can switch to using a command line and enter SAS commands directly. As you learn SAS, we recommend that you use the menu choices. On PCs, SAS software automatically starts in display manager mode.

If your site doesn't have interactive capabilities, you need to use batch or noninteractive mode. You will find a SAS program in the "Example" summary at the end of each chapter. This program produces all the output shown in the chapter. For batch mode, you need to add any necessary operating-system specific information to the program.

If your site has interactive capabilities, you can use either interactive line mode or display manager mode. If you are learning to use SAS software for the first time, we recommend display manager mode. Most people prefer this mode once they are familiar with SAS software. Display Manager is the default mode on PCs. Appendix 1 gives an introduction to the SAS Display Manager System.

Getting Started with SAS Software

This section assumes you know the basics about your computing environment. Specifically, you need to know the answers to the questions in the last two sections.

Summarizing the Structure of SAS Software

In analyzing data, there are two basic steps you perform. First, you organize your data. This allows you to find missing information and to summarize the information that you have. Second, you perform some analysis on the organized data. For example, you might collect all your paycheck stubs for the year (organizing) and then add the net salary from each to find your total spendable income for the year (analyzing).

SAS software is designed along the lines of these two basic steps. First, there is a *DATA step* where you organize your data by creating a SAS data set. Second, there are *PROC steps*, which use SAS procedures to analyze your data. Once you create a SAS data set, you can use any SAS procedure without re-creating the data set.

Chapter 3 discusses the DATA step. The rest of the book discusses a series of PROC steps that correspond to the different procedures that you use for different methods of analysis.

The DATA and PROC steps consist of *SAS statements*. Most statements have one or more keywords that must be spelled exactly as shown. Depending on the statement, keywords may be followed by additional information that you supply. When we give the general form of SAS statements, keywords and required punctuation appear in bold type and the information that you need to supply appears in italic type.

Syntax and Spacing Conventions

The DATA and PROC steps are part of the SAS language. Like any language, it has its own vocabulary and syntax. Some words have special meaning, and there are rules about how words are put together. Fortunately, there are very few restrictions.

Syntax

There is just one basic syntax rule you must always follow: **SAS statements must end with a semicolon.** The semicolon tells the software that you have completed one statement and that the next word starts a new statement. If you complete a statement and forget the semicolon,

SAS software continues to read your program as one statement. When the software finds something it doesn't understand, you receive an error message. However, in most cases, the error message won't tell you that you have forgotten a semicolon. Anytime you get an error message, you should first look to see that all statements end with a semicolon.

Spacing

With some computer languages, the spacing of your statements and of parts of statements is important. This isn't true with SAS software. You can put several statements on one line. You can spread one statement out over several lines. You can put spaces between statements or not. You can indent statements or not. The key point is that semicolons, not spacing, determine where SAS statements start and end. As an example, three SAS statements are shown below. Each of the several methods of spacing the statements has the same result. You can choose whatever spacing works best for you.

```
data new; input x; datalines;


data new;input
x;
datalines;


data      new;
    input    x;
datalines;


data new;input x;datalines;


data new;
input x;
datalines;


data new;
    input x;
    datalines;
```

The final example shows the form used in this book. This form is used simply for convenience and readability. You may choose whatever spacing works best for you in your situation.

Notice that the sample SAS statements are in lowercase type. You can use either lowercase or uppercase in SAS statements. This book uses lowercase in sample programs, and uppercase to show you the general form of SAS statements.

Output Produced by SAS Software

After you run a SAS program, you receive output. The output is in two parts: the *log* and the *procedure output*. The log

- shows the program you submitted
- tells you what the software did with the program
- prints any error or warning messages.

For example, if your program creates a data set, the log tells you that the data set is created and gives you some information about the data set. The procedure output gives the results of your program. For example, if your program calculates and prints the average of a group of numbers in your data set, the procedure output contains the printed averages.

In this book, the log is shown only for the sample program later in this chapter. However, you need to remember that the log exists. If you run into problems, the first step you should take is to look at the log to find error messages and figure out where the mistakes are. Also, as a general strategy, it's a good idea to look at the log to verify that the program ran as expected. For all examples in this book, the procedure output appears in a labeled box.

Whether output from your programs is printed or simply sent to your terminal depends on your computer and the way you use SAS software. See Table 2.1.

Table 2.1 **Where SAS Output Appears**

Mode	Where Output Appears
Batch	Printed or sent to file, depending on system statements (for example, JCL)
Noninteractive	Printed, sent to your terminal, or sent to files on the system as you request
Interactive line	Sent to your terminal
Display manager	Displays in LOG and OUTPUT windows

Releases of SAS Software

SAS software is available in several different releases, which give the same results but may differ slightly in appearance. All the output shown in this book is from Release 6.12 of SAS software.

In most cases, the differences between Release 6.12 output and output from other releases are cosmetic (such as different spacing between columns of information in the output). In cases where there are important differences between releases, the differences are discussed. For example, if Release 6.12 output is substantially different from output for earlier releases, a box with the heading "Releases Before 6.12" explains the differences. Table 2.2 tells you how to find out which release of SAS software you are using.

Table 2.2   **Figuring Out the SAS Software Release You Have**

If you are using...	then look at...
Batch mode	the message on the first line of the log
Noninteractive mode	the message on the first line of the log
Interactive line mode	the message that appears before the first prompt (1?)
Display manager mode	the message at the top of the LOG window

Example of a Simple SAS Program

This section summarizes the information from previous sections and shows you an example of a SAS program. The program, log, and procedure output are all shown. For now, don't be concerned about the individual statements in the program or look for a detailed explanation of the output. These are all presented in later chapters.

One indicator of an individual's fitness is the percent of body fat, which is measured with a special set of calipers. (Calipers look something like pliers that have a dial on them.) The calipers are placed at three or four different places on the body to measure the amount of skin that can easily be pinched off. Women are measured on the triceps, the abdomen, and near the hips. Men are measured on the chest, the abdomen, near the hips, and at the mid-axillary line. This skin-fold measure is then averaged across the different places to provide a measure of the percent of body fat. Depending on whose guidelines you look at, the normal range for men is 15-20% body fat, and the normal range for women is 20-25% body fat. Table 2.3 shows percent body fat for several men and women. These people participated in unsupervised aerobic exercise or weight training (or both) about three times per week for a year. Then they were measured for the percent of body fat.

Table 2.3 **Body Fat Data**

Gender	Body Fat (%)	Gender	Body Fat (%)
Male	13.3	Female	22
Male	19	Female	26
Male	20	Female	16
Male	8	Female	12
Male	18	Female	21.7
Male	22	Female	23.2
Male	20	Female	21
Male	31	Female	28
Male	21	Female	30
Male	12	Female	23
Male	16		
Male	12		
Male	24		

* Data is from the Recreation and Fitness Center at SAS Institute Inc.

The SAS statements below create a data set that contains the body fat data, print the data set, and calculate average body fat for men and women. The large braces are not part of the program but are an aid to show you the DATA and PROC steps in the program.

```
options pagesize=60 linesize=80 nodate;
data bodyfat;
   input gender $ fatpct @@;
   datalines;
m 13.3 f 22 m 19 f 26 m 20 f 16 m 8 f 12 m 18 f 21.7
m 22 f 23.2 m 20 f 21 m 31 f 28 m 21 f 30 m 12 f 23
m 16 m 12 m 24
;

proc print data=bodyfat;
   title 'Body Fat Data for Fitness Program';
   footnote '1986 Measurements';
run;

proc means data=bodyfat;
   class gender;
   var fatpct;
   title 'Body Fat Averages in Fitness Program';
   run;
```

The statements above produce the log shown in Output 2.1 and the procedure output shown in Output 2.2 and Output 2.3.

Note that the second line of the log shows you the release of SAS software used. From the output, the average body fat for women in the fitness program is 22.29%, and the average body fat for men in the fitness program is 18.18%.

Output 2.1   Log for Body Fat Data

```
LOG - [Untitled]                                                          _ □ ×
NOTE: Copyright (c) 1989-1996 by SAS Institute Inc., Cary, NC, USA.
NOTE: SAS (r) Proprietary Software Release 6.12  TS020
      Licensed to SANDRA D. SCHLOTZHAUER, Site 0032899001.


1     options pagesize=60 linesize=80 nodate;
2     data bodyfat;
3       input gender $ fatpct @@;
4       datalines;
NOTE: SAS went to a new line when INPUT statement reached past the end of a
      line.
NOTE: The data set WORK.BODYFAT has 23 observations and 2 variables.
NOTE: The DATA statement used 2.02 seconds.

8     ;
9
10    proc print data=bodyfat;
11    title 'Body Fat Data for Fitness Program';
12    footnote '1986 Measurements';
13    run;

NOTE: The PROCEDURE PRINT used 0.6 seconds.


14
15    proc means data=bodyfat;
16      class gender;
17      var fatpct;
18      title 'Body Fat Averages in Fitness Program';
19    run;

NOTE: The PROCEDURE MEANS used 0.33 seconds.
```

Output 2.2   Procedure Output for Body Fat Data

```
            Body Fat Data for Fitness Program              1

              OBS    GENDER    FATPCT

               1       m       13.3
               2       f       22.0
               3       m       19.0
               4       f       26.0
               5       m       20.0
               6       f       16.0
               7       m        8.0
               8       f       12.0
               9       m       18.0
              10       f       21.7
              11       m       22.0
              12       f       23.2
              13       m       20.0
              14       f       21.0
              15       m       31.0
              16       f       28.0
              17       m       21.0
              18       f       30.0
              19       m       12.0
              20       f       23.0
              21       m       16.0
              22       m       12.0
              23       m       24.0


                  1986 Measurements
```

Output 2.3   **Procedure Output for Body Fat Data** (Continued)

```
                    Body Fat Averages in Fitness Program                    2

    Analysis Variable : FATPCT

    GENDER   N Obs   N        Mean       Std Dev      Minimum       Maximum
    -----------------------------------------------------------------------
    f           10   10   22.2900000     5.3196596   12.0000000    30.0000000

    m           13   13   18.1769231     6.0324337    8.0000000    31.0000000
    -----------------------------------------------------------------------



                              1986 Measurements
```

Introducing Several SAS Statements

This section explains the OPTIONS, TITLE, FOOTNOTE, RUN, and END-SAS statements. These statements are not exclusively part of the DATA step or of a PROC step but can be used in either. Four of these statements are shown in the program in the previous section. One statement is used to exit from SAS. You may want to skip this section until you are ready to run your own SAS program.

The TITLE Statement

The TITLE statement provides a title on the top line of each page of output. The TITLE statement is not required. If you don't specify a title, each page of output has the following default title: The SAS System.

In the TITLE statement, enclose the text of the title in single quotes or double quotes. The text that is typed between the quotes appears as the title for the output. For example, if you use all uppercase, the output title will print in uppercase. If your title contains an apostrophe, enclose the title text in double quotes and use a single quote to get an apostrophe. Or, enclose the title text in single quotes and use two single quotes to get the apostrophe. Examples of valid TITLE statements are shown below:

```
title 'PRODUCTION SUMMARY FOR FY 1993';
title 'Experiment to Test Emotions under Hypnosis';
title 'Children''s Reading Scores';
title "Children's Reading Scores";
```

Each time you use a TITLE statement, the previous title is replaced with the new one. Look again at Output 2.2 and Output 2.3, and notice how the title for the second page is different from that for the first. This is a result of including the second TITLE statement in the program.

In addition, you can specify up to ten levels of titles. For a second title to appear on a line below the first, type TITLE2, followed by the title text enclosed in single quotes. For example,

```
title 'BODY FAT DATA';
title2 'Men and Women in Fitness Program';
title3 'Data Property of SAS Institute Inc.';
```

You may find that using two or three levels of titles is more informative than using just one long title.

Finally, you can suppress both the default title (The SAS System) and titles that are specified in previous TITLE statements. To do so, omit the quotes and the title text from the TITLE statement. For example, to suppress all three titles shown above, type

```
title;
```

To suppress the second and third titles, type

```
title2;
```

Similarly, you can suppress a title and all titles below it in the output by typing TITLE*x*, where *x* is the first title you want to suppress.

The general form of the TITLE statement is shown below:

> **TITLE**_n_ _'title text'_;
>
> where _n_ is a number between 1 and 10 for titles 1 through 10. For the first title, both TITLE1 and TITLE can be used. To suppress titles, omit both the quotes and the _title text_.

The FOOTNOTE Statement

Text shown in a FOOTNOTE statement appears at the bottom of the page of output. Unlike titles, there is no default footnote.

The syntax of the FOOTNOTE statement is very similar to that of the TITLE statement. The footnote text is enclosed in single quotes, and apostrophes are indicated by using two single quotes together. Or, enclose the footnote text in double quotes and use a single quote for apostrophes. You can specify up to ten levels of footnotes. A new FOOTNOTE statement replaces a previous one. You can suppress footnotes by simply omitting the quotes and footnote text from the FOOTNOTE statement.

Look again at Outputs 2.2 and 2.3. The footnote at the bottom of each page is produced by the FOOTNOTE statement in the program. (To save space, several of the blank lines between the output and the footnote have been omitted.)

The general form of the FOOTNOTE statement is shown below:

> **FOOTNOTE**_n_ _'footnote text'_;
>
> where _n_ is a number between 1 and 10 for footnotes 1 through 10. For the first footnote, both FOOTNOTE1 and FOOTNOTE can be used. To suppress footnotes, omit both the quotes and the _footnote text_.

The RUN Statement

The RUN statement executes the statement or group of statements immediately above it. If you use batch or noninteractive mode, you don't need to use this statement. However, if you use SAS software interactively, you need to use the RUN statement.

If you use interactive line mode, you should use a RUN statement at the end of each DATA or PROC step. If you use display manager mode, you only need a RUN statement at the end of each group of statements that you submit. However, using a RUN statement at the end of each DATA or PROC step helps to identify where one step ends and another step begins and to find errors in a program that doesn't run.

The general form of the RUN statement is shown below:

RUN;

The OPTIONS Statement

The OPTIONS statement allows you to set certain system options. Although there are many system options, this book uses only three. Your site may have set these three options already and may also have set some of the many other system options that are available. Although you can override the default settings with an OPTIONS statement, your site probably has these options set in the best way for your computer system. In the sample program in the previous section, the first SAS statement is

```
options pagesize=60 linesize=80 nodate;
```

This statement begins with the keyword OPTIONS. Then the PAGESIZE= keyword is followed by the number 60, which sets the page size to 60 lines. Next, the LINESIZE= keyword is followed by the number 80, which sets the line size to 80 spaces. You can think of the PAGESIZE= option as giving the number of lines of text on a page and the LINESIZE= option as giving the number of spaces in each line of text.

Next, the NODATE keyword suppresses the date that is normally printed on the same line as the page number. Finally, the statement ends with a semicolon.

The OPTIONS statement above was used to produce all output shown in this book. For your own programs, you want to be able to look at the output and see when you ran the program, so you probably don't want to use NODATE. The setting of 60 for PAGESIZE= works well for 11-inch-long paper printed with 6 lines per inch. If your site uses a different paper size or lines per inch, you will want to use another setting. Typical settings for LINESIZE= are 80 for terminal screens, 78 for 8.5-inch-wide paper, and 132 for output printed on 14-inch-wide paper.

Statements for Exiting from SAS Software

If you use batch or noninteractive mode, you don't need to read this section. After your system runs your SAS job, the system exits from SAS automatically.

If you use interactive line mode or display manager mode, you need to know how to exit from SAS and return to your computer's operating system. Submitting the ENDSAS statement accomplishes this task. The general form of the ENDSAS statement is shown below:

ENDSAS;

If you use the automatic menus in display manager mode, choosing File and then Exit ends the SAS session. You typically see a message window asking if you are sure you want to exit; just select Yes. If you have switched from the menus to a command line in display manager mode, you can simply type "bye" on any command line to exit SAS. Or, you can select Exit from the File menu bar.

Summary

Key Ideas

- The SAS language consists of DATA steps, which organize your data by creating a SAS data set, and PROC steps, which analyze your data. These steps consist of SAS statements, which contain keywords and additional information about your data.

- All SAS statements must end with a semicolon.

- SAS statements can start anywhere on a line and can continue for several lines. Several SAS statements can be put on one line. Either uppercase or lowercase text can be used.

- SAS output consists of the log and the list. The log displays the program and messages. The list contains the results of the program.

Syntax

- To produce a title for your output,

    TITLE*n* '*title text* ';

    where *n* is one of the numbers 1 through 10, and *title text* contains the title.

- To produce a footnote for your output,

    FOOTNOTE*n* '*footnote text* ';

    where *n* is one of the numbers 1 through 10, and *footnote text* contains the footnote.

- To execute one or more statements,

    RUN;

- To provide the options to reproduce the output shown in this book,

    OPTIONS PAGESIZE=60 LINESIZE=80 NODATE;

    However, you will probably want to use the default options at your site.

- To exit from SAS software and return to the operating system,

    ENDSAS;

    or in display manager mode, either type BYE on any command line or select Exit from the File menu bar.

Example

The program below produces all output shown in this chapter:

```
options pagesize=60 linesize=80 nodate;
data bodyfat;
   input gender $ fatpct @@;
   datalines;
m 13.3 f 22 m 19 f 26 m 20 f 16 m 8 f 12 m 18 f 21.7
m 22 f 23.2 m 20 f 21 m 31 f 28 m 21 f 30 m 12 f 23
m 16 m 12 m 24
;
```

```
proc print data=bodyfat;
title 'Body Fat Data for Men and Women in Fitness Program';
footnote '1986 Measurements';
run;

proc means data=bodyfat;
   class gender;
   var fatpct;
title 'Body Fat Averages for Men and Women in Fitness Program';
run;
```

Further Reading

You do not need to refer to the manuals below as you use this book. However, as you become an experienced user, you may find them helpful in showing you how to use SAS software with your operating system most efficiently. For information on how to order these manuals, turn to Appendix 3, "Additional Information."

For more information about your operating system, see one of these manuals:

- *SAS® Companion for the CMS Environment, Version 6, First Edition*
- *SAS® Companion for the Macintosh, Version 6, First Edition*
- *SAS® Companion for the Microsoft Windows Environment, Version 6, Second Edition*
- *SAS® Companion for the Microsoft Windows NT Environment Version 6, First Edition*
- *SAS® Companion for the MVS Environment, Version 6, First Edition*
- *SAS® Companion for the OpenVMS Environment, Version 6, Second Edition*
- *SAS® Companion for the OS/2 Environment, Version 6, Second Edition*
- *SAS® Companion for the UNIX Environment: Language, Version 6, First Edition*
- *SAS® Companion for the UNIX Environment: User Interfaces, Version 6, First Edition*
- *SAS® Companion for the VSE Environment, Version 6, First Edition*

In addition, there may be technical reports that contain updated information for a given release.

To learn more about the SAS Display Manager System or about available SAS options, see one of these books:

- *SAS® Language and Procedures: Introduction, Version 6, First Edition* gives an introduction to display manager in Appendix 1.

- *SAS® Language: Reference, Version 6, First Edition* gives details about display manager in Chapters 17 and 18, and details about options in Chapter 16.

- *SAS® Language and Procedures: Syntax, Version 6, First Edition* gives a syntax summary for display manager in Chapter 8, and summarizes options in Chapter 7.

- *The Little SAS® Book: A Primer* discusses several commonly used commands in display manager, and also discusses several commonly used options.

Chapter 3 **Creating SAS® Data Sets**

The first two chapters of this book have given you an introduction and a list of things you need to know about your computer system before you start to use SAS software. This chapter assumes you know the answers to all the questions in Chapter 2. Now you'll start to use SAS software to solve problems. In this chapter, you learn about

- creating a SAS data set
- printing a data set
- sorting a data set.

At the end of the chapter, "Advanced Topics" shows how to use labels to make your printed output more complete.

Contents

What Is a Data Set?

You see data sets every day when you read the stock market results in the newspaper or, if you're a student, when you look at the list of test grades and social security numbers posted by your professor. These lists or tables are collections of information that you can store in a computer. You may think of these as lists or tables instead of data sets.

An example of a data set is shown in Table 3.1. This data was originally printed in *Newsweek*. The table shows the speeding ticket fines for driving 65 miles per hour in each of the 50 states. The data was collected when the speed limit on state and interstate highways was 55 mph. The next section shows how to create a SAS data set and uses the speeding ticket data as an example.

Understanding the SAS DATA Step

A *SAS data set* has some specific characteristics and rules that must be followed so that the data can be analyzed using SAS software. Fortunately there are only a few simple rules to remember. Recall that the SAS language is divided into DATA and PROC steps. The process of creating a SAS data set is the DATA step. Once you create a SAS data set, it can be used with any SAS procedure.

The speeding ticket data, like most data, consists of pieces of information that are recorded for each of several units. In this case, the pieces of information include the name of the state and the amount of the speeding ticket fine. You could think of a spreadsheet with two columns for the names of the states and the speeding ticket amounts. Each row contains all the information for a state. When you use SAS software, the columns are called *variables* and the rows are called *observations*. In general, variables are the specific pieces of information you have, and observations are the units you have measured. In Table 3.1, there are fifty observations, one for each state, and two variables, the name of the state and the speeding ticket amount for the state. For example, the first observation has the value "Alabama" for the variable "state," and the value "60" for the variable "amount."

Table 3.1   Speeding Ticket Fines across the U.S.
(Amounts shown are for driving 65 mph* in a 55 mph zone.)

State	Fine	State	Fine
Alabama	$60	Hawaii	$35
Delaware	$31.50	Illinois	$20
Alaska	$20	Connecticut	$60
Arkansas	$47	Iowa	$33
Florida	$44	Kansas	$28
Arizona	$15	Indiana	$50
California	$50	Louisiana	$45
Georgia	$45	Montana	$5
Idaho	$12.50	Kentucky	$65
Colorado	$64	Maine	$40
Nebraska	$10	Massachusetts	$50
Maryland	$40	Nevada	$5
Missouri	$50	Michigan	$40
New Mexico	$20	New Jersey	$50
Minnesota	$44	New York	$28
North Carolina	$47.50	Mississippi	$39.50
North Dakota	$10	Ohio	$100
New Hampshire	$33	Oregon	$26
Oklahoma	$56	South Carolina	$45
Rhode Island	$30	Pennsylvania	$72.50
Tennessee	$40	South Dakota	$10
Texas	$48	Vermont	$35
Utah	$28	West Virginia	$60
Virginia	$40	Wyoming	$15
Washington	$38	Wisconsin	$44.50

* Data from *Newsweek*, July 21, 1986. Used with permission.

Summarizing the SAS DATA Step

Table 3.2 uses an example to summarize the parts of a SAS DATA step.

Table 3.2   **Summarizing Parts of a SAS DATA Step**

DATA Step	Summary
`data tickets;`	The DATA statement gives a name to the data set.
`input state $ 1-2` `    amount 4-8;`	The INPUT statement tells SAS software what the variable names are, whether the variables have numeric or character values, and where the variables are located.
`datalines;`	The DATALINES statement tells the software that the data lines follow. Do not put a blank line between the DATALINES statement and the start of the data.

`AL 60`
`HI 35`
`DE 31.50`
`AK 20`
	The data lines contain the data. Only four states are shown here, but all could be entered this way.

`;`	After the data lines, a null statement (semicolon alone) ends the data lines.
`run;`	The RUN statement executes the DATA step.

The only output produced by this DATA step is a note on the log. This note tells you that the data set has been created. It also gives the name of the data set, the number of variables, and the number of observations.

The next six sections give details on the parts of a DATA step. It is important to understand these statements now since they are used repeatedly in this book.

Assigning Names

Before you can name the data set or name variables, you need to choose names that are acceptable to SAS. These names must follow three simple rules as shown in Table 3.3.

Table 3.3

Rules for SAS Names

• SAS names must start with a letter or an underscore. The remaining characters in a SAS name can be letters, numbers, or underscores.

• The total length of a SAS name must be eight characters or less.

• SAS names must not contain any embedded blanks. For example, DOLAMT is a valid SAS name, but DOL AMT is not.

For the speeding ticket data, use the name TICKETS to identify the data set, the name STATE to identify the state, and the name AMOUNT to identify the dollar amount of the speeding ticket.

The DATA Statement

The first statement in a DATA step is the DATA statement. Its purpose is to start the DATA step and to assign a name to the data set. For the speeding ticket data, use

```
data tickets;
```

The general form for the DATA statement is shown below:

> **DATA** *data-set-name*;
> where *data-set-name* is the name of the data set.

If you need to create another data set with a different name, then substitute the name of your choice.

If you don't give a data set name, SAS chooses the name for you. The first data set is automatically named DATA1, the second DATA2, and so on. It's better to give the data set a meaningful name than to use the automatic names.

The INPUT Statement

The next statement in the DATA step is the INPUT statement. This statement tells SAS software

- what to use as variable names
- whether the variables contain numbers or letters
- where the variables are located.

The software can handle very complex data sets, and a complete description of all you can do with the INPUT statement would take many pages. However, this chapter covers only the situations needed for this book. Table 3.4 gives a step-by-step approach to writing an INPUT statement. It uses the speeding ticket data as an example. You'll use these steps throughout this book and in analyzing your own data.

Identifying Missing Data Values

If you don't have the value of a variable for a particular observation, you can leave the columns blank or you can enter a period in the columns for the variable. It's better to enter a period for missing numeric variables. For the speeding ticket data, you don't have the amount for Washington, DC. In your data, you have

```
DC  .
```

for Washington, DC.

Table 3.4   **How to Write an INPUT Statement**

Step	INPUT Statement
1	Begin with the word INPUT. `input`
2	Choose a name for the first variable. (Remember the rules for names as shown in Table 3.3.) `input state`
3	Look to see whether the values of the variable are character or numeric. If the values are all numbers, the variable is a *numeric variable*, and you can go on to the next step. Otherwise, the variable is a *character variable* and you need to put a dollar sign ($) after the variable name. `input state $`
4	Enter column numbers for the data values. Enter the beginning column, then a dash, and then the last column. If you have a variable that uses only one column, enter the number for that column. `input state $ 1-2`
5	Repeat steps 2 through 4 for each variable in your data set. The speeding ticket data has one more variable, AMOUNT, which is numeric since the values are all numbers. If the values are in columns 4 through 8 of the data, then the INPUT statement looks like this: `input state $ 1-2 amount 4-8`
6	End the INPUT statement with a semicolon. The final INPUT statement is `input state $ 1-2 amount 4-8;`

Omitting the Column Location for Variables

There is a simple form of the INPUT statement that doesn't require you to specify the columns for variables. This form is shown below:

```
input state $ amount;
```

To use this simple form, the data must satisfy the following conditions:

• Each value on the data line is separated from the next value by at least one blank.

• Any missing numeric values are represented by a period instead of blanks.

• Values for all character variables are eight characters or less and don't contain any embedded blanks.

When your data meets these conditions, you can write the INPUT statement as follows:

• list variable names in the INPUT statement in the order that they appear in the data lines

• follow character variable names with a dollar sign ($)

• end the INPUT statement with a semicolon (;).

Putting Several Short Observations on One Line

You may have data similar to the speeding ticket data, with only a few variables for each observation. It may seem like a waste of effort to enter only two variables on each line. If you omit column locations for variables, you can also put several observations on a line. To do this,

• your data must satisfy the three conditions for omitting column locations for variables.

• you may have several observations on a data line and differing numbers of observations on different data lines.

• use the INPUT statement without column locations and type two at (@@) signs just before the semicolon (;).

For the speeding ticket data, the form of the INPUT statement is

```
input state $ amount @@;
```

The @@ tells the software to continue reading data from the same line instead of moving to the next line. Without the @@, the software assumes one observation appears on each data line. With the @@, you tell the software to ignore the assumption and to look for multiple observations on each line. (See the example in "Creating the Speeding Ticket Data Set" later in this chapter.)

The DATALINES Statement

The DATALINES statement is placed immediately before the lines of data. The general form of the DATALINES statement is shown below:

DATALINES;

In some SAS programs, you may see a CARDS statement instead of the DATALINES statement. The two statements perform the same task.

The Data Lines

After the DATALINES statement, enter the data lines according to the INPUT statement. Do not insert a blank line between the DATALINES statement and the data. If you specify certain columns for variables, enter the values of those variables in the correct columns. If you don't specify columns in the INPUT statement, put a period in places where there are missing values.

Existing Data Lines: Using the INFILE Statement

Suppose your data already exists in an ASCII text file. You don't have to re-enter the data lines. Instead, you can access the data lines by using the INFILE statement instead of the DATALINES statement. The INFILE statement tells the software to use the file identified as the data lines. Place the INFILE statement between the DATA statement (which names the data set) and the INPUT statement (which tells how to read the information in the file). Suppose the speeding ticket data is stored in the ticket.dat file in the c:\example directory on your PC. Then, the DATA step looks like this:

```
data tickets;
    infile 'c:\example\ticket.dat';
    input state $ amount @@ ;
```

Note that you can use the various forms of the INPUT statement (discussed in earlier sections) with the INFILE statement. Of course, the INPUT statement must match the appearance of the data in the external file.

Here are sample INFILE statements for several operating systems:

PC   INFILE 'c:\example\ticket.dat';

UNIX   INFILE '/usr/yourid/example/ticket.dat';

VMS   INFILE '[yourid.data]ticket.dat';

OS/390   INFILE ' yourid.ticket.dat';

The general form of the INFILE statement is shown below.

> **INFILE** *file-name*;
> where *file-name* is the file that contains the data lines.

The Null Statement

After the last data line, enter a semicolon (;) alone, on a new line. This is called a *null statement*, and it ends the data lines. The null statement must be on a different line from the data. If you use the INFILE statement, described in the previous section, you don't need the null statement.

Creating the Speeding Ticket Data Set

This section uses the DATA, INPUT, and DATALINES statements to create a data set for the speeding ticket data. In the program that is shown, notice that the INPUT statement omits column locations, and it places several observations on each line. The values of STATE are the two-letter codes used by the U.S. Postal Service.

```
data tickets;
    input state $ amount @@;
    datalines;
AL 60 HI 35 DE 31.50 IL 20 AK 20 CT 60 AR 47
IA 33 FL 44 KS 28 AZ 15 IN 50 CA 50 LA 45 GA 45
MT 5 ID 12.50 KY 65 CO 64 ME 40 NE 10 MA 50
MD 40 NV 5 MO 50 MI 40 NM 20 NJ 50 MN 44 NY 28
NC 47.50 MS 39.50 ND 10 OH 100 NH 33 OR 26 OK 56
SC 45 RI 30 PA 72.50 TN 40 SD 10 TX 48 VT 35 UT 28
WV 60 VA 40 WY 15 WA 38 WI 44.5 DC .
;
```

Look at the next to last line of the program above. Notice that the missing value for Washington, DC, is created by putting a period where SAS software expects to find the value for the variable AMOUNT.

Before you run this program, read the next section.

Printing a Data Set

All the DATA step does in this example is create a SAS data set. To do anything else, you need to use a SAS procedure. This section shows you how to print your data set with the PRINT procedure (PROC PRINT). To print the speeding ticket data, add the following statements to the end of the program that creates the data set:

```
proc print data=tickets;
    title 'Speeding Ticket Data';
run;
```

Now if you run the program, the TICKETS data set is created and printed.

Your output should look like Output 3.1. The output is in three columns. The first column is labeled *OBS* and represents the *observation number*, which you can think of as the order of the observation in the data set. For example, Alabama is the first observation in the speeding ticket data set, and the OBS for AL is 1. The second column of output is labeled *STATE*. This column gives the values for the variable STATE. The third column is labeled *AMOUNT* and gives the values for the variable AMOUNT.

In general, when you print a data set, the first column is labeled *OBS*. Other columns are labeled with the variable names given in the INPUT statement. The variables appear in the order they were listed in the INPUT statement.

Output 3.1   **PROC PRINT for the Speeding Ticket Data**

```
             Speeding Ticket Data                    1
             OBS      STATE      AMOUNT
               1       AL         60.0
               2       HI         35.0
               3       DE         31.5
               4       IL         20.0
               5       AK         20.0
               6       CT         60.0
               7       AR         47.0
               8       IA         33.0
               9       FL         44.0
              10       KS         28.0
              11       AZ         15.0
              12       IN         50.0
              13       CA         50.0
              14       LA         45.0
              15       GA         45.0
              16       MT          5.0
              17       ID         12.5
              18       KY         65.0
              19       CO         64.0
              20       ME         40.0
              21       NE         10.0
              22       MA         50.0
              23       MD         40.0
              24       NV          5.0
              25       MO         50.0
              26       MI         40.0
              27       NM         20.0
              28       NJ         50.0
              29       MN         44.0
              30       NY         28.0
              31       NC         47.5
              32       MS         39.5
              33       ND         10.0
              34       OH        100.0
              35       NH         33.0
              36       OR         26.0
              37       OK         56.0
              38       SC         45.0
              39       RI         30.0
              40       PA         72.5
              41       TN         40.0
              42       SD         10.0
              43       TX         48.0
              44       VT         35.0
              45       UT         28.0
              46       WV         60.0
              47       VA         40.0
              48       WY         15.0
              49       WA         38.0
              50       WI         44.5
              51       DC          .
```

Printing Only Some of the Variables

If you have a data set with many variables, you may not want to print all of them. Suppose you conducted a survey that asked opinions about nuclear power plants and collected some demographic information (age, sex, race, and income). If you don't want to print all of the variables, you can use a VAR statement with PROC PRINT. Suppose the data set is named NUCPOWER and you want to print only the variables AGE and INCOME. To do so, type

```
proc print data=nucpower;
    var age income;
run;
```

The resulting printout contains three columns: the first for OBS, the second for AGE, and the third for INCOME. The general form for printing a data set is shown below:

> **PROC PRINT DATA=***data-set-name***;**
> **VAR** *variables***;**
>
> where *data-set-name* is the name of the data set and *variables* are the names of one or more variables in the data set. To print all of the variables in the data set, omit the VAR statement.

Sorting a Data Set

Notice that PROC PRINT prints the data in the order the values were entered. Suppose you want to see the data sorted by AMOUNT. In other words, you want to see the data with the smallest AMOUNT first and the largest AMOUNT last. Fortunately, you don't have to figure this out by hand and re-enter the data. You can simply type

```
proc sort data=tickets;
    by amount;
run;
```

SAS software then sorts the data set, reordering the observations so that the observation with the smallest value for AMOUNT is first. To see the re-ordered data set, run another PROC PRINT. Simply type

```
proc print data=tickets;
    title 'Speeding Ticket Data: Sorted by AMOUNT';
run;
```

After you add the six lines above to the program that creates the data set, your output should look like that in Output 3.2.

Notice that the observation for DC is first. When you sort a data set, observations with missing values are at the beginning of the sorted data set. The general form for PROC SORT is shown below:

PROC SORT DATA=_data-set-name_;
    BY _sorting-variables_;

where _data-set-name_ is the name of the data set to be sorted and _sorting-variables_ are the names of one or more variables that are used to sort the data set.

Output 3.2   PROC PRINT of Sorted Data

```
            Speeding Ticket Data: Sorted by AMOUNT        2
                    OBS     STATE     AMOUNT
                     1       DC          .
                     2       MT         5.0
                     3       NV         5.0
                     4       NE        10.0
                     5       ND        10.0
                     6       SD        10.0
                     7       ID        12.5
                     8       AZ        15.0
                     9       WY        15.0
                    10       IL        20.0
                    11       AK        20.0
                    12       NM        20.0
                    13       OR        26.0
                    14       KS        28.0
                    15       NY        28.0
                    16       UT        28.0
                    17       RI        30.0
                    18       DE        31.5
                    19       IA        33.0
                    20       NH        33.0
                    21       HI        35.0
                    22       VT        35.0
                    23       WA        38.0
                    24       MS        39.5
                    25       ME        40.0
                    26       MD        40.0
                    27       MI        40.0
                    28       TN        40.0
                    29       VA        40.0
                    30       FL        44.0
                    31       MN        44.0
                    32       WI        44.5
                    33       LA        45.0
                    34       GA        45.0
                    35       SC        45.0
                    36       AR        47.0
                    37       NC        47.5
                    38       TX        48.0
                    39       IN        50.0
                    40       CA        50.0
                    41       MA        50.0
                    42       MO        50.0
                    43       NJ        50.0
                    44       OK        56.0
                    45       AL        60.0
                    46       CT        60.0
                    47       WV        60.0
                    48       CO        64.0
                    49       KY        65.0
                    50       PA        72.5
                    51       OH       100.0
```

Summaries

Key Ideas

- SAS names must start with a letter or an underscore, be eight characters or less, and cannot contain any embedded blanks.
- SAS data sets consist of variables, with one or more observations for each variable.
- In a SAS DATA step, use the DATA statement to assign the data set a name. Use the INPUT statement to assign variable names and describe the data. Then use the DATALINES statement, include the data lines, and end with a semicolon on a line by itself.
- Use PROC PRINT to print data sets and PROC SORT to sort them.

Syntax

The DATA Step

In a DATA step, use the statements shown below:

1. **DATA** *data-set-name*;

    where *data-set-name* gives the name of the data set.

2. One of these INPUT statements:

    INPUT *variable* $ *location* ... ;
    INPUT *variable* $ ... ;
    INPUT *variable* $ ... @@ ;

    where *variable* is a variable name, $ is used for character variables and omitted for numeric variables, and *location* gives the starting and ending columns for the variable. When used, the @@ looks for multiple observations on each line of data.

3. **DATALINES;** (if the lines of data appear in the program).

4. **data lines** (if the lines of data appear) **or an INFILE statement** that identifies the external file that contains the data lines.

5. a null statement (;) to end the lines of data.

Printing

To print a data set,

> **PROC PRINT DATA=** *data-set-name*;

where *data-set-name* is the name of the data set. To print only some of the variables in a data set, add

> **VAR** *variables*;

where *variables* are the names of one or more variables to be printed.

Sorting

To sort a data set,

> **PROC SORT DATA=***data-set-name*;
>   **BY** *sorting-variables*;

where *data-set-name* is the name of the data set and *sorting-variables* is the name of one or more variables that are used to sort by.

Example

The program below produces all the output in this chapter:

```
data tickets;
    input state $ amount @@;
    datalines;
AL 60 HI 35 DE 31.50 IL 20 AK 20 CT 60 AR 47
IA 33 FL 44 KS 28 AZ 15 IN 50 CA 50 LA 45 GA 45
MT 5 ID 12.50 KY 65 CO 64 ME 40 NE 10 MA 50
MD 40 NV 5 MO 50 MI 40 NM 20 NJ 50 MN 44 NY 28
NC 47.50 MS 39.50 ND 10 OH 100 NH 33 OR 26 OK 56
SC 45 RI 30 PA 72.50 TN 40 SD 10 TX 48 VT 35 UT 28
WV 60 VA 40 WY 15 WA 38 WI 44.5 DC .
;

proc print data=tickets;
    title 'Speeding Ticket Data';
run;

proc sort data=tickets;
    by amount;
run;

proc print data=tickets;
    title 'Speeding Ticket Data: Sorted by AMOUNT';
run;
```

Advanced Topics

This section shows how to customize output from PROC PRINT. Specifically, you may want to attach labels to the variable names, to the values of variables, or to both. One way to do this is to attach a label in the DATA step, and use PROC PRINT to print the data with the label. Labels that are attached in the DATA step are printed with many SAS procedures.

Labeling Variables

In the speeding ticket example, the variable names you have used are fairly descriptive. However, sometimes the eight-character length of a variable name isn't long enough to describe the variable.

You can attach labels to variable names in the DATA step by using a LABEL statement between the INPUT and DATALINES statements. For the speeding ticket data, type

```
data tickets;
    input state $ amount @@;
    label state='State Where Ticket Received'
                 amount='Cost of Ticket to Driver';
    datalines;
```

Follow these statements with the lines of data. It is important to enclose the label in quotes. (This is similar to the TITLE statement, where the title text must be enclosed in quotes.) This DATA step doesn't produce any printed output. To print the labels you have attached to your variables, you need to add the LABEL option to the PROC PRINT statement. This option tells SAS software to print the variable labels instead of the variable names. For the speeding ticket data, type

```
proc print data=tickets label;
    title 'Speeding Ticket Data: Variables Labeled';
run;
```

Using both the DATA step with the LABEL statement and the LABEL option in PROC PRINT produces Output 3.3.

Output 3.3   Using LABELS in PROC PRINT

```
          Speeding Ticket Data: Variables Labeled            1
                          State
                          Where        Cost of
                          Ticket      Ticket to
              OBS        Received       Driver
               1           AL           60.0
               2           HI           35.0
               3           DE           31.5
               4           IL           20.0
               5           AK           20.0
               6           CT           60.0
               7           AR           47.0
               8           IA           33.0
               9           FL           44.0
              10           KS           28.0
              11           AZ           15.0
              12           IN           50.0
              13           CA           50.0
              14           LA           45.0
              15           GA           45.0
              16           MT            5.0
              17           ID           12.5
              18           KY           65.0
              19           CO           64.0
              20           ME           40.0
              21           NE           10.0
              22           MA           50.0
              23           MD           40.0
              24           NV            5.0
              25           MO           50.0
              26           MI           40.0
              27           NM           20.0
              28           NJ           50.0
              29           MN           44.0
              30           NY           28.0
              31           NC           47.5
              32           MS           39.5
              33           ND           10.0
              34           OH          100.0
              35           NH           33.0
              36           OR           26.0
              37           OK           56.0
              38           SC           45.0
              39           RI           30.0
              40           PA           72.5
              41           TN           40.0
              42           SD           10.0
              43           TX           48.0
              44           VT           35.0
              45           UT           28.0
              46           WV           60.0
              47           VA           40.0
              48           WY           15.0
              49           WA           38.0
              50           WI           44.5
              51           DC             .
```

In summary, to print variable labels, first attach labels to the variable names using a LABEL statement in the DATA step. Then use PROC PRINT with the LABEL option. Both steps are needed. If you create labels in the DATA step and don't use the LABEL option, the variable names appear in the output. The general form of the statements for attaching labels to variable names and then printing the data set is shown at the end of the "Advanced Topics" sections.

Formatting Values of Variables

You may want to attach labels to the individual values of variables. To distinguish between labels for variable names and labels for variable values, labels for values are called *formats*. This section discusses creating your own formats and using existing formats.

Creating Your Own Formats

To print a data set with formats, you first need to define the formats and then use the formats in a DATA step. The SAS procedure that allows you to attach formats to values of variables is PROC FORMAT. The statements to create formats for values of the STATE variable are shown below:

```
proc format;
    value $names 'AL'='Alabama' 'HI'='Hawaii'
                 'DE'='Delaware' 'IL'='Illinois'
                 'AK'='Alaska' 'CT'='Connecticut'
                 'AR'='Arkansas' 'IA'='Iowa'
                 'FL'='Florida' 'KS'='Kansas'
                 'AZ'='Arizona' 'IN'='Indiana'
                 'CA'='California' 'LA'='Louisiana'
                 'GA'='Georgia' 'MT'='Montana'
                 'ID'='Idaho' 'KY'='Kentucky'
                 'CO'='Colorado' 'ME'='Maine'
                 'NE'='Nebraska' 'MA'='Massachusetts'
                 'MD'='Maryland' 'NV'='Nevada'
                 'MO'='Missouri' 'MI'='Michigan'
                 'NM'='New Mexico' 'NJ'='New Jersey'
                 'MN'='Minnesota' 'NY'='New York'
                 'NC'='North Carolina' 'MS'='Mississippi'
                 'ND'='North Dakota' 'OH'='Ohio'
```

```
                         'NH'='New Hampshire' 'OR'='Oregon'
                         'OK'='Oklahoma' 'SC'='South Carolina'
                         'RI'='Rhode Island' 'PA'='Pennsylvania'
                         'TN'='Tennessee' 'SD'='South Dakota'
                         'TX'='Texas' 'VT'='Vermont'
                         'UT'='Utah' 'WV'='West Virginia'
                         'VA'='Virginia' 'WY'='Wyoming'
                         'WA'='Washington' 'WI'='Wisconsin'
                         'DC'='Washington DC'
     ;
     run;
```

There are only two SAS statements in the previous example: the PROC FORMAT and the VALUE statements. Notice the semicolon at the end of the list in the VALUE statement. The VALUE statement is like all other SAS statements in that you must end it with a semicolon.

Use PROC FORMAT before a DATA step, and then include a FORMAT statement in the DATA step. The FORMAT statement attaches the formats to the values of a variable. In the FORMAT statement in the DATA step, the format name must end in a period. For the speeding ticket data, add the FORMAT statement to the DATA step as follows:

```
data tickets;
    input state $ amount @@;
    format state $names.;
    datalines;
```

This creates the TICKETS data set, and assigns the format for the STATE variable. The example uses a format that you have created.

Using Existing Formats

SAS software includes many existing formats. In fact, if you want to format your output, it's a good idea to see if there is already a format that will work for you. Suppose you want to format AMOUNT to show dollars and cents. The DOLLAR format will do this for you. With this format, you specify the length of the variable and the number of places after the decimal point. For AMOUNT, the statement below specifies a length of 8 with two characters after the decimal point.

```
format amount dollar8.2;
```

You can assign existing formats in the DATA step. This formats the variable in output for all procedures, and works just as described above for the build-your-own formats.

Or, you can use a FORMAT statement with many procedures. This formats the variable for the output from that procedure. This example uses the DOLLAR format with the PRINT procedure. If you use the PROC FORMAT and the DATA step outlined above and add the statements below, your output will look like Output 3.4.

```
proc print data=tickets;
    format amount dollar8.2;
    title 'Speeding Ticket Data: Formatted Values';
run;
```

In summary, to print a data set with formats for the values of a variable, you have some choices.

- If there isn't an existing format that works for you, first create the formats using PROC FORMAT, attach the formats to the variable values, and then print the data set with PROC PRINT.

- If there is an existing format that works for you, add a FORMAT statement to the PROC PRINT step.

The general form of the statements for this process is shown at the end of the next section, which shows how to combine labeling and formatting.

Output 3.4   **Formatted Variable Values**

```
         Speeding Ticket Data:   Formatted Values          2

            OBS    STATE                AMOUNT

             1     Alabama              $60.00
             2     Hawaii               $35.00
             3     Delaware             $31.50
             4     Illinois             $20.00
             5     Alaska               $20.00
             6     Connecticut          $60.00
             7     Arkansas             $47.00
             8     Iowa                 $33.00
             9     Florida              $44.00
            10     Kansas               $28.00
            11     Arizona              $15.00
            12     Indiana              $50.00
            13     California           $50.00
            14     Louisiana            $45.00
            15     Georgia              $45.00
            16     Montana               $5.00
            17     Idaho                $12.50
            18     Kentucky             $65.00
            19     Colorado             $64.00
            20     Maine                $40.00
            21     Nebraska             $10.00
            22     Massachusetts        $50.00
            23     Maryland             $40.00
            24     Nevada                $5.00
            25     Missouri             $50.00
            26     Michigan             $40.00
            27     New Mexico           $20.00
            28     New Jersey           $50.00
            29     Minnesota            $44.00
            30     New York             $28.00
            31     North Carolina       $47.50
            32     Mississippi          $39.50
            33     North Dakota         $10.00
            34     Ohio                $100.00
            35     New Hampshire        $33.00
            36     Oregon               $26.00
            37     Oklahoma             $56.00
            38     South Carolina       $45.00
            39     Rhode Island         $30.00
            40     Pennsylvania         $72.50
            41     Tennessee            $40.00
            42     South Dakota         $10.00
            43     Texas                $48.00
            44     Vermont              $35.00
            45     Utah                 $28.00
            46     West Virginia        $60.00
            47     Virginia             $40.00
            48     Wyoming              $15.00
            49     Washington           $38.00
            50     Wisconsin            $44.50
            51     Washington DC           .
```

Table 3.5 describes several commonly-used formats that are automatically provided with SAS. All the formats shown are for numeric variables. Use these in a FORMAT statement either in the DATA step (as with the NAMES format) or in a PROC step (as with the DOLLAR format). The names end in a period, as is required in the FORMAT statement.

Table 3.5   **Selected SAS Formats**

Format	Description
COMMA$w.d$	formats numbers with commas and decimal points. The total width is w, and d is 0 for no decimal points or 2 for decimal values. Useful for dollar amounts.
DOLLAR$w.d$	formats numbers with dollar signs, commas, and decimal points. The total width is w, and d is 0 for no decimal points or 2 for decimal values. Useful for dollar amounts.
E$w.$	formats numbers in scientific notation. The total width is w.
FRACT$w.$	formats numbers as fractions. The total width is w. Example: 0.333333 formats as 1/3.
PERCENT$w.d$	formats numbers as percents. The total width is w, and the number of decimal places is d. Example: 0.15 formats as 15%.

Combining: Labeling and Formatting

You can combine the two techniques of labeling variables and formatting values of variables. To do so, use

- PROC FORMAT before the DATA step to build your own formats
- both the LABEL and FORMAT statements in the DATA step

- PROC PRINT with the LABEL option to use the variable labels

- FORMAT statements in PROC PRINT to use existing formats.

The resulting output shows both the labels for the variables and the formats for the values of variables. For the speeding ticket data, first use PROC FORMAT to build the format values for state names, and then use the following DATA step and PROC PRINT:

```
data tickets;
    input state $ amount @@;
    format state $names.;
    label state='State Where Ticket Received'
          amount='Cost of Ticket to Driver';
    datalines;
data lines
;

proc print data=tickets label;
    format amount dollar8.2;
    title 'Speeding Ticket Data with Labels and Formats';
run;
```

These statements produce Output 3.5. In the DATA step, both the LABEL and FORMAT statements appear between the INPUT and DATALINES statements. The order of the LABEL and FORMAT statements is not important.

Output 3.5   **Using Labels and Formats**

```
              Speeding Ticket Data with Labels and Formats      2
                 OBS          State              Cost of
                              Where             Ticket to
                              Ticket             Driver
                             Received

                  1       Alabama               $60.00
                  2       Hawaii                $35.00
                  3       Delaware              $31.50
                  4       Illinois              $20.00
                  5       Alaska                $20.00
                  6       Connecticut           $60.00
                  7       Arkansas              $47.00
                  8       Iowa                  $33.00
                  9       Florida               $44.00
                 10       Kansas                $28.00
                 11       Arizona               $15.00
                 12       Indiana               $50.00
                 13       California            $50.00
                 14       Louisiana             $45.00
                 15       Georgia               $45.00
                 16       Montana                $5.00
                 17       Idaho                 $12.50
                 18       Kentucky              $65.00
                 19       Colorado              $64.00
                 20       Maine                 $40.00
                 21       Nebraska              $10.00
                 22       Massachusetts         $50.00
                 23       Maryland              $40.00
                 24       Nevada                 $5.00
                 25       Missouri              $50.00
                 26       Michigan              $40.00
                 27       New Mexico            $20.00
                 28       New Jersey            $50.00
                 29       Minnesota             $44.00
                 30       New York              $28.00
                 31       North Carolina        $47.50
                 32       Mississippi           $39.50
                 33       North Dakota          $10.00
                 34       Ohio                 $100.00
                 35       New Hampshire         $33.00
                 36       Oregon                $26.00
                 37       Oklahoma              $56.00
                 38       South Carolina        $45.00
                 39       Rhode Island          $30.00
                 40       Pennsylvania          $72.50
                 41       Tennessee             $40.00
                 42       South Dakota          $10.00
                 43       Texas                 $48.00
                 44       Vermont               $35.00
                 45       Utah                  $28.00
                 46       West Virginia         $60.00
                 47       Virginia              $40.00
                 48       Wyoming               $15.00
                 49       Washington            $38.00
                 50       Wisconsin             $44.50
                 51       Washington DC            .
```

To label variables and format values, use the general form shown below:

```
PROC FORMAT;
   VALUE format name      value=format
                          value=format
                              .
                              .
                              .
                          value=format ;
DATA statement
   INPUT statement
   FORMAT variable format-name. ;
   LABEL variable='label' ;
   DATALINES statement
   data lines
;
PROC PRINT DATA=data-set-name LABEL ;
   FORMAT variable format-name. ;
```

where

format-name   is a SAS name you assign to the list of formats. If
               the variable has character values, this name must
               begin with a dollar sign ($). The next six characters
               of the name can be letters or numbers. The seventh
               character must be a letter. For formats you build,
               you choose the *format-name*. For existing formats,
               use the *format-name* for the format you want.

value   is the value of the variable you want to format.

format   is the format you want to attach to the value of the
               variable. This must be 200 characters or less in
               length. Note that blanks count as characters.

variable   is the name of the variable with the values to be
               formatted or labeled.

label   is the label for the variable, enclosed in single
               quotes. The label can be up to 40 characters long.
               Note that blanks count as characters.

data-set-name is the name of a data set

If a *value* or *format* contains letters or blanks, you must enclose
it in single quotes. In the FORMAT statement in the DATA and

(continued)

PROC PRINT steps, **the period immediately following the format name is required.**

You can associate formats with several variables in one FORMAT statement, and associate labels with several variables in one LABEL statement. The order of the FORMAT and LABEL statements in the DATA step may be reversed.

The general DATA, INPUT, and DATALINES statements shown above must end with a semicolon when the specific information for a data set is provided.

Labeling Values Using SAS Functions

The previous sections showed how to label the values for variables using formats. In some situations, *SAS functions* provide another way to do this. You can use SAS functions to create new variables whose values are based on an existing variable. For the speeding ticket data, type

```
data tickets;
    input state $ amount @@;
    label state='State Where Ticket Received'
          amount='Cost of Ticket to Driver';
    statext = stnamel(state);
    datalines;
AL 60 HI 35 DE 31.50 IL 20 AK 20 CT 60 AR 47
IA 33 FL 44 KS 28 AZ 15 IN 50 CA 50 LA 45 GA 45
MT 5 ID 12.50 KY 65 CO 64 ME 40 NE 10 MA 50
MD 40 NV 5 MO 50 MI 40 NM 20 NJ 50 MN 44 NY 28
NC 47.50 MS 39.50 ND 10 OH 100 NH 33 OR 26 OK 56
C 45 RI 30 PA 72.50 TN 40 SD 10 TX 48 VT 35 UT 28
WV 60 VA 40 WY 15 WA 38 WI 44.50 DC .
;

proc print data=tickets label;
    format amount dollar8.2;
    title 'Speeding Ticket Data';
run;
```

The statements above use the LABEL statement in the DATA step and use a FORMAT statement in PROC PRINT as discussed earlier. The statements also use the STNAMEL function to create a new variable, STATEXT, which contains the text for state names. These statements produce Output 3.6.

Output 3.6   **Using Functions for the State Name**

```
                                  Speeding Ticket Data                    1

                    State
                    Where           Cost of
                    Ticket          Ticket to
           OBS      Received        Driver          STATEXT

            1       AL              $60.00          Alabama
            2       HI              $35.00          Hawaii
            3       DE              $31.50          Delaware
            4       IL              $20.00          Illinois
            5       AK              $20.00          Alaska
            6       CT              $60.00          Connecticut
            7       AR              $47.00          Arkansas
            8       IA              $33.00          Iowa
            9       FL              $44.00          Florida
           10       KS              $28.00          Kansas
           11       AZ              $15.00          Arizona
           12       IN              $50.00          Indiana
           13       CA              $50.00          California
           14       LA              $45.00          Louisiana
           15       GA              $45.00          Georgia
           16       MT               $5.00          Montana
           17       ID              $12.50          Idaho
           18       KY              $65.00          Kentucky
           19       CO              $64.00          Colorado
           20       ME              $40.00          Maine
           21       NE              $10.00          Nebraska
           22       MA              $50.00          Massachusetts
           23       MD              $40.00          Maryland
           24       NV               $5.00          Nevada
           25       MO              $50.00          Missouri
           26       MI              $40.00          Michigan
           27       NM              $20.00          New Mexico
           28       NJ              $50.00          New Jersey
           29       MN              $44.00          Minnesota
           30       NY              $28.00          New York
           31       NC              $47.50          North Carolina
           32       MS              $39.50          Mississippi
           33       ND              $10.00          North Dakota
           34       OH             $100.00          Ohio
           35       NH              $33.00          New Hampshire
           36       OR              $26.00          Oregon
           37       OK              $56.00          Oklahoma
           38       SC              $45.00          South Carolina
           39       RI              $30.00          Rhode Island
           40       PA              $72.50          Pennsylvania
           41       TN              $40.00          Tennessee
           42       SD              $10.00          South Dakota
           43       TX              $48.00          Texas
           44       VT              $35.00          Vermont
           45       UT              $28.00          Utah
           46       WV              $60.00          West Virginia
           47       VA              $40.00          Virginia
           48       WY              $15.00          Wyoming
           49       WA              $38.00          Washington
           50       WI              $44.50          Wisconsin
           51       DC                  .           District of Columbia
```

The new variable STATEXT gives the text for the state names. Because the LABEL statement in the DATA step doesn't give a label for STATEXT, the variable name appears in the output.

SAS includes many functions which can often save you the effort of using PROC FORMAT. Table 3.6 lists selected SAS functions. For more information, see the references in "Further Reading."

Table 3.6   **Selected SAS Functions**

Function	Description
ABS(*variable*)	takes the absolute value of the variable. *variable* must be numeric.
LOG(*variable*)	takes the natural logarithm of the variable. *variable* must be numeric.
ROUND(*variable, unit*)	rounds the *variable.variable* must be numeric. *unit* gives the round-off details. Example: round(amount,1) rounds AMOUNT to the nearest whole number.
LOWCASE(*variable*)	takes mixed-case text and converts it to all lowercase. *variable* must be character.
STATNAMEL(*variable*)	converts the postal codes to state names. *variable* must be the character 2-letter postal codes.
UPCASE(*variable*)	takes mixed-case text and converts it to all uppercase. *variable* must be character.

In general, use functions in a DATA step to create new variables that recode values for existing variables. The general form for using functions in this way is shown below:

DATA statement
    INPUT statement
    new-variable = function(existing-variable);
    DATALINES statement
data lines
;

where *new-variable* is the new variable, *function* is a SAS function, and *existing-variable* is an appropriate variable in the INPUT statement.

The semicolon at the end of the statement is required.

Advanced Topics Summaries

Key Ideas

- To attach labels to variables, first use the LABEL statement in the DATA step, and then use PROC PRINT with the LABEL option.

- To attach formats to values of variables, first use PROC FORMAT to build your own format values, then use the FORMAT statement in the DATA step, and then use PROC PRINT.

- To attach formats using existing formats, use a FORMAT statement with PROC PRINT.

- To attach labels to variables and attach formats to values of variables, first use PROC FORMAT if you need to build your own format values, then use both the LABEL and FORMAT statements in the DATA step, and then use PROC PRINT with the LABEL option. To use existing formats, use a FORMAT statement with PROC PRINT.

- To assign labels to values of variables, another approach is to use SAS functions to create a new variable that recodes values of the existing variable.

Syntax

The sections below give syntax for labeling variables, creating your own formats, and using existing formats. Combine labeling and formatting by combining the statements summarized below.

Labeling Variables

To label variables,

> DATA statement
>   INPUT statement
>   **LABEL** *variable='label'* ;
>   DATALINES statement
> *data lines*
> ;

> **PROC PRINT DATA=***data-set-name* **LABEL;**

where *variable* is the variable you want to label, *label* is the label you want for the variable, and *data-set-name* is the name of a data set. The label must be enclosed in single quotes and can be up to 40 characters long. (Note that blanks count as characters.)

Creating Your Own Formats

To create your own formats,

> **PROC FORMAT;**
> **VALUE** *format name   value=format*
>   *value=format*
>
>   .
>   .
>   .
>
>   *value=format*;
> DATA statement
>   INPUT statement
>   **FORMAT** variable *format-name.* ;
>   DATALINES statement
> *data lines*
> ;

where *format-name* is a SAS name you assign to the list of formats. If the variable has character values, this name must begin with a dollar sign ($). The next six characters of the name can be letters or numbers. The seventh character must be a letter. In the VALUE statement, *value* is the value of the variable you want to format, and *format* is the format you want to attach to the value. The format can be up to 200 characters long. (Note that blanks count as characters.) In the FORMAT statement in the DATA step, *variable* is the name of the variable with values to be formatted.

Using Existing Formats

To use existing formats,

    PROC PRINT DATA=*data-set-name.* **;**
        FORMAT *variable format-name.* **;**

where items in italic are as described above.

Using SAS Functions

To use SAS functions in a DATA step:

    DATA statement
      INPUT statement
      new-variable = function(*existing-variable*)**;**
      DATALINES statement
    data lines
    ;

where *new-variable* is the new variable, *function* is a SAS function, and *existing-variable* is an appropriate variable in the INPUT statement. **The semicolon at the end of the statement is required.**

Example

The program below produces Output 3.5. For Output 3.4, delete the LABEL statement from the DATA step and the LABEL option from PROC PRINT. For Output 3.3, delete PROC FORMAT, the FORMAT statement in the DATA step, and the FORMAT statement in PROC PRINT. For Outputs 3.3 and 3.4, you also need to change the TITLE statement.

```
proc format;
    value $names 'AL'='Alabama' 'HI'='Hawaii'
                 'DE'='Delaware' 'IL'='Illinois'
                 'AK'='Alaska' 'CT'='Connecticut'
                 'AR'='Arkansas' 'IA'='Iowa'
                 'FL'='Florida' 'KS'='Kansas'
                 'AZ'='Arizona' 'IN'='Indiana'
                 'CA'='California' 'LA'='Louisiana'
                 'GA'='Georgia' 'MT'='Montana'
```

```
                        'ID'='Idaho' 'KY'='Kentucky'
                        'CO'='Colorado' 'ME'='Maine'
                        'NE'='Nebraska' 'MA'='Massachusetts'
                        'MD'='Maryland' 'NV'='Nevada'
                        'MO'='Missouri' 'MI'='Michigan'
                        'NM'='New Mexico' 'NJ'='New Jersey'
                        'MN'='Minnesota' 'NY'='New York'
                        'NC'='North Carolina' 'MS'='Mississippi'
                        'ND'='North Dakota' 'OH'='Ohio'
                        'NH'='New Hampshire' 'OR'='Oregon'
                        'OK'='Oklahoma' 'SC'='South Carolina'
                        'RI'='Rhode Island' 'PA'='Pennsylvania'
                        'TN'='Tennessee' 'SD'='South Dakota'
                        'TX'='Texas' 'VT'='Vermont'
                        'UT'='Utah' 'WV'='West Virginia'
                        'VA'='Virginia' 'WY'='Wyoming'
                        'WA'='Washington' 'WI'='Wisconsin'
                        'DC'='Washington DC'
   ;
run;
data tickets;
   input state $ amount @@;
   label state='State Where Ticket Received'
         amount='Cost of Ticket to Driver';
   format state $names.;
   datalines;
AL 60 HI 35 DE 31.50 IL 20 AK 20 CT 60 AR 47
IA 33 FL 44 KS 28 AZ 15 IN 50 CA 50 LA 45 GA 45
MT 5 ID 12.50 KY 65 CO 64 ME 40 NE 10 MA 50
MD 40 NV 5 MO 50 MI 40 NM 20 NJ 50 MN 44 NY 28
NC 47.50 MS 39.50 ND 10 OH 100 NH 33 OR 26 OK 56
SC 45 RI 30 PA 72.50 TN 40 SD 10 TX 48 VT 35 UT 28
WV 60 VA 40 WY 15 WA 38
WI 44.50 DC .
   ;

proc print data=tickets label;
   format amount dollar8.2;
   title 'Speeding Ticket Data with Labels and Formats';
run;
```

The program below produces Output 3.6.

```
data tickets;
      input state $ amount @@;
      label state='State Where Ticket Received'
            amount='Cost of Ticket to Driver';
      statext = stnamel(state);
      datalines;
AL 60 HI 35 DE 31.50 IL 20 AK 20 CT 60 AR 47
IA 33 FL 44 KS 28 AZ 15 IN 50 CA 50 LA 45 GA 45
MT 5 ID 12.50 KY 65 CO 64 ME 40 NE 10 MA 50
MD 40 NV 5 MO 50 MI 40 NM 20 NJ 50 MN 44 NY 28
NC 47.50 MS 39.50 ND 10 OH 100 NH 33 OR 26 OK 56
SC 45 RI 30 PA 72.50 TN 40 SD 10 TX 48 VT 35 UT 28
WV 60 VA 40 WY 15 WA 38
WI 44.50 DC .
;

proc print data=tickets label;
    format amount dollar8.2;
    title 'Speeding Ticket Data';
run;
```

Further Reading

For more detail about the DATA step and the procedures that are presented in this chapter, see one of the following books:

- *SAS® Language and Procedures: Introduction, Version 6, First Edition* gives an introduction to the DATA step in Chapter 3.

- *SAS® Language: Reference, Version 6, First Edition* gives details about the DATA step in Chapter 2, functions in Chapter 11, and formats in Chapter 14.

- *SAS® Language and Procedures: Syntax, Version 6, First Edition* lists functions in Chapter 3, formats in Chapter 5 and gives a syntax summary of procedures in Chapter 10.

- *SAS® Procedures Guide, Version 6, Third Edition* discusses the PRINT and SORT procedures in Chapters 27 and 31

- *The Little SAS® Book: A Primer* discusses the DATA step in Chapter 2, functions and formats in Chapter 4, and the PRINT and SORT procedures in Chapter 5.

Although there may also be technical reports with updated information for various releases, the best source of the most recent information is the online help and online documentation. These are most appropriate in display manager mode.

Chapter 4 # Summarizing Data

Now that you've learned how to create a data set, the next step is to learn how to summarize a data set. This chapter first explains the concept of levels of measurement. Depending on the level of measurement, a variable may be summarized as follows:

- using descriptive statistics, such as the average
- generating frequencies or counts of values for a variable
- creating vertical or horizontal bar charts
- using exploratory data analysis (EDA) plots.

This chapter uses the speeding ticket data from Chapter 3.

Contents

Levels of Measurement

Chapter 3 discussed character and numeric variables. Character variables have values containing characters, and numeric variables have values containing numbers only.

Another way to classify variables is based on the level of measurement. The level of measurement is important since some methods of summarizing or analyzing data are based on the level of measurement. Levels of measurement can be *nominal*, *ordinal*, *interval*, or *ratio*. In addition, variables can be measured on a *discrete* or a *continuous* scale.

Types of Variables

Nominal Measurements

Nominal measurements give names to the values of a variable. For example, gender is a nominal measurement with "male" and "female" as values. You could also code the values as "1" and "2," but the numbers would only name the values. They would not have any meaning as numbers. The type of car you drive is another example of a nominal measurement. You could code the values as "Toyota," "Chevrolet," "Volkswagen," and so on. You could also set up a coding system where you assigned a "1" to Toyotas, a "2" to Chevrolets, a "3" to Volkswagens, and so on, but the numbers would have no meaning other than to associate a name with a value of the variable.

Ordinal Measurements

Ordinal measurements have an inherent ordering that corresponds to the values of a variable. Opinion polls often use an ordinal scale with the following values: strongly agree, agree, no opinion, disagree, strongly disagree. People are given a statement such as, "I think the new tax law is an improvement over the old law." Then they are asked to choose a point on the scale to represent their opinion. As another example, in clinical trials for new drugs, patients may experience side effects, or adverse events. These are typically classified into three categories: mild, moderate, and severe. In both these examples, there is an inherent ordering to the values of the variable.

As with nominal data, you can assign numbers to the values. With ordinal data, the numbers you assign need to match the order of the values. The specific numbers you assign are not important. For the adverse events example, you could assign 1, 2, and 3 to the values, or you could assign 1, 10, and 100. If you choose an analysis appropriate for an ordinal variable, the analysis is based only on the order of the values, not on the numeric values of the variable.

Interval Measurements

Interval measurements are numeric and also have an inherent ordering. In addition to the order being important, differences between values are important. Consider temperature in degrees Fahrenheit (F). A temperature of 120°F is 20° warmer than one of 100°F. Similarly, a temperature of 170°F is 20° warmer than one of 150°F. Contrast this with an ordinal measurement where the numeric difference between values isn't meaningful. For the ordinal measurement in the adverse events example, the difference between 2 and 1 does not necessarily have the same meaning as the difference between 3 and 2.

Ratio Measurements

Ratio measurements are numeric, have an inherent order, and differences between values are important. In addition, the value of 0 is meaningful. For example, the weight of gold is a ratio measurement. Also, the number of calories in a meal is a ratio measurement. A meal with 2000 calories has twice as many calories as one with 1000 calories. Contrast this with temperature: it doesn't make sense to say that a temperature of 100°F is twice as hot as one of 50°F because 0° on a Fahrenheit scale is just an arbitrary reference point.

Types of Response Scales

Variables can also be classified according to whether they are measured on a discrete or a continuous scale. Discrete scales have only a limited number of values, and continuous scales have conceptually an infinite number of values. In practice, many continuous variables are measured on a discrete scale. The next two sections describe these scales in more detail.

Discrete Scale

Variables measured on a *discrete scale* have a limited number of numeric values in any given range. The number of times you wash your hair each week is a variable measured on a discrete scale. You can simply not wash your hair at all, which gives a value of 0, or you can wash your hair 1,

2, or 7 times, which give values of 1, 2, and 7, respectively. You can't wash your hair 3.5 times in one week, however. The discrete values for this variable are the numbers 0, 1, 2, 3, and so on, up to a common-sense maximum of about 14. Test scores are another example of a variable measured on a discrete scale. With a range of scores from 0 to 100, the possible values are 0, 1, 2, and so on.

Continuous Scale

Variables measured on a *continuous scale* have conceptually an unlimited number of values. As an example, your exact body temperature is measured on a continuous scale. A thermometer doesn't measure your exact temperature but measures your approximate body temperature. Body temperature conceptually can take on any value within a specific range, say 95° to 105°F. In this range, conceptually there are an unlimited number of values for your exact body temperature (98.6001, 98.6002, 98.60021, and so on), but in reality, you can measure only a limited number of values (98.6, 98.7, 98.8, and so on). Contrast this with the number of times that you wash your hair each week. Conceptually and in reality, there are a limited number of values to represent the number of times you wash your hair each week.

The important idea that underlies a continuous scale is that the variable can theoretically take on an unlimited number of values. In reality, the number of values for the variable is limited by your ability to measure.

Types of Variables and Response Scales

Nominal and ordinal variables are usually measured on a discrete scale. However, for ordinal variables the discrete scale is sometimes one that separates a continuous scale into categories. For example, a person's age is often classified according to categories (0-21, 22-45, 46-65, and over 65, for example).

Interval and ratio variables are measured on discrete and continuous scales. The number of times you wash your hair in a given week is a ratio measurement on a discrete scale. Conceptually, your weight is a ratio measurement on a continuous scale. In reality, the ability to measure weight is limited by the measuring device, so the actual variable is discrete. You usually measure your weight in pounds rather than to the nearest tenth of an ounce.

Summary Methods for Types of Variables

Table 4.1 shows the relationship between the levels of measurement and the summary methods explained in this chapter. For example, descriptive statistics are appropriate for ratio measurements but not for nominal ones.

Table 4.1   Relationship between Levels of Measurement and Summary Methods

	Methods for Summarizing Data			
Level of Measurement	Descriptive Statistics	Frequency Tables	Bar Charts	EDA Plots
Nominal		X	X	
Ordinal	X	X	X	
Interval	X	X	X	X
Ratio	X	X	X	X

An X indicates the method is appropriate for the level of measurement. In this table and in the rest of this book, EDA is used as an abbreviation for exploratory data analysis. This abbreviation is also commonly used in statistics texts.

Examining Data for Errors

Before you make any decisions based on a summary of a data set, examine the data set to make sure there aren't any errors. Many of the descriptive methods presented in this chapter can help you with this task. You can use the same SAS procedures to check your data for errors and to summarize the data.

For very short data sets, compare the data values with the original data using output from PROC PRINT. Simply look to see that all the values in the printed data set match the values you originally collected.

This process of verifying your data against a printout is tedious, so short-cut methods can be used. Here are some other ways to verify your data:

- For numeric variables, look at the maximum and minimum values. Are there any that seem odd? For example, you don't expect to see a value of 150° for a person's temperature.

- For nominal and ordinal variables, are there duplicate values that are just misspellings? For example, do you have both "test" and "gest" as values for a variable?

- For nominal and ordinal variables, are there too many values? If you have coded answers to an opinion poll as 1 to 5, all your values should be 1, 2, 3, 4, or 5. If you find a 6, you know it's an error.

Many of the methods in the next several sections can help you verify your data as well as summarize it. In each section, methods to verify data are discussed where appropriate.

Descriptive Statistics

You use descriptive statistics to summarize data in everyday life. When you fill out a tax return each year, you summarize your total earnings for the year rather than enter the amount of each paycheck. When you buy a new car, you keep track of the miles per gallon for the first few tankfuls, take the average, and tell your friends you get "25 miles per gallon on the average." You probably don't tell them what you got for the first tank, then the second, then the third, and so on.

Most descriptive statistics require variables to be interval or ratio. This is because most descriptive statistics summarize numerical values, but with nominal or ordinal variables, the actual numerical values (and differences between values) don't have any real meaning. Some exceptions occur for ordinal variables, where descriptive statistics that summarize the ranking of values are appropriate.

Descriptive statistics are always appropriate for variables measured on a continuous scale. These statistics are also useful for discrete variables that have many values. For example, the variable AMOUNT in the speeding ticket data (introduced in Chapter 3) is discrete. However, there are many distinct values for AMOUNT. Descriptive statistics, such as the average, would be useful in summarizing AMOUNT. Consider, as a counterexample, the number of times people wash their hair each day. This variable will likely have three values: 0, 1, and 2. Descriptive statistics would not be as useful in summarizing this variable; a frequency table would be more appropriate.

Descriptive Statistics from PROC UNIVARIATE

Several SAS procedures provide descriptive statistics, but PROC UNIVARIATE gives the most extensive summary. To get a summary of the speeding ticket data, type

```
proc univariate data=tickets;
    var amount;
    id state;
    title 'Summary of Speeding Ticket Data';
run;
```

The PROC UNIVARIATE statement requests a summary for the TICKETS data set, the VAR statement lists variables to be summarized, and the ID statement names a variable that identifies observations in one part of the output. These statements produce Output 4.1.

The output is in four sections, with headings: *Moments, Quantiles, Extremes,* and *Missing Value.* The *Moments* and *Quantiles* sections summarize the numeric values of a variable. Use these sections for interval or ratio variables. The *Extremes* and *Missing Value* sections are useful for all levels of measurement.

Output 4.1   **PROC UNIVARIATE Results for Speeding Ticket Data**

```
               Summary of Speeding Ticket Data            1

                     Univariate Procedure

Variable=AMOUNT

                          Moments

      N                 50   Sum Wgts            50
      Mean            38.5   Sum               1925
      Std Dev     18.79318   Variance      353.1837
      Skewness    0.446814   Kurtosis      1.133682
      USS          91418.5   CSS              17306
      CV          48.81346   Std Mean      2.657757
      T:Mean=0     14.4859   Pr>|T|          0.0001
      Num ^= 0          50   Num > 0             50
      M(Sign)           25   Pr>=|M|         0.0001
      Sgn Rank       637.5   Pr>=|S|         0.0001


                     Quantiles(Def=5)

      100% Max          100   99%              100
       75% Q3            50   95%               65
       50% Med           40   90%               60
       25% Q1            28   10%            11.25
        0% Min            5   5%                10
                              1%                 5
      Range             95
      Q3-Q1             22
      Mode              40


                          Extremes

      Lowest      ID       Highest      ID
           5(NV     )          60(WV     )
           5(MT     )          64(CO     )
          10(SD     )          65(KY     )
          10(ND     )        72.5(PA     )
          10(NE     )         100(OH     )


          Missing Value            .
          Count                    1
          % Count/Nobs          1.96
```

The Moments Section

First look at the section labeled *Moments*. This book doesn't discuss *Sum Wgts*, *USS*, *CSS*, *M(Sign)*, or *Pr>=|M|*. Discussions about *T:Mean=0*, *Pr>|T|*, *Sgn Rank*, and *Pr>=|S|* are in Chapter 7.

The rest of the *Moments* section is discussed below:

N   is the number of observations with nonmissing values for the variable being summarized. There are 50 nonmissing observations for AMOUNT. These observations correspond to the 50 states.

Sum   is the sum of values for all observations.

Mean   the arithmetic average. This is calculated as *Sum/N*. The mean for AMOUNT is 38.5, so the average speeding ticket fine for the 50 states is $38.50. The mean is one measure used to describe the center of a distribution of values. Other measures used include the mode and the median, which are printed in the *Quantiles* section (discussed later).

Variance is the most commonly used measure of dispersion or variability, around the mean. When all the values are close to the mean, the variance is small. When the values are scattered widely from the mean, the variance is larger. The variance is never less than 0, and it is 0 only if all the values are the same. (Chapter 5 gives a theoretical discussion and a formula for variance.) The variance for AMOUNT is about 353.18 (rounded off from the output shown).

Std Dev   is the standard deviation. For AMOUNT, this is about 18.79 (rounded off from the output shown). The standard deviation is the square root of the variance. Like the variance, it is a measure of dispersion about the mean, but it is easier to interpret because the units of measurement for the standard deviation are the same as the units of measurement for the data.

Skewness is a measure of the tendency for the distribution of values to be more spread out on one side than the other. Positive skewness indicates that values located to the right of the mean are more spread out than the values located to the left of the mean. Negative skewness indicates the opposite. You may understand skewness better after seeing charts of the distribution of values (discussed later in this chapter). The skewness for AMOUNT is about 0.447 (rounded off from the output shown).

Kurtosis	is another measure of the shape of the distribution of values. Another way to think of kurtosis is of measuring how "peaked" or "flat" the shape of the distribution of values is. Large values for kurtosis indicate the distribution has "heavy tails" or is "flat." This means that the data contains some values that are very distant from the mean, as compared to most of the other values in the data set. You may understand kurtosis better after seeing charts of the distribution of values (discussed later in this chapter). The kurtosis for AMOUNT is about 1.134 (rounded off from the output).
CV	is the coefficient of variation. This is calculated as the standard deviation divided by the mean and multiplied by 100 [(*Std Dev/Mean*)×100]. The CV for AMOUNT is about 48.81 (rounded off).
Std Mean	is the standard error of the mean. This is calculated as the standard deviation divided by the square root of the sample size (*Std Dev*/$\sqrt{n}$). For more discussion, see Chapter 6. The standard error of the mean for AMOUNT is about 2.66 (rounded off from the output).
Num ^= 0	is the number of nonmissing values not equal to 0. In the TICKETS data, none of the 50 nonmissing values for AMOUNT are 0. A caret (^) is SAS shorthand for "not." You may see this in other output also.
Num>0	is the number of nonmissing values greater than 0. In the TICKETS data, all of the 50 nonmissing values for AMOUNT are greater than 0.

The Quantiles Section

The section labeled *Quantiles* gives you more information about the distribution of values. The 0th percentile is the lowest value, and the 100th percentile is the highest value. The 75th percentile, also called the *third quartile*, is greater than 75% of the values. For the speeding ticket data, the 75th percentile for AMOUNT is 50, so a speeding ticket amount of $50.00 is greater than 75% of the values in the data set. The 25th percentile, also called the *first quartile*, is greater than 25% of the values. The 50th percentile is the *median*. Half the data values are above the median, and half are below. The median is one measure used to describe the center of a distribution of values. It is especially appropriate for ordinal data. The median is also less sensitive than the mean to skewness and is often used with skewed data. The 1st, 5th, 10th, 90th, 95th, and 99th percentiles are larger than 1%, 5%, 10%, 90%, 95%, and 99% of the values, respectively. SAS has five different definitions to determine percentiles. This book uses the default definition. See the "Further Reading" section at the end of the chapter for details on where to find the definitions in the manuals.

Range is the difference between the highest and lowest values. The range of values for AMOUNT is 95, with values from 5 to 100. *Q3-Q1* is the difference between the 75th percentile and the 25th percentile. This is also called the *interquartile range*, and it is sometimes used as a measure of dispersion. For the speeding ticket data, the interquartile range is 22. Contrast this with the standard deviation (another measure of dispersion), which is about 18.79.

Mode is the data value with the largest associated number of observations. In the example, the mode is 40. This indicates that more states give speeding tickets of $40.00 than of any other amount.

Some data sets have several values with the same "largest" associated number of observations. For this case of multiple modes, PROC UNIVARIATE lists the mode with the lowest value. In the TICKETS data set, a second mode occurs at 50. This can be discovered by looking at the frequency of data values, which is discussed later in this chapter in "Frequency Tables with PROC UNIVARIATE" and "Frequency Tables with PROC FREQ."

The Extremes Section

Now look at the *Extremes* section. This section lists the five *Lowest* and five *Highest* values. However, two observations with the same lowest value appear in this section. This section doesn't give the lowest five distinct values. For example, two states have an AMOUNT of 5, and two of the lowest values show this. The five highest values for AMOUNT are 60, 64, 65, 72.5, and 100.

The result of using the ID statement is seen in the *Extremes* section. The lowest and highest values are identified by the value of STATE. If you don't use the ID statement, PROC UNIVARIATE identifies observations with their observation number.

The Missing Value Section

Missing Value shows how missing values are coded, *Count* gives the number of missing values, and % *Count/Nobs* gives the percent of missing data. For the speeding ticket data, missing values are coded with a period; one of fifty-one values, or about 2% of the data, is missing.

Examining the Data for Errors

For all levels of measurement, use the *Extremes* section to look for incorrect values. Suppose you measured the weights of dogs and find that your *Highest* value is listed as 200 pounds. Although this value is potentially valid, it is unusual enough that you should check it before you use it: perhaps the dog really weighs 20 pounds and an extra 0 has been added.

The *Missing Values* section is also useful when looking for errors. If the value of *Count* is higher than you expect, perhaps your INPUT statement is incorrect, so the values of the variables are wrong. For example, you may have used incorrect columns for a variable in the INPUT statement, so several values of your variable are listed as missing.

The information about the number of nonmissing values greater than 0 and not equal to 0 in the *Moments* section is also useful in looking for errors. In the speeding ticket data, a value less than 0 would be incorrect (because it would imply that drivers were paid for speeding). You can look for this error by verifying that *Num>0* matches the number of non-missing values. In this example, it is potentially valid for some values to equal 0. These would correspond to states that have no fine for speeding. However, in the weights of dogs example, all dogs should have nonzero weights. In general, you can look for the number of nonzero values (*Num^=0*) to match the number of nonmissing values in the data.

Summarizing PROC UNIVARIATE

The general form of the statements for using PROC UNIVARIATE to get descriptive statistics is shown below:

> **PROC UNIVARIATE DATA=***data-set-name* ;
>   **VAR** *measurement-variables* ;
>   **ID** *id-variable* ;
>
> where *data-set-name* is the name of a SAS data set, *measurement-variables* is the name of one or more variables in the data set, and *id-variable* is the name of one variable to use to identify the extreme values.

You can use PROC UNIVARIATE without a VAR or an ID statement. While the VAR statement is not required, you should use it. Otherwise, all numeric variables in the data set are summarized. If you don't use an ID statement, extreme values are identified with their observation numbers.

Descriptive Statistics from PROC MEANS

You may not need all the information you get from PROC UNIVARIATE. If you want just a few descriptive statistics or you want a concise summary for several variables, you may want to use PROC MEANS.

To get a brief summary of the speeding ticket data, type

```
proc means data=tickets;
    var amount;
    title 'Brief Summary of Speeding Ticket Data';
run;
```

Your output should look like Output 4.2.

Output 4.2   **PROC MEANS Results for Speeding Ticket Data**

```
Brief Summary of Speeding Ticket Data                              1

   Analysis Variable : AMOUNT

   N          Mean        Std Dev       Minimum       Maximum
   ------------------------------------------------------------
   50     38.5000000    18.7931816     5.0000000    100.0000000
   ------------------------------------------------------------
```

From this summary, you learn the following:

- The TICKETS data set contains 50 observations with nonmissing values for AMOUNT (*N*)

- The average value of AMOUNT (*Mean*) is 38.50, so the average amount of a speeding ticket for driving 65 mph is $38.50.

- The standard deviation (*Std Dev*) of AMOUNT is about 18.79 (rounded off from output).

- The *Minimum* value of AMOUNT is 5.00.

- The *Maximum* value of AMOUNT is 100.00.

Notice how brief the PROC MEANS output is. If there were several variables in the TICKETS data set, and you wanted to get only these few descriptive statistics for each variable, PROC MEANS would produce a line of output for each variable. PROC UNIVARIATE would produce a page of output for each variable.

The general form for PROC MEANS is shown below:

PROC MEANS DATA=*data-set-name* ;
   VAR *measurement-variables* ;

where *data-set-name* is the name of a SAS data set, and *measurement-variables* is the name of one or more variables in the data set.

Like PROC UNIVARIATE, PROC MEANS allows several variables in the VAR statement and also allows you to omit the VAR statement. However, you should use a VAR statement because all numeric variables are summarized when it is omitted.

This section presented PROC UNIVARIATE and PROC MEANS, both of which give descriptive statistics. PROC UNIVARIATE gives a much more complete summary than PROC MEANS. As a general guideline, use PROC MEANS when you want a brief summary for each variable.

Frequency Tables

For nominal and ordinal variables, you may want to know the frequency
of each value. In addition, for interval or ratio variables measured on a
discrete scale, you may also want to know the frequency of each value.
For example, you may want to know how many of the states give speeding tickets of $10.

Frequency Tables with PROC UNIVARIATE

To produce a frequency table, add the FREQ option to PROC UNIVARIATE.
For the speeding ticket data, type

```
proc univariate data=tickets freq;
   var amount;
   title 'Summary of Speeding Ticket Data';
run;
```

The first page of your output looks like Output 4.1, and the second page
looks like Output 4.3.

Look at Output 4.3. The column labeled *Value* shows values for the variable
AMOUNT. The column labeled *Count* shows you the number of observations that have a given value. For example, there are 2 states (observations)
with an AMOUNT of 5, 3 states with an AMOUNT of 10, and so on. Notice
the two observations with *Count*=5. These correspond to 40 and 50, the
two modes for this data. The two columns labeled *Percents* give the percent
(*Cell*) and cumulative percent (*Cum*) for each value. For example, from the
Cell column you see that 4% of the states have an AMOUNT of 5, 6% have
an AMOUNT of 10, and 2% have an AMOUNT of 12.5. From the *Cum* column, you see that 12% (=4+6+2) of the observations have an AMOUNT of
12.5 or less.

Output 4.3   Using the FREQ Option in PROC UNIVARIATE

```
                    Summary of Speeding Ticket Data                    2

                         Univariate Procedure

Variable=AMOUNT


                           Frequency Table


                    Percents                        Percents
        Value  Count  Cell   Cum      Value  Count  Cell    Cum
            5    2    4.0    4.0         44    2    4.0   60.0
           10    3    6.0   10.0       44.5    1    2.0   62.0
         12.5    1    2.0   12.0         45    3    6.0   68.0
           15    2    4.0   16.0         47    1    2.0   70.0
           20    3    6.0   22.0       47.5    1    2.0   72.0
           26    1    2.0   24.0         48    1    2.0   74.0
           28    3    6.0   30.0         50    5   10.0   84.0
           30    1    2.0   32.0         56    1    2.0   86.0
         31.5    1    2.0   34.0         60    3    6.0   92.0
           33    2    4.0   38.0         64    1    2.0   94.0
           35    2    4.0   42.0         65    1    2.0   96.0
           38    1    2.0   44.0       72.5    1    2.0   98.0
         39.5    1    2.0   46.0        100    1    2.0  100.0
           40    5   10.0   56.0
```

The general form of the statements for producing frequency tables using PROC UNIVARIATE with the FREQ option is shown below:

PROC UNIVARIATE DATA=_data-set-name_ **FREQ** ;
  VAR _measurement-variables_ ;
  ID _id-variable_ ;

where items in italic are defined earlier in this chapter.

Frequency Tables with PROC FREQ

PROC FREQ provides another approach to get a frequency table. This second approach is especially useful for nominal and ordinal variables, where you may not want the descriptive statistics produced by PROC UNIVARIATE. For the speeding ticket data, type

```
proc freq data=tickets;
   tables amount;
      title 'Frequency Table for Speeding Ticket Data';
run;
```

These statements produce Output 4.4.

Output 4.4   PROC FREQ Results for Speeding Ticket Data

```
Frequency Table for Speeding Ticket Data                         1

                                     Cumulative   Cumulative
     AMOUNT   Frequency    Percent    Frequency     Percent

         5        2         4.0           2           4.0
        10        3         6.0           5          10.0
      12.5        1         2.0           6          12.0
        15        2         4.0           8          16.0
        20        3         6.0          11          22.0
        26        1         2.0          12          24.0
        28        3         6.0          15          30.0
        30        1         2.0          16          32.0
      31.5        1         2.0          17          34.0
        33        2         4.0          19          38.0
        35        2         4.0          21          42.0
        38        1         2.0          22          44.0
      39.5        1         2.0          23          46.0
        40        5        10.0          28          56.0
        44        2         4.0          30          60.0
      44.5        1         2.0          31          62.0
        45        3         6.0          34           8.0
        47        1         2.0          35          70.0
      47.5        1         2.0          36          72.0
        48        1         2.0          37          74.0
        50        5        10.0          42          84.0
        56        1         2.0          43          86.0
        60        3         6.0          46          92.0
        64        1         2.0          47          94.0
        65        1         2.0          48           6.0
      72.5        1         2.0          49          98.0
       100        1         2.0          50         100.0

                 Frequency Missing = 1
```

In Output 4.4, *Frequency* is the same as *Count* in PROC UNIVARIATE output and gives the number of observations for each value. *Cumulative Frequency* gives the cumulative frequency. For example, 6 observations have values of 12.5 or less, corresponding to the six states with speeding tickets of $12.50 or less. *Percent* is the same as *Cell* in PROC UNIVARIATE output and gives the percent of observations for each value. *Cumulative Percent* is the same as *Cum* in PROC UNIVARIATE output and gives the cumulative percent.

Notice that the PROC FREQ output gives you essentially the same information as the *Extremes* section, the *Missing Value* section, and the frequency table produced by the FREQ option in PROC UNIVARIATE output. The *Frequency Missing* shows the number of observations with missing values. The frequency counts can be used to find the extremes in the data set. For example, the 5 lowest values in the speeding ticket data are two values of 5 and three values of 10.

One advantage of frequency tables with PROC UNIVARIATE is that you can use the ID option and Extreme Values section of output to identify which states are associated with the highest and lowest values. This feature isn't available with frequency tables from PROC FREQ.

The general form of the statements for getting a frequency table using PROC FREQ is shown below:

> **PROC FREQ DATA=***data-set-name* ;
>   **TABLES** *variables*;
>
> where *data-set-name* is the name of a SAS data set, and *variables* is the name of one or more variables in the data set.

Several variables can be listed in the TABLES statement. PROC FREQ produces a frequency table for each variable. For the speeding ticket data, you already know there is only one observation for each state, so STATE is not listed in the TABLES statement; only AMOUNT is listed. PROC FREQ can be run without the TABLES statement; then it produces a frequency table for every variable in the data set. However, you should always use a TABLES statement.

> ## Releases before 6.12
>
> For SAS software releases before 6.12, PROC FREQ truncates char-
> acter values at 16 characters. If some values are identical for the
> first 16 characters and differ after the 16ᵗʰ character, the procedure,
> in prior releases, groups them together.
>
> Consider the following values for the variable NAME:
>
> Schwichtenberg Mary
>
> Schwichtenberg Michael
>
> Schwichtenberg Miguel
>
> Schwichtenberg Mona
>
> The values of NAME are identical for the first 16 characters.
> Release 6.12 will distinguish between these four values; previous
> releases will not.

Checking for Errors Using Frequency Tables

Because a frequency table lists all the values for a variable, it can be a
useful tool in looking for errors. Look at the values, and see if all the
values seem reasonable. If you know the possible values for a variable are
between 0 and 100 (scores on a test, for example) and the frequency table
contains values greater than 100, you know there are errors in the data.

This section discussed two ways to get a frequency table. For interval or
ratio variables measured on a discrete scale, use the FREQ option in
PROC UNIVARIATE. For nominal or ordinal variables, use PROC FREQ.
Frequency tables aren't used to summarize interval or ratio variables
measured on a continuous scale.

Bar Charts

The most frequently used graphic representation of the distribution of
values for a variable is the bar chart. Bar charts are very similar to histo-
grams. They can be used to summarize variables with all levels of
measurement. For nominal and ordinal variables, you usually want a bar
for each value of the variable. For interval or ratio variables, you usually
want to group values together. Sometimes interval or ratio variables are

measured on a discrete scale, and you may want a bar for each value of the variable.

For variables with character values, SAS software automatically produces a bar for each value. For nominal or ordinal variables with numeric values, you need to tell the software to produce a bar for each value. For continuous data, use the charts produced automatically, or customize the bar chart by listing the number of bars or by specifying which values to include in each bar. This section starts with the simplest bar chart produced automatically by SAS software and then presents options for customizing bar charts.

Vertical Bar Charts with PROC GCHART

In vertical bar charts, the horizontal axis shows the values of a variable, and the vertical axis shows the frequency counts for the variable. The bars rise vertically from the horizontal axis.

This section discusses using PROC GCHART, which requires that SAS/GRAPH software has been installed at your site. PROC GCHART generates a high-resolution graph, which can be displayed on all PCs and most terminals. Most printers can also print this type of graph. However, if you have a terminal or a printer that cannot display or print high-resolution graphs, you can use the CHART procedure to produce low-resolution graphs, as shown for one chart in this section.

To produce charts, two additional general statements are important: the GOPTIONS and PATTERN statements.

The GOPTIONS statement sets options for graphs. This is similar to how the OPTIONS statement sets options for regular, or text, output. The SAS statements shown for the plots in this chapter also show the GOPTIONS statements for the plots generated. Because some graphics options depend on the hardware, you may need to change the options shown. Typically, the only option specified is DEVICE=WIN, which identifies the graphics device as a monitor. If you do not use SAS in Display Manager mode, you will probably need to specify a different device.

The second important statement for charts is the PATTERN statement, which specifies the fill pattern for bars. The charts in this section specify a solid fill (v=solid) of color gray (color=gray). You may want different colors or patterns. The "Further Reading" section at the end of the chapter identifies the manuals that have more information.

To produce a vertical bar chart for the speeding ticket data, use the PROC GCHART statement and the VBAR statement. Type

```
goptions device=win;
pattern v=solid color=gray;
proc gchart data=tickets;
    vbar amount;
    title 'Default Bar Chart for Speeding Ticket Data';
run;
```

The resulting bar chart is shown in Output 4.5.

Output 4.5   **Vertical Bar Chart for Speeding Ticket Data**

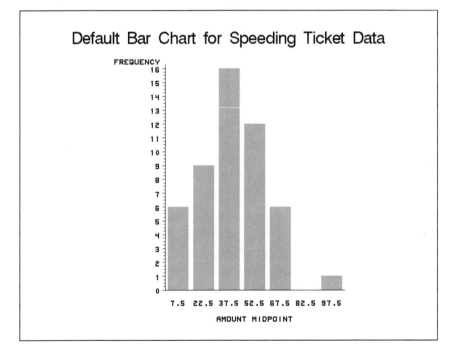

The vertical axis on the bar chart shows the *FREQUENCY*, which is the number of observations in each bar. The horizontal axis gives the *AMOUNT MIDPOINT* for each bar. In this example, PROC GCHART chose the number of bars and the midpoint for each bar. Rather than

labeling each bar with the range of values included, PROC GCHART labels the bar with the midpoint of the range of values. The following table shows the range of values for AMOUNT included in each bar and the number of values in each bar. You can check the frequencies by referring to Output 4.4.

Midpoint	Range of Values	Frequency
7.5	$0 \leq$ AMOUNT < 15	6
22.5	$15 \leq$ AMOUNT < 30	9
37.5	$30 \leq$ AMOUNT < 45	16
52.5	$45 \leq$ AMOUNT < 60	12
67.5	$60 \leq$ AMOUNT < 75	6
82.5	$75 \leq$ AMOUNT < 90	0
97.5	$90 \leq$ AMOUNT < 105	1

Notice that the last bar contains values less than 105. In reality, the maximum value in the data set is 100, so the maximum potential value contained in the last bar is 100.

The CHART procedure syntax is almost identical. This procedure does not require SAS/GRAPH and it prints on all printers. To produce a low-resolution vertical bar chart, type

```
proc chart data=tickets;
    vbar amount;
    title 'Default Bar Chart for Speeding Ticket Data';
run;
```

The resulting output is shown in Output 4.6. The rest of this book uses PROC GCHART for bar charts. You can substitute PROC CHART in all cases and generate a low-resolution bar chart instead.

Output 4.6   **PROC CHART Results for Speeding Ticket Data**

Default Bar Chart for Speeding Ticket Data

Customizing Vertical Bar Charts

The default chart produced by SAS software may not be what you want to use to summarize the data. For example, you may want to produce a chart with fewer bars. There are several options that allow you to customize a chart to meet your needs. Options in the VBAR statement allow you to specify the values to be included in each bar, specify the number of bars, and specify that a bar be produced for each value of the variable. The next three sections discuss these options.

The MIDPOINTS= Option

This option allows you to specify the values to be included in each bar on the chart. To do so, you specify the midpoint of each bar as in the following statements:

```
goptions device=win;
pattern v=solid color=gray;
proc gchart data=tickets;
    vbar amount / midpoints=10 30 50 70 90;
    title 'Bar Chart with MIDPOINTS= Option';
    title2 'Speeding Ticket Data';
run;
```

The chart produced is shown in Output 4.7.

Output 4.7 **Customizing with the MIDPOINTS= Option**

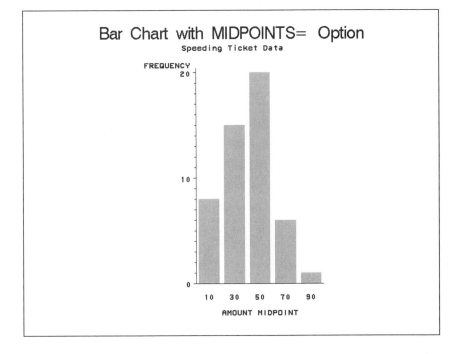

The first bar includes values of AMOUNT greater than or equal to 0 and less than 20 (0≤Value<20). This range of values has a midpoint of 10, which corresponds to your request in the MIDPOINTS= option. The second bar includes values greater than or equal to 20 and less than 40 (20≤Value<40). This range of values has a midpoint of 30, corresponding to your request in the MIDPOINTS= option.

The LEVELS= option

This option allows you to specify the number of bars on the chart. For the speeding ticket data, type

```
goptions device=win;
pattern v=solid color=gray;
proc gchart data=tickets;
    vbar amount / levels=5;
    title 'Bar Chart with LEVELS= Option';
run;
```

In the statements above, you specify 5 bars. The chart produced is shown in Output 4.8.

Output 4.8   **Customizing with the LEVELS= Option**

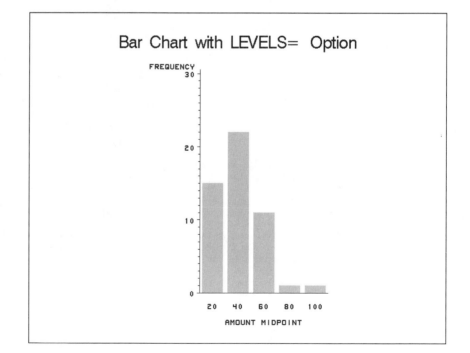

In Output 4.8, PROC GCHART picked the midpoints for the bars. You asked for 5 bars, and the midpoints picked for the 5 bars are 20, 40, 60, 80, and 100. The values in the first bar are between MIN (5) and 30. The values in the second bar are greater than or equal to 30 and less than 50 (30≤Value<50). When you use the LEVELS= option, PROC GCHART doesn't always choose intervals of equal length. In Output 4.8, the first bar contains values in a 25-dollar-wide interval, and the second bar contains values in a 20-dollar-wide interval.

To make sure that you understand this chart, you may want to examine the frequencies that are shown in the bar with the PROC FREQ output that is shown in Output 4.4. For example, Output 4.4 shows the cumulative frequency of 15 for an AMOUNT of 28. The next value of AMOUNT is 30, which wouldn't be included in the first bar in Output 4.8. Thus, the first bar of Output 4.8 should have a frequency of 15, which it does.

The DISCRETE option

The MIDPOINTS= and LEVELS= options are most useful in customizing a chart for continuous data. The DISCRETE option allows you to specify that a variable is numeric, and that it has a limited number of values. PROC GCHART produces a bar chart with a bar for each value. This type of chart is useful for a discrete variable, such as the number of times people wash their hair each week. You also want this type of chart for a nominal or ordinal variable with numeric values. For example, you may have used numbers as values for the types of cars people drive, and now, you want a separate bar to represent each type of car.

To use the DISCRETE option for the speeding ticket data, type

```
goptions device=win;
pattern v=solid color=gray;
proc gchart data=tickets;
    vbar amount / discrete;
    title 'Bar Chart with DISCRETE Option';

run;
```

The chart produced is shown in Output 4.9.

Output 4.9   **Customizing with the DISCRETE Option**

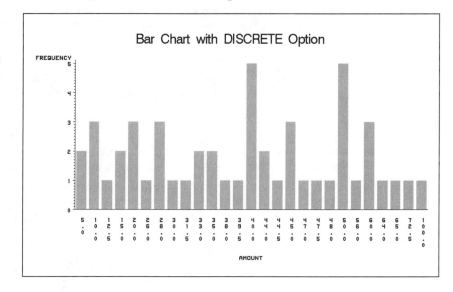

Compare the bar chart in Output 4.9 with the frequency table produced by PROC UNIVARIATE or PROC FREQ. Notice how each distinct numeric value in the data set is represented by a bar in the chart above. Notice also how this chart shows the two modes at 40 and 50. Finally, notice how values are not proportionally spaced on the horizontal line. For example, the bars for 72.5 and 100 are as close together as the bars for 10.0 and 12.5.

Summarizing Vertical Bar Charts

The general form of the statements for producing a vertical bar chart is shown below:

PROC GCHART DATA=*data-set-name* ;
 VBAR *variables* / *option* ;

where

data-set-name   is the name of a SAS data set

variables   is the name of one or more variables in the data set. A vertical bar chart is produced for each variable named in the VBAR statement.

/   separates the names of the variables and the option. If no options are specified, omit the slash.

option   specifies an option that customizes a bar chart. *option* is either omitted or is one of the three options MIDPOINTS=, LEVELS=, or DISCRETE. The form for each option is shown below:

MIDPOINTS=*list-of-numbers*
where *list-of-numbers* gives the midpoints for the bars. This option produces a bar chart with the specified midpoints.

LEVELS=*number*
where *number* gives the number of bars in the chart. This option produces a bar chart with the specified number of bars.

DISCRETE
produces a bar for each variable value. Use this option with discrete numeric variables or with nominal or ordinal variables with numeric values.

The VBAR statement is required, but only one of the options listed above can be used in a given VBAR statement.

Additional options allow you to customize charts even more. See the "Further Reading" section at the end of this chapter for references about PROC GCHART.

Horizontal Bar Charts with PROC GCHART

You may want to summarize data using a horizontal bar chart instead of a vertical bar chart. PROC GCHART also produces horizontal bar charts. Instead of a VBAR statement, you use an HBAR statement. For the speeding ticket data, type

```
goptions device=win;
pattern v=solid color=gray;
proc gchart data=tickets;
    hbar amount;
    title 'Horizontal Bar Chart';
run;
```

These statements produce Output 4.10.

Output 4.10   Horizontal Bar Chart from PROC GCHART

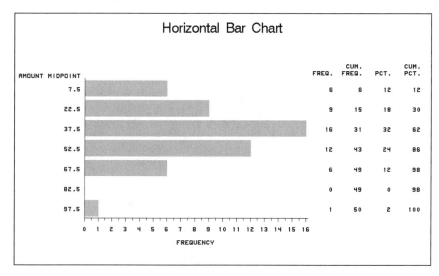

Notice that PROC GCHART chose the same midpoints as those chosen for the first vertical bar chart you produced (see Output 4.5). Note also that you can produce a low-resolution horizontal bar chart with the HBAR statement in PROC CHART.

Customizing Horizontal Bar Charts

The MIDPOINTS=, LEVELS=, and DISCRETE options that can be used with the VBAR statement can also be used with the HBAR statement. You may want to use the options to produce customized horizontal bar charts for the speeding ticket data. Remember that you must use the options one at a time: don't specify more than one of these three options for a given chart.

The NOSTAT Option

In addition to the horizontal bar chart, Output 4.10 shows the frequency, cumulative frequency, percent, and cumulative percent for the values in each bar. To suppress this statistical summary, use the NOSTAT option. Type

```
goptions device=win;
pattern v=solid color=gray;
proc gchart data=tickets;
    hbar amount / nostat;
run;
```

When you use the NOSTAT option, the scale for frequencies may be expanded. Since the summary has been omitted, there is more room on the page for the horizontal bar chart. The resulting chart is shown in Output 4.11.

Output 4.11   **Customizing with the NOSTAT Option**

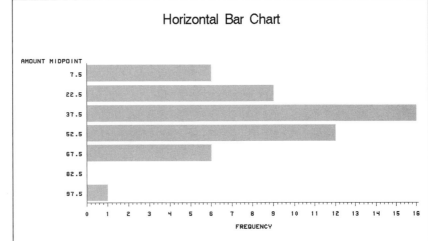

The DESCENDING and the SUMVAR= Options

The DESCENDING option orders the bars on the chart from the maximum to minimum value and is useful in customizing a chart for numeric or character data. The SUMVAR= option identifies a second variable, so that the length of the bars represents the sum of this second variable instead of the frequency counts for the first variable. Using these two options together produces an ordered chart for a categorical variable, where the lengths of the bars give information on a numeric variable. For example, in the speeding ticket data, each state (a categorical variable) is associated with a numeric variable (the speeding ticket amount). To produce a chart that shows the speeding ticket amount for each state, use the DESCENDING and SUMVAR= options together. Type

```
goptions device=win;
pattern v=solid color=gray;
proc gchart data=tickets;
    hbar state / nostat descending sumvar=amount;
run;
```

The resulting output is shown in Output 4.12.

Output 4.12   **Customizing with Several Options**

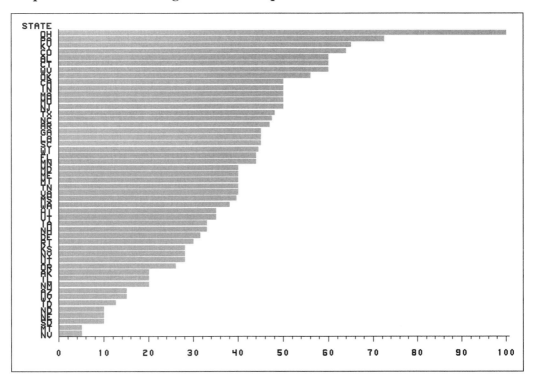

Notice an important difference between this bar chart and previous
bar charts: the variable STATE is identified as the variable to summarize.
Without the SUMVAR= option, PROC GCHART would produce a
frequency bar chart, which would have a bar with a length of 1 for each
state. With SUMVAR=AMOUNT, the bars for each state have a length that
corresponds to the amount of the speeding ticket for that state. Without
the DESCENDING option, the bars on the chart would be ordered by
STATE. While this chart might make it easier to find a particular state,
it is not as useful when trying to compare the speeding ticket amounts
for different states.

The "Advanced Topics" section in Chapter 3 discusses using formats for variable values. If the format $NAME. is assigned to the variable STATE in a data set, the plot created with the preceding statements automatically uses the format. The resulting plot appears in Output 4.13.

Output 4.13   Customized Chart Using Formats

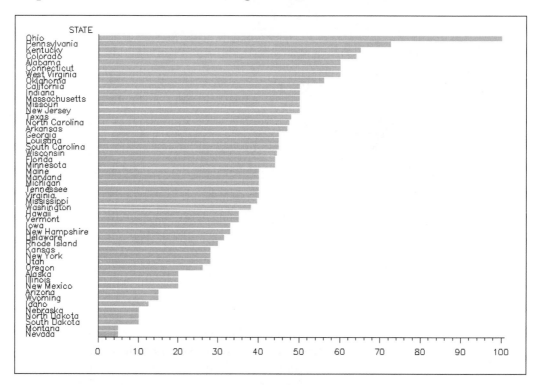

Summarizing Horizontal Bar Charts

The general form of the statements for producing a horizontal bar chart is shown below:

PROC GCHART DATA=*data-set-name* ;
  HBAR *variables* / *option* ;

where

data-set-name   is the name of a SAS data set

variables   is the name of one or more variables in the data set. A horizontal bar chart is produced for each variable named in the HBAR statement.

/   separates the names of the variables and the option. If no options are specified, omit the slash.

option   specifies an option that customizes a bar chart. *option* is either omitted; is one of the three options **MIDPOINTS=**, **LEVELS=**, or **DISCRETE,** discussed for vertical bar charts earlier; or, *option* is one or more of: **NOSTAT**, **DESCENDING,** and **SUMVAR=**, discussed below. The form for the other three options is shown in "Summarizing Vertical Bar Charts" earlier in this chapter.

NOSTAT
suppresses summary statistics for a horizontal bar chart.

DESCENDING
produces a chart with the values ordered from maximum to minimum.

SUMVAR=*sum-variable*
produces a chart with bar lengths corresponding to the values of the *sum-variable* for each *variable* listed in the HBAR statement. Used with the DESCENDING option, the chart is ordered from maximum to minimum values for the *sum-variable.*

The HBAR statement is required. The MIDPOINTS=, LEVELS=, and DISCRETE options cannot be used in combination with one another. The NOSTAT option can be used in combination with the other options.

This section showed how to produce vertical and horizontal bar charts using PROC GCHART. Depending on your choice of options, you can produce either the default charts or customized charts. Additional options are available for both kinds of charts. See the "Further Reading" section at the end of this chapter for references.

Exploratory Data Analysis: Simple Plots

Exploratory Data Analysis (EDA) techniques available in SAS software are box plots and stem-and-leaf plots. As with descriptive statistics, these EDA plots are appropriate for interval and ratio variables. (Note that SAS/QC and SAS/INSIGHT software contain several EDA techniques. See "Using SAS/INSIGHT Features" later in this chapter; for SAS/QC reference, see "Further Reading" at the end of this chapter.)

EDA plots are obtained by using the PLOT option in PROC UNIVARIATE. For the speeding ticket data, type

```
proc univariate data=tickets plot;
    var amount;
    title 'Summary of Speeding Ticket Data';
run;
```

The first part of your output should be identical to the output shown in Output 4.1. The second part of your output should look similar to that in Output 4.14. Your output should show three plots, labeled as *Stem Leaf*, *Boxplot*, and *Normal Probability Plot*. The normal probability plot is discussed in Chapter 5 and was omitted from Output 4.14. The other two plots are covered in the next two sections.

Output 4.14   EDA Plots from PROC UNIVARIATE

```
Variable=AMOUNT

            Stem Leaf                    #            Boxplot
             10 0                        1               0
              9
              9
              8
              8
              7
              7 2                        1               |
              6 5                        1               |
              6 0004                     4               |
              5 6                        1               |
              5 00000                    5           +-----+
              4 555788                   6           |     |
              4 000000444                9           *-----*
              3 558                      3           |  +  |
              3 0233                     4           |     |
              2 6888                     4           +-----+
              2 000                      3               |
              1 55                       2               |
              1 0002                     4               |
              0 55                       2               |
                ----+----+----+----+
              Multiply Stem.Leaf by 10**+1
```

Unlike the bar charts previously discussed, you cannot control the appearance of the EDA plots produced by PROC UNIVARIATE.

Stem-and-Leaf Plots

Look at the stem-and-leaf plot, labeled as *Stem Leaf* on the output. The stem-and-leaf plot is similar to a horizontal bar chart in that both show a plot of distribution of data values. However, the stem-and-leaf plot also shows the value of the variable for each observation.

Finding the Values of a Variable

Notice the instructions at the bottom of the plot: *Multiply Stem.Leaf by 10**+1*. These instructions vary from plot to plot depending on your data, but instructions always appear, with one exception. If you need to multiply *Stem.Leaf* by 1, no instructions appear. You can use these instructions to calculate the values of the variable.

For the speeding ticket data, look at the lowest stem. Take 0.5 (*Stem.Leaf*) and multiply it by $10^{**}{+}1$ (= 10^1 = 10) to get 5 (0.5×10=5). As another example, take the *Stem.Leaf* of 4.8. Calculate 4.8×10=48 to get the AMOUNT value of 48.

Now suppose the instructions were: *Multiply Stem.Leaf by $10^{**}{+}2$*. Then, figure out that $10^{**}{+}2$ = 10^2 = 100. Using a *Stem.Leaf* of 4.8, calculate 4.8×100=480 to get the value of 480. If no instructions appeared on this plot, the values in the plot would be 0.5, 0.5, 1.0, and so on.

In general, follow the instructions at the bottom of the stem-and-leaf plot to figure out the values of the variable. Sometimes PROC UNIVARIATE rounds the values. This happens if a variable has many digits. If your data set contains a variable PRICE with selling prices of homes as values, and the range of values is between 50,000 and 150,000, the value of 89,950 would be rounded to 90,000 in the stem-and-leaf plot. For the speeding ticket data, PROC UNIVARIATE has rounded some values. As an example, the value of 47.50 has been rounded to 48 in the stem-and-leaf plot.

Using a Stem-and-Leaf Plot
PROC UNIVARIATE usually groups the data so that about 20 stems are produced. The stem-and-leaf plot shows the distribution of values and points out unusual values in the data.

For the speeding ticket data, the lowest stem is for the values from 5 to 9, the second is for the values from 10 to 14, the third is for the values from 15 to 19, and so on. The plot is roughly mound-shaped if you look at it sideways. The highest part of the mound is in the 40s. Recall that the modes are 40 and 50, and notice that there are more values of 40 and 50 in the data than of any other values. Notice also that the value of 39.5 has been rounded to 40 in the stem-and-leaf plot.

The plot also shows a slight skewness, or sidedness. Notice that the values at the higher end of the scale (near 100) are more spread out than the values at the lower end (near 0). The data are slightly skewed to the right—in the direction where more values trail out to the end of the distribution of sample values. You also saw this slight skewness in the skewness value of 0.447 in Output 4.1. The plot shows one unusual value of 100. Notice how much farther away this value is from the rest of the data. This extremely high value causes the positive kurtosis of 1.13. The right tail of the distribution of values is "heavy."

Between the stem-and-leaf plot and the box plot is a column labeled with a pound sign, #. This column gives the frequency of observations in each bar in the stem-and-leaf plot. For example, there are 2 observations in the "5 to 9" bar for the speeding ticket data.

If you have more than 48 observations in a single bar, PROC UNIVARIATE produces a horizontal bar chart instead of a stem-and-leaf plot. This generally occurs with large data sets and continuous variables.

Box Plots

Now look at the box plot, labeled as *Boxplot* on the output. The upper and lower ends of the box indicate the 25th percentile and the 75th percentile (using the scale on the stem-and-leaf plot). The line inside the box (with an asterisk at each end) indicates the median (the 50th percentile). The length of the box is one interquartile range. Remember the interquartile range is the difference between the 75th and the 25th percentiles. The plus sign (+) indicates the mean, which may be the same as the median but usually is not. If the median and the mean are close to each other, the plus sign (+) falls on the line inside the box. The central vertical lines are called *whiskers*. Each whisker extends up to 1.5 interquartile ranges from the end of the box. Values outside the whiskers are marked with a 0 or an asterisk (*). A 0 is used if the value is between 1.5 and 3 interquartile ranges of the box, and an asterisk (*) is used if the value is farther away. Values that are far away from the rest of the data are called *outliers*.

The box plot for the speeding ticket data shows all but one of the values inside the whiskers. There is one outlier shown by the 0 corresponding to the value of 100. The mean and the median are not equal but are fairly close together. Notice that the line for the median is not exactly in the middle of the box. This indicates a small amount of skewness or sidedness, to the data values. (You also saw this slight skewness from looking at the stem-and-leaf plot.)

Summarizing EDA Plots

The general form of the statements to produce EDA plots in PROC
UNIVARIATE is shown below:

> **PROC UNIVARIATE DATA=***data-set-name* **PLOT**;
>   **VAR** *measurement-variables*;
>
> Items in italic are defined earlier in this chapter. A summary
> and EDA plots are produced for each variable in the list.

While the VAR statement is not required, you should use it. Otherwise,
PROC UNIVARIATE produces a summary and EDA plots for every numeric
variable in the data set.

The PLOT and FREQ options in PROC UNIVARIATE can be used at the
same time. For example, you can type

```
proc univariate data=tickets freq plot;
    var amount;
    title 'Summary of Speeding Ticket Data';
run;
```

The output from the statements above is the same as that shown in
Output 4.1, Output 4.3, and Output 4.14.

Using SAS/INSIGHT Software

SAS/INSIGHT provides an interactive graphics and statistics tool that
can perform all of the analyses in this book. The last section in most
chapters shows how to reproduce the analyses in the chapter by using
SAS/INSIGHT software. The explanations of results, however, are not
repeated.

Basic Concepts

One basic concept for SAS/INSIGHT software is the *data window*. This
window displays the active SAS data set, which is available for summarizing,
graphing, or analyzing. You can hide this window, which can be helpful if
you want to avoid having many windows display at the same time on your
monitor screen.

Another basic concept involves the *graph windows* and *analysis windows*. Depending on the analysis, the results tables and graphs may appear in multiple windows or in the same window.

A final concept is the *tools palettes*. Because of its interactive nature, you can dynamically change the colors, symbols, and so on in graphs by making choices in the tools palettes.

Starting SAS/INSIGHT Software

To start SAS/INSIGHT software, you can

- select `Globals` on the menu bar and then select `Interactive data analysis`

- type INSIGHT on a command line

- submit a PROC INSIGHT statement, with additional statements as needed.

This book uses the third choice, because that provides a way for you to replicate the analyses shown in the example data. In addition, the book briefly summarizes the choices in the interactive windows that will produce the same analyses. The "Further Reading" section at the end of this chapter provides information about the SAS/INSIGHT manuals, which discuss interactive use in detail.

Summarizing the Speeding Ticket Data

This chapter summarized the tickets data with descriptive statistics, a frequency table, a bar charts, and a box plot. The following statements generate everything except the frequency table:

```
proc insight data=tickets;
   dist amount;
run;
```

Output 4.15 shows a portion of the data window.

Output 4.15   **SAS/INSIGHT Data Window**

Both variables are shown, but only some of the observations appear. To see the rest of the observations, scroll down in the window. The window identifies that the data set has 51 observations and 2 variables; see the left corner of the window. Also, STATE is automatically assigned to be a nominal variable. This is indicated by "Nom" in the heading for STATE. Similarly, AMOUNT is automatically assigned to be an interval variable as indicated by "Int" in the heading.

The graphs are shown in Output 4.16.

Output 4.16   **SAS/INSIGHT Graphs**

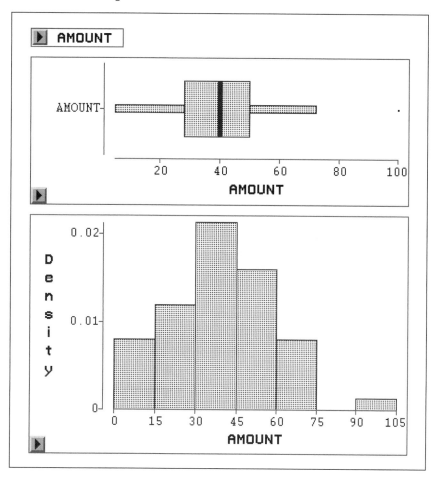

The boxplot in SAS/INSIGHT displays horizontally, rather than vertically as in PROC UNIVARIATE. Also, SAS/INSIGHT displays a special form of the bar chart called a histogram. The X-axis scale differs from that for the bar charts in PROC GCHART. Also, the Y-axis does not measure frequencies directly. For more detail, see the references for SAS/INSIGHT in the "Further Reading" section at the end of the chapter.

The descriptive statistics are displayed below the graphs in the Distribution window and are shown in Output 4.17.

Output 4.17   **SAS/INSIGHT Descriptive Statistics**

Moments			
N	50.0000	Sum Wgts	50.0000
Mean	38.5000	Sum	1925.0000
Std Dev	18.7932	Variance	353.1837
Skewness	0.4468	Kurtosis	1.1337
USS	91418.5000	CSS	17306.0000
CV	48.8135	Std Mean	2.6578

Quantiles			
100% Max	100.0000	99.0%	100.0000
75% Q3	50.0000	97.5%	72.5000
50% Med	40.0000	95.0%	65.0000
25% Q1	28.0000	90.0%	60.0000
0% Min	5.0000	10.0%	11.2500
Range	95.0000	5.0%	10.0000
Q3-Q1	22.0000	2.5%	5.0000
Mode	40.0000	1.0%	5.0000

These results match those from PROC UNIVARIATE, discussed earlier.

To produce the frequency table, select Tables on the menu bar (the set of words that appears across the top of the window). From the pull-down menu, select Frequency Table. This generates the frequency table, which appears below the Quantiles table, as shown in Output 4.18.

Output 4.18   SAS/INSIGHT Frequency Table

Frequency Table			
Value	Count	Cell Percent	Cum Percent
5.0000	2	4.0	4.0
10.0000	3	6.0	10.0
12.5000	1	2.0	12.0
15.0000	2	4.0	16.0
20.0000	3	6.0	22.0
26.0000	1	2.0	24.0
28.0000	3	6.0	30.0
30.0000	1	2.0	32.0
31.5000	1	2.0	34.0
33.0000	2	4.0	38.0
35.0000	2	4.0	42.0
38.0000	1	2.0	44.0
39.5000	1	2.0	46.0
40.0000	5	10.0	56.0
44.0000	2	4.0	60.0
44.5000	1	2.0	62.0
45.0000	3	6.0	68.0
47.0000	1	2.0	70.0
47.5000	1	2.0	72.0
48.0000	1	2.0	74.0
50.0000	5	10.0	84.0
56.0000	1	2.0	86.0
60.0000	3	6.0	92.0
64.0000	1	2.0	94.0
65.0000	1	2.0	96.0
72.5000	1	2.0	98.0
100.0000	1	2.0	100.0

These results match those shown earlier for PROC FREQ.

An important feature of SAS/INSIGHT software is that when you select a point in any plot, it is automatically selected in all windows. For example, if you select the outlier (100) in the bar chart, the corresponding row is highlighted in the data window, as is the outlier in the box plot. This can be very useful both for summarizing data and for examining data for errors.

The general form of the statements to use SAS/INSIGHT to summarize data is shown below.

> **PROC INSIGHT DATA=***data-set-name* ;
>   **DIST** *variables* ;
>
> where *data-set-name* is the name of a SAS data set, and *variables* is the name of one or more variables in the data set. You can put more than one variable name in a DIST statement. However, for valid normal plots, use only interval or ratio variables.

Summaries

Key Ideas

- The four levels of measurement for variables are nominal, ordinal, interval, and ratio. The choice of an appropriate analysis for a variable often is based on the level of measurement for the variable.

- The table below gives the SAS procedure for a specific level of measurement and method of summarizing data. If the method is inappropriate for the level of measurement, no procedure is listed.

	SAS Procedures for Summarizing Data			
Level of Measurement	**Descriptive Statistics**	**Frequency Tables**	**Bar Charts**	**EDA Plots**
Nominal		FREQ	GCHART or CHART	
Ordinal	UNIVARIATE or MEANS	FREQ	GCHART or CHART	
Interval and Ratio	UNIVARIATE or MEANS	FREQ or UNIVARIATE	GCHART or CHART	UNIVARIATE or INSIGHT

Notes:

1. Use PROC MEANS for a brief summary, or use PROC UNIVARIATE for a complete summary.

2. For interval and ratio variables, use PROC FREQ when you need only a frequency table. Use PROC UNIVARIATE with the FREQ option when you want both descriptive statistics and a frequency table.

3. You can use several options in PROC GCHART to customize charts. For low-resolution charts, the same statements and options are available with PROC CHART.

4. You can use PROC INSIGHT in SAS/INSIGHT software to produce all of the summary information provided by the other procedures.

Syntax

A summary for all of the SAS procedures discussed in this chapter is given below:

• For a brief summary containing descriptive statistics,

> **PROC MEANS DATA**=*data-set-name* ;
>   **VAR** *measurement-variables* ;

where *data-set-name* is the name of a data set and *measurement-variables* are the variables that you want to summarize.

• For an extensive summary containing descriptive statistics, a frequency table, and EDA plots,

> **PROC UNIVARIATE DATA**=*data-set-name* **FREQ PLOT;**
>   **VAR** *measurement-variables* ;
>   **ID** *id-variables* ;

The first two items in italic are as defined earlier. *id-variable* is the variable to identify the highest and lowest values in the output. To suppress the frequency table, omit the FREQ option; to suppress EDA plots, omit the PLOT option.

• To produce a frequency table,

> **PROC FREQ DATA**=*data-set-name* ;
>   **TABLES** *variables* ;

The first item in italic is defined earlier. *variables* are the variables that you want to include in the table.

- For vertical bar charts,

    PROC GCHART DATA=*data-set-name* ;
        VBAR *variables / option*;

    The first two items in italic are as defined earlier. *option* is either omitted or is one of the following:

    MIDPOINTS=*list-of-numbers*
    for a chart with bar midpoints as specified in the list of numbers.

    LEVELS=*number*
    for a chart with a specified number of bars.

    DISCRETE
    for a chart with a bar for every value of the variable.

- For horizontal bar charts,

    PROC GCHART DATA=*data-set-name* ;
        HBAR *variables / options*;

    where *data-set-name* and *variables* are as defined earlier. *options* is either omitted or is one or more of the following:

    MIDPOINTS=, LEVELS=, or DISCRETE
    as defined for vertical bar charts earlier. Only one of these three options can be used at one time.

    NOSTAT
    to suppress summary statistics on the chart. **NOSTAT** can be used in combination with other options.

    DESCENDING
    to produce a chart with the values ordered from maximum to minimum.

    SUMVAR=*sum-variable*
    to produce a chart with bar lengths that correspond to the values of the *sum-variable* for each variable that is listed in the HBAR statement. Used with the option DESCENDING, the chart is ordered from maximum to minimum values for the *sum-variable*.

- For EDA plots and descriptive statistics using SAS/INSIGHT,

    PROC INSIGHT DATA=*data-set-name* ;
        DIST *measurement-variables* ;

    where items in italic are as defined earlier.

Example

The following statements produce all output shown in this chapter:

```
data tickets;
   input state $ amount @@;
   datalines;
AL 60 HI 35 DE 31.50 IL 20 AK 20 CT 60 AR 47
IA 33 FL 44 KS 28 AZ 15 IN 50 CA 50 LA 45 GA 45
MT 5 ID 12.50 KY 65 CO 64 ME 40 NE 10 MA 50
MD 40 NV 5 MO 50 MI 40 NM 20 NJ 50 MN 44 NY 28
NC 47.50 MS 39.50 ND 10 OH 100 NH 33 OR 26 OK 56
SC 45 RI 30 PA 72.50 TN 40 SD 10 TX 48 VT 35 UT 28
WV 60 VA 40 WY 15 WA 38 WI 44.5 DC .
;

proc means data=tickets;
   var amount;
   title 'Brief Summary of Speeding Ticket Data';
run;

proc univariate data=tickets freq plot;
   var amount;
   id state;
title 'Summary of Speeding Ticket Data';
run;

proc freq data=tickets;
   tables amount;
   title 'Frequency Table for Speeding Ticket Data';
run;

goptions device=win;
pattern v=solid color=gray;
proc gchart data=tickets;
   vbar amount;
   title 'Default Bar Chart for Speeding Ticket Data';
run;

proc chart data=tickets;
   vbar amount;
   title 'Default Bar Chart for Speeding Ticket Data';
run;
```

```
goptions device=win;
pattern v=solid color=gray;
proc gchart data=tickets;
    vbar amount / midpoints=10 30 50 70 90;
    title 'Bar Chart with MIDPOINTS= Option';
    title2 'Speeding Ticket Data';
run;

goptions device=win;
pattern v=solid color=gray;
proc gchart data=tickets;
    vbar amount / levels=5;
    title 'Bar Chart with LEVELS= Option';
run;

goptions device=win;
pattern v=solid color=gray;
proc gchart data=tickets;
    vbar amount / discrete;
    title 'Bar Chart with DISCRETE Option';
run;

goptions device=win;
pattern v=solid color=gray;
proc gchart data=tickets;
    hbar amount;
    title 'Horizontal Bar Chart';
    run;

goptions device=win;
pattern v=solid color=gray;
proc gchart data=tickets;
    hbar amount / nostat;
    title 'Horizontal Bar Chart';
    run;

goptions device=win;
pattern v=solid color=gray;
proc gchart data=tickets;
    hbar state / nostat descending sumvar=amount;
    title 'Horizontal Bar Chart';
    run;

proc insight data=tickets;
    dist amount;
run;
```

Further Reading

For more information about how to produce effective charts and for discussions of EDA plots, see the following:

- Cleveland, W. S. (1985), *The Elements of Graphing Data*, Monterey, CA: Wadsworth.

- Hartwig, F. and Dearing, B.E. (1979), " Exploratory Data Analysis," Sage *University Paper Series on Quantitative Applications in the Social Sciences*, 07 016. Beverly Hills: Sage Publications.

- Schmid, C. F. (1983), *Statistical Graphics*, New York: John Wiley & Sons, Inc.

- Tufte, E.R. (1983), *The Visual Display of Quantitative Information*, Cheshire, CT: Graphics Press.

- Tufte, E.R. (1990), *Envisioning Information*, Cheshire, CT: Graphics Press.

- Tufte, E.R. (1996), *Visual Explanations*, Cheshire, CT: Graphics Press.

- Tukey, J.W. (1977), *Exploratory Data Analysis*, Reading, MA: Addison-Wesley.

- Velleman, P.F. and Hoaglin, D.C. (1981), *Applications, Basics, and Computing of Exploratory Data Analysis*, North Scituate, MA: Duxbury Press.

For a nontechnical discussion of how statistics can be used incorrectly, see the following:

- Gonick, L. and Smith, W. (1993), *The Cartoon Guide to Statistics*, New York: Harper Collins Publishers, Inc.

- Hooke, R. (1983), *How to Tell the Liars from the Statisticians*, New York: Marcel Dekker Inc.

- Huff, D. *How to Lie with Statistics*, New York: Norton.

- Jaffe, A.J. and Spirer, H.F. (1987), *Misused Statistics*, New York: Marcel Dekker, Inc.

For more information about the procedures that are presented in this chapter, see the following:

- *SAS/INSIGHT® Users' Guide, Version 6, Third Edition* gives details about the software.

- *SAS/GRAPH® Software: Reference, Version 6, First Edition, Volumes 1 and 2* give details about the software.

- *SAS/GRAPH® Software: Syntax, Version 6, First Edition* summarizes syntax for GOPTIONS and PATTERN statements and the GCHART procedure.

- *SAS/GRAPH® Software: Examples, Version 6, First Edition* provides how-to examples for several types of charts and plots.

- *SAS® Language and Procedures: Introduction, Version 6, First Edition* gives an introduction to the CHART, FREQ, and MEANS procedures in Chapters 9, 10, and 11, respectively.

- *SAS® Language and Procedures: Syntax, Version 6, First Edition* gives a syntax summary of procedures in Chapter 10.

- *SAS® Procedures Guide, Version 6, Third Edition* discusses the CHART, FREQ, MEANS, and UNIVARIATE procedures in Chapters 9, 20, 21 and 42, respectively. The chapter on PROC UNIVARIATE discusses the different ways that SAS defines percentiles.

- *SAS/QC® Software: Usage and Reference, Version 6, First Edition, Volumes 1 and 2* give details about the EDA plots that are provided by the software.

- *The Little SAS® Book: A Primer* discusses the MEANS and FREQ procedures in Chapter 5.

Although there may also be technical reports with updated information for various releases, the best source of the most recent information is the online help and online documentation. These are most appropriate in display manager mode.

Part 2 **Statistical Background**

Chapter 5 **Understanding Some Basic Statistical Concepts**

The focus of this chapter is more on statistical concepts than on using SAS software. The major analysis tool discussed is testing for normality. This chapter also discusses hypothesis testing, which is the foundation of many statistical analyses. The major topics are

- understanding populations and samples
- understanding the normal distribution
- defining parametric and nonparametric statistical methods
- testing for normality
- building hypothesis tests
- understanding statistical and practical significance.

Testing for normality is appropriate for interval and ratio variables. However, the general concepts presented in this chapter apply to all types of variables.

Contents

Populations and Samples

Definitions

A *population* is a collection of values that has one value for every member in the group of interest. For example, Chapters 3 and 4 use a data set that contains speeding ticket amounts in the United States. If you consider only the 50 states (and ignore the District of Columbia), you have the speeding ticket amounts for the entire group of 50 states. You have a collection of values that contains one value for every member in the group of interest (the 50 states), so you have the entire population of speeding ticket amounts.

This definition of a population as a collection of values may be different from the one you are more familiar with. That is, you may think of a population as a group of people, as in "the population of Detroit." In statistics, think of a population as a collection of measurements on people or things.

A *sample* is also a collection of values, but it does not represent the entire group of interest. For the speeding ticket data, a sample could be the collection of values for speeding ticket amounts for the states located in the Southeast U.S. Notice how this sample differs from the population. Both are collections of values, but the population represents the entire set of interest (all 50 states), and the sample represents only a subgroup (states located in the Southeast U.S.).

Consider another example. Suppose you are interested in estimating the average price of new homes sold in the U.S. during 1996, and you have the prices for a few homes in several cities. You have only a sample of the values. To have the entire population of values, you would need the price for every new home sold in the U.S. in 1996.

Figure 5.1 shows the relationship between a population and a sample.

Figure 5.1   **Relationship between a Population and a Sample**

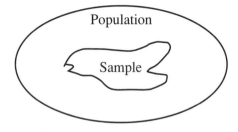

For a final example, think about opinion polls. You often see the results of these polls published in newspapers and magazines, yet most people have never been asked to participate in one of these polls. Rather than ask every person in the country (collect a population of values for the group of interest), the companies that conduct these polls ask a small number of people. They collect a sample of values for the group of interest.

Random Samples

Most of the time you can't collect the entire population of values. Instead, you collect a sample. To make a valid decision about the population based on a sample, the sample must be representative of the population. This is usually done by collecting a random sample.

A sample is a *simple random sample* if the process used in collecting the sample ensures that any one sample is as likely to be selected as any other sample. For example, the companies that conduct opinion polls often collect random samples. Any group of people (and their associated sample values) is as likely to be selected as any other group of people. In contrast, the collection of speeding ticket amounts for states located in the Southeast U.S. is not a random sample from the population of speeding ticket amounts for all of the 50 states. This is because the Southeastern states were deliberately chosen to be in the sample.

In many cases, the process of collecting a random sample is complicated and requires the help of a qualified statistician. Simple random samples are only one type of sampling scheme. In many cases, other sampling schemes are preferable. Suppose you conduct a survey to find out the students' opinions of their professors. At first, you decide to randomly sample students on campus, but then you realize that seniors may have different opinions from freshmen, sophomores from juniors, and so on. Seniors have developed opinions about what they expect in professors, and freshmen haven't yet had the chance to do that. With a simple random sample, your results could be affected by the differences between students in the different classes. Thus, you decide to group students according to class and get a random sample from each class (seniors, juniors, sophomores, and freshmen). This *stratified random sampling* gives you a better idea about the students' opinions and tells you about the differences in opinions for different classes. Before you conduct a survey, you should consult a statistician to develop the best sampling scheme for your survey.

Describing Parameters and Statistics

Another difference between populations and samples is the way you refer to summary measures that are calculated for each. Summary measures for a population are called *parameters*; summary measures for a sample are called *statistics*. As an example, suppose you calculate the average for a set of data. If the data set is a population of values, the average is a parameter, which we call the *population mean*. However, if the data set is a sample of values, the average is a statistic, which we call the *sample average* (or the *average* for short). The rest of this book uses "mean" to indicate the population mean and "average" to indicate the sample average.

To help distinguish between summary measures for populations and samples, different statistical notation is used. In general, population parameters are denoted by letters of the Greek alphabet. For now, consider only three summary measures: the mean, the variance, and the standard deviation. Recall that the mean is a measure that describes the center of a distribution of values, the variance is a measure that describes the dispersion of values around the mean, and the standard deviation is the square root of the variance. The average of a sample is denoted as $\overline{X}$ and is called x bar. The population mean is denoted as μ and is called mu. The sample variance is denoted as s^2 and is called s-squared. The population variance is denoted as σ^2 and is called sigma-squared. Because the standard deviation is the square root of the variance, it is denoted as s for a sample and σ for a population. These differences in notation are shown in Table 5.1.

Table 5.1   **Symbols Used for Populations and Samples**

	Average	**Variance**	**Standard Deviation**
Population	μ	σ^2	σ
Sample	$\overline{X}$	s^2	s

In the case of the average, the same formula applies to calculations for the population parameter and the sample statistic. This is not necessarily the case for other summary measures. An important example is the sample variance and the population variance. Some authors use different formulas for the sample variance and the population variance. SAS procedures automatically calculate the sample variance, not the population variance. Because you almost never have measurements on the whole population, SAS software gives summary statistics, such as the variance, that are appropriate for a sample.

Technical Details

To calculate the sample variance for a variable:

1. Find the average.

2. For each observation, calculate the difference between the observation and the average.

3. Square these differences.

4. Sum the squares.

5. Divide by n -1, where n is the number of differences.

For example, suppose your sample values are 10, 11, 12, and 15. The sample size is 4, and the average is 12. The variance is calculated as

$$s^2 = \frac{(10-12)^2 + (11-12)^2 + (12-12)^2 + (15-12)^2}{4-1}$$

$$= 14/3 = 4.67$$

More generally, the formula is:

$$s^2 = \frac{\sum (X_i - \overline{X})^2}{(n-1)}$$

where Σ stands for sum, X_i represents each sample value, $\overline{X}$ represents the sample average, and n represents the sample size.

The difference between computing the sample variance and the population variance is in the denominator of the formula above. The population variance uses n instead of n-1.

The Normal Distribution

Definition and Properties

Many methods of statistical analysis assume the data is a sample from a population with a normal distribution. The *normal distribution* is a theoretical distribution of values for a population. This distribution has a precise mathematical definition. Rather than give this complex defini-

tion, this book describes some of the properties and characteristics of
the normal distribution.

Figure 5.2 shows several normal distributions. Notice that μ (the population mean) and σ (the standard deviation of the population) are different. The two graphs with μ=100 have the same scaling on both axes as
do the three graphs with μ=30.

Figure 5.2   **Graphs of Several Normal Distributions**

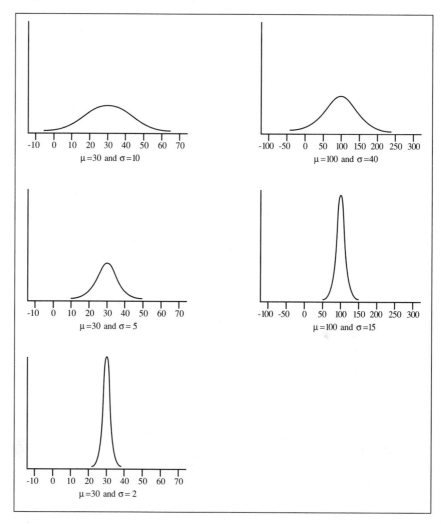

The normal distribution

- **is completely defined by its mean and standard deviation.** In other words, for a given mean and standard deviation, there is only one normal distribution whose graph you can draw.

- **has mean=mode=median.** Recall that mode is the most frequently occurring value, and that the median is greater than half of the values and less than half of the values. In other words, if you draw a graph of the distribution and fold the graph in half, the center of the distribution (the fold) is the mean, the mode, and the median of the distribution.

- **is symmetric.** If you draw a graph of the distribution and fold the graph in half, each side of the distribution looks the same. A symmetric distribution has a skewness of 0, so a normal distribution has a skewness of 0. The distribution doesn't lean to one side or the other, but is even on both sides.

- **is smooth.** From the highest point at the center of the distribution out to the ends of the distribution (the "tails"), there are no irregular bumps.

- **has a kurtosis of 0,** as calculated in SAS. (There are different formulas for kurtosis; in some formulas, a normal distribution has a kurtosis of 3.) Kurtosis describes the "heaviness of the tails" of a distribution. Extremely nonnormal distributions may have high positive or negative kurtosis values, while nearly normal distributions will have kurtosis values close to 0. Kurtosis is positive if the tails are "heavier" than for a normal distribution and negative if the tails are "lighter" than for a normal distribution.

Because the plots of the normal distribution are smooth and symmetric, and thus resemble the outlines of a bell, the normal distribution is sometimes said to have a bell-shaped curve.

You may be wondering about the use of the word "normal." Does this mean that data from a nonnormal distribution is abnormal in some way? The answer is no. The normal distribution is one of many distributions that occur. For example, the time to failure for computer chips does not have a normal distribution. Experience has shown that chips fail more often early (often on their first use) and then have failure times slowly decreasing for the length of use. This distribution is not symmetrical.

The Empirical Rule

If data is from a normal distribution, the Empirical Rule gives a quick and easy way to summarize the data. This rule says

• 68% of the values are within one standard deviation of the mean

• 95% of the values are within two standard deviations of the mean

• more than 99% of the values are within three standard deviations of the mean.

Figure 5.3 shows a normal distribution. About 68% of the values occur between $\mu-\sigma$ and $\mu+\sigma$, corresponding to the Empirical Rule.

Figure 5.3   **The Normal Distribution and the Empirical Rule**

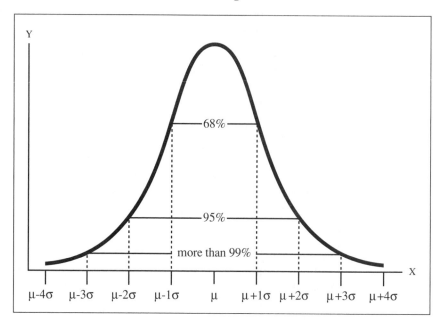

To understand the Empirical Rule better, consider an example. Suppose the population of weights for 12-year old girls is normally distributed with a mean of 86 pounds and a standard deviation of 10 pounds. Using the Empirical Rule, you would find that

• 68% of the weights are between 76 and 96 pounds

• 95% of the weights are between 66 and 106 pounds

• more than 99% of the weights are between 56 and 116 pounds.

Parametric and Nonparametric Statistical Methods

Many statistical methods rely on the assumption that the data is a sample from a normal distribution. Other statistical methods rely on an assumption of some other distribution of the data. Methods that rely on assumptions about distributions are called *parametric methods*.

Another group of statistical methods does not assume a particular distribution for the data. Methods that don't rely on assumptions about the specific distribution of the data are called *nonparametric methods*.

This distinction is important in later chapters, which explain both parametric and nonparametric methods for solving problems. Use the parametric method if your data meets the assumptions, and use the nonparametric method if it doesn't. Later chapters provide detail about the assumptions that are needed for both the nonparametric and parametric tests.

Testing for Normality

A normal distribution is a theoretical distribution for a population. Many statistical methods assume the values in a data set are a sample from a normal distribution. For a given sample, you need to decide if this assumption is reasonable or not. Because you only have a sample, you can never be absolutely sure that the assumption is correct. What you can do is test the assumption and, based on the results of testing, decide whether the assumption is reasonable. This testing-and-decision process is called *testing for normality*.

Statistical Test for Normality

When testing for normality, you start with the idea that the sample is from a normal distribution. Then you verify whether the data agrees or disagrees with the idea. Using the sample, you calculate a statistic and use this statistic to try to verify the idea. Since this statistic tests the idea, it is called a *test statistic*. The test statistic compares the shape of the sample distribution and the shape of a normal distribution.

The result of this comparison is a number called a *p-value*, which describes how doubtful the idea is in terms of a probability. *p*-values can range from 0 to 1. A *p*-value close to 0 means the idea is very doubtful and provides evidence against the idea. If you find enough evidence to reject the idea of normality, you decide that the data is not a sample from a normal distribution. If you can't find enough evidence to reject the idea of normality, you proceed with the analyses based on the assumption that the data is a sample from a normal distribution.

The formal test for normality is obtained by using the NORMAL option in PROC UNIVARIATE. To illustrate the test, data collected about the heights of aeries, or nests, for prairie falcons in North Dakota are used. (Data used with permission of Dr. George T. Allen, U.S. Fish and Wildlife Service, Billings, Montana.)

```
data falcons;
    input aerieht @@;
    label aerieht='Aerie Height in Meters';
    datalines;
15.00 3.50 3.50 7.00 1.00 7.00 5.75 27.00 15.00 8.00
4.75 7.50 4.25 6.25 5.75 5.00 8.50 9.00 6.25 5.50
4.00 7.50 8.75 6.50 4.00 5.25 3.00 12.00 3.75 4.75
6.25 3.25 2.50
;

proc univariate data=falcons normal;
    var aerieht;
    title 'Normality Test for Prairie Falcon Data';
run;
```

This program produces one page of output. Output 5.1 shows a portion of this page.

In Output 5.1, the bottom line shows the results of the formal test for normality. The column labeled *W:Normal* gives the value of the test statistic. The test statistic, *W*, is greater than 0 and less than or equal to 1 ($0<W\leq1$). Values of *W* that are too small indicate that the data is not a sample from a normal distribution. The second column, labeled *Prob<W*, contains the probability value, which describes how doubtful the idea of normality is. Probability values (*p*-values) can range from 0 to 1 ($0\leq Prob\leq1$). Values very close to 0 indicate the data is not a sample from

a normal distribution and produce the most doubt in the idea. For the prairie falcon data, you conclude that the aerie heights are not normally distributed.

Output 5.1   **Testing for Normality of Falcon Data**

```
        Normality Test for Prairie Falcon Data                 1

                        UNIVARIATE Procedure

Variable=AERIEHT        Aerie Height in Meters

                            Moments

            N               33  Sum Wgts            33
            Mean      6.878788  Sum                227
            Std Dev   4.791807  Variance      22.96141
            Skewness  2.651782  Kurtosis      9.276307
            USS        2296.25  CSS           734.7652
            CV        69.66063  Std Mean      0.834146
            T:Mean=0  8.246499  Pr>|T|          0.0001
            Num ^= 0        33  Num > 0             33
            M(Sign)       16.5  Pr>=|M|         0.0001
            Sgn Rank     280.5  Pr>=|S|         0.0001
            W:Normal  0.752119  Pr<W            0.0001
```

The general form of the statements to test for normality are shown below:

> **PROC UNIVARIATE DATA=**=*data-set-name*   **NORMAL**;
>   **VAR** *variables*;
>
> where *data-set-name* is the name of a SAS data set, and *variables* is the name of one or more variables in the data set. For valid normality tests, you may only use either interval or ratio variables in the VAR statement.

PROC UNIVARIATE performs different tests for normality based on the sample size. The interpretation of values in the output is the same, but the output is slightly different. PROC UNIVARIATE performs the Shapiro-Wilk test if the sample size (N) is less than 2000 and performs the Kolmogorov test for larger sample sizes. The output for the Shapiro-Wilk test looks like Output 5.1. In the output for the Kolmogorov test, the columns in the bottom line are labeled *D:Normal* and *Prob>D*.

Other Methods of Checking for Normality

In addition to the formal test for normality, other methods for checking for normality can be used. These should be used in addition to the formal test to increase your understanding about the distribution of the sample values. These methods include looking at a bar chart of the data, checking the values of skewness and kurtosis, and looking at a normality plot of the data.

Skewness and kurtosis

Output 5.1 also shows the skewness and kurtosis for the prairie falcon data. Recall that for a normal distribution, the skewness is 0. Also, as calculated in SAS, the kurtosis for a normal distribution is 0. For the prairie falcon data, neither of these values is close to 0. This confirms the results of the formal test that led you to reject the idea of normality.

Normal plot

To look at a normal plot for a set of data, use the PLOT option in PROC UNIVARIATE. For the prairie falcon data, type

```
proc univariate data=falcons plot;
   var aerieht;
   title 'Normality Test for Prairie Falcon Data';
run;
```

This program produces two pages of output. The first page contains descriptive statistics. Output 5.1 shows a portion of this first page of output for the prairie falcon data. The second page of output contains three plots. Two of these plots, the box plot and the stem-and-leaf plot, are explained in detail in Chapter 4. The third plot is the normal plot, which is discussed in detail below. Output 5.2 shows the portion of output that contains the normal plot.

Output 5.2   Normal Plot for Falcon Data

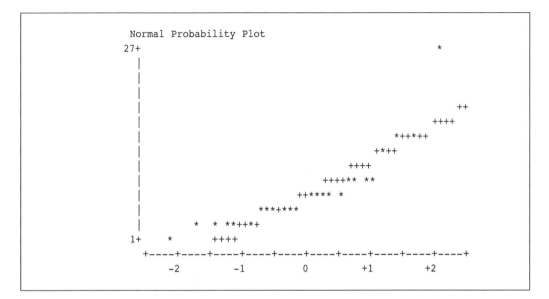

Notice that the normal plot in Output 5.2 shows both asterisks (*) and plus signs (+). The plus signs form a straight line. The asterisks represent the sample. If the sample is from a normal distribution, the asterisks (*) also form a straight line and thus cover most of the plus signs (+). When using the plot, first look to see if the asterisks (*) form a straight line. This indicates a normal distribution. Then, look to see if there are few visible plus signs (+). Because the asterisks in the plot for the prairie falcon data don't form a straight line or cover most of the plus signs, you again conclude that the data isn't a sample from a normal distribution.

Figure 5.4 shows several patterns that can occur in normal plots and gives the interpretation for these patterns. Compare the patterns in Figure 5.4 to the asterisks (*) in the normal plot in Output 5.2. The closest match occurs for the pattern for a distribution that is skewed to the right. (Remember that the positive skewness measure also indicates that the data are skewed to the right.)

Figure 5.4   How to Interpret Patterns in Normal Plots

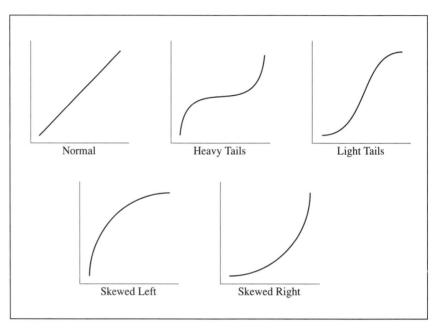

The general form of the statements to generate a normal plot are shown below:

PROC UNIVARIATE DATA=*data-set-name* **PLOT**;
   VAR *variables* ;

where *data-set-name* is the name of a SAS data set, and *variables* is the name of one or more variables in the data set. You can put more than one variable name in a VAR statement. However, for valid normal plots, use only interval or ratio variables.

You can request the PLOT option and the NORMAL option (described earlier in this chapter) in the same PROC UNIVARIATE statement. You can also request the FREQ option (described in Chapter 4) in the same PROC UNIVARIATE statement.

Bar charts

Another way to check for normality is to look at a bar chart. To produce a simple bar chart for the prairie falcon data, type

```
goptions device=win;
pattern v=solid color=gray;
proc gchart data=falcons;
    vbar aerieht;
    title 'Bar Chart for Prairie Falcon Data';
run;
```

These statements produce Output 5.3. If you don't have access to PROC GCHART, use the same VBAR statement with PROC CHART. This gives a low-resolution chart. Notice that the chart does not show the general bell-shape of a normal distribution. Once again, this indicates the sample isn't from a normal distribution.

Output 5.3   **Bar Chart for Falcon Data**

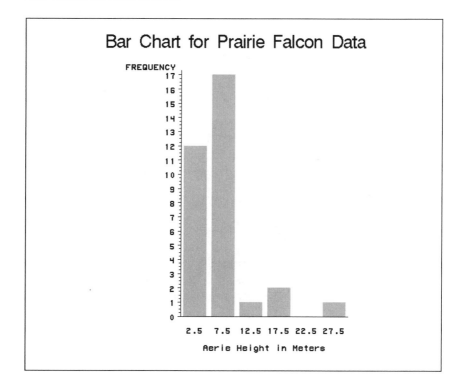

The general form of the statements for producing a simple bar chart like the one in Output 5.3 is shown below:

> **PROC GCHART DATA=**_data-set-name_ ;
>   **VBAR** _variables_ ;
>
> where _data-set-name_ is the name of a SAS data set, and _variables_ is the name of one or more variables in the data set.

In addition, you can produce customized bar charts and horizontal bar charts with PROC GCHART. Or, you can use PROC CHART instead. The statements and options that you need for this are presented in Chapter 4.

Using Stem-and-Leaf Plots

When you use the PLOT option in PROC UNIVARIATE, your output contains a stem-and-leaf plot. This portion of the output for the prairie falcon data is shown in Output 5.4.

Notice that there is a bell-shaped grouping at the lower end of the distribution of values. Four values (12, 14, 14, and 26) are separated from this main grouping. Perhaps these values represent an unusual situation: prairie falcons may have been using a nest built by another type of bird, for example. If your data looks like this, you should carefully examine the outliers to avoid incorrectly concluding the data isn't a sample from a normal distribution. If we had identified the four large values as values that should not be included (eagle nests recorded as falcon nests by mistake, for example) and then deleted them, the _Prob<W_ would be about 0.88. Without these four large values, you could proceed with analyses based on the assumption that the data is a sample from a normal distribution.

However, this is an example only. In general, values should not be deleted from the data. As discussed in later chapters, there are analysis methods appropriate for both normal and nonnormal data.

Output 5.4   **Stem-and-Leaf Plot for Falcon Data**

```
             Stem Leaf                    #
              26 0                        1
              24
              22
              20
              18
              16
              14 00                       2
              12 0                        1
              10
               8 0580                     4
               6 22250055                 8
               4 0028802588              10
               2 502558                   6
               0 0                        1
                 ----+----+----+----+
```

Using SAS/INSIGHT to Check Normality

You can also check normality by using SAS/INSIGHT. Since this software is interactive, you start by submitting some statements and then make selections from the menu bar. To follow the examples in this section, you need to use Display Manager mode.

For the prairie falcon data, submit the statements below to start working with SAS/INSIGHT software:

```
proc insight;
   open falcons / nodisplay;
   dist aerieht;
run;
```

These statements generate Output 5.5.

Output 5.5   **SAS/INSIGHT Plots for Falcon Data**

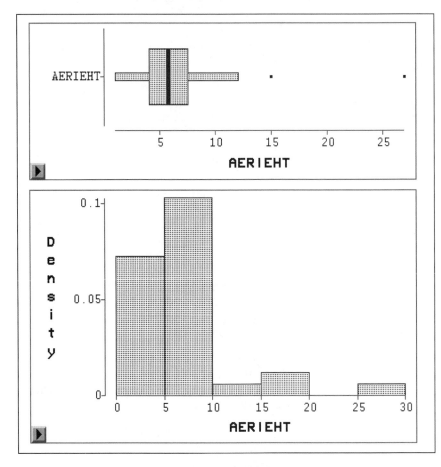

Output 5.5 first shows a horizontal box plot of the data. These plots are described in Chapter 4. For the prairie falcon data, you see that there are outliers in the data. These are identified by the blocks at the right side of the graph.

Interactive tip: Click on one of the outliers, and you see the observation numbers for the outliers. Also, the bars associated with these observations highlight in the bar chart.

The bar chart from SAS/INSIGHT is similar to the bar chart generated earlier in the chapter. The differences are in the labels for the bars. Both charts show bars in the ranges 0-5, 5.01-10, 10.01-15, and so on. The first bar chart labels the midpoints of the bars as 2.5, 7.5, and so on. The SAS/INSIGHT bar chart labels the edges of the bars as 0, 5, 10, and so on.

The SAS/INSIGHT bar chart leads to a similar conclusion as the PROC GCHART bar chart — that the data is not a sample from a normal distribution.

The statements shown above also generate a table of Moments in SAS/INSIGHT. The values for skewness and kurtosis are the same as those from PROC UNIVARIATE.

Adding the Normality Test and Normal Plot

You can add both the normal plot and the statistical test for normality by making selections from the menu bar. Select Curves and then select Test for Distribution... and the Test for Distribution window appears. In this window, Normal is selected automatically, and you can just select the OK button. Two new boxes appear in the SAS/INSIGHT output as shown in Output 5.6 .

Output 5.6   Testing for Normality in SAS/INSIGHT

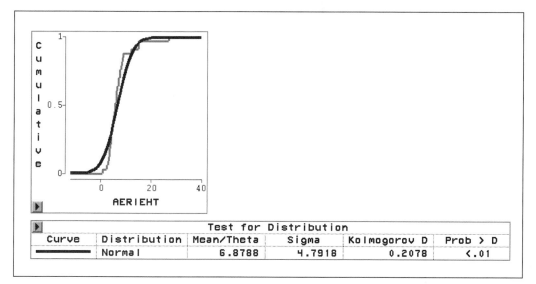

This output shows the normal plot for the data, where the smooth curve is the normal distribution and the stair-step curve is the actual data. From this plot, you conclude the data is not from a normal distribution.

This output also shows the results of a normality test. PROC INSIGHT uses the Kolmogorov test for all sample sizes. (Recall that PROC UNIVARIATE uses this test only for samples larger than 2000.) The column labeled *Prob>D* gives the results of the test. Values that are very close to 0 indicate that the data is unlikely to be a sample from a normal distribution. For the prairie falcon data, you conclude that the aerie heights are not normally distributed.

Adding a Normal Curve to the Bar Chart

With PROC INSIGHT, you can add a normal curve to the bar chart. This helps you see how similar or different the data are from the expected normal curve. To do so, select `Curves` from the menu bar. Then select `Parametric Density...` and the Parametric Density Estimation window appears. In this window, the Normal distribution and Sample Estimates are automatically selected. You can just select `OK`, and the curve is added to the bar chart. This changes the bar chart in your PROC INSIGHT output to the one shown in Output 5.7. The only difference between this chart and the one in Output 5.5 is the normal curve.

Output 5.7   **Adding a Normal Curve to the Bar Chart**

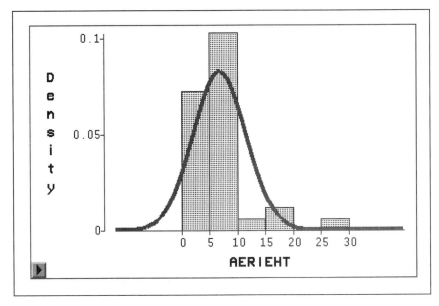

Here is the general form of the statements when using SAS/INSIGHT to check for normality.

> **PROC INSIGHT**;
>   **OPEN** *data-set-name* / **NODISPLAY**;
>   **DIST** *variables* ;
>
> where *data-set-name* is the name of a SAS data set, and *variables* is the name of one or more variables in the data set. **NODISPLAY** suppresses the data table and is optional. If **NODISPLAY** is omitted, omit the slash also.
>
> You can put more than one variable name in a DIST statement. However, for valid normal plots, use either interval or ratio variables only.
>
> To add a normal plot and normality test, select `Curves` from the menu bar. Then select `Test for Distribution...` and when the Test for Distribution window appears, select `OK`. The Normal distribution should be automatically selected.
>
> To add a normal curve to the bar chart, select `Curves` from the menu bar. Then select `Parametric Density...` and when the Parametric Density Estimation window appears, select `OK`. The Normal Distribution and Sample Estimates should be automatically selected.

For an example of the data table in SAS/INSIGHT, see Output 4.15 in Chapter 4.

Building a Hypothesis Test

Earlier in this chapter, you saw how to test for normality to determine whether you could assume your data is a sample from a normal distribution or not. The process used in testing for normality is one example of a statistical method used in many types of analysis. This process is called *performing a hypothesis test*, usually abbreviated to *hypothesis testing*. This section describes the general method of hypothesis testing. In discussions of analyses in later chapters, the hypotheses tested are discussed in relation to the general framework shown here.

Recall the statistical test for normality: you start with the idea that the sample is from a normal distribution and verify whether the data agrees or disagrees with the idea. This concept is basic to hypothesis testing. In building a hypothesis test, you work with an idea called the *null hypothesis*, which describes one idea about the population. The null hypothesis provides a frame of reference that is contrasted with the *alternative hypothesis*, which describes an alternative idea about the population. For the test for normality, the null hypothesis is that the data is a sample from a normal distribution; the alternative hypothesis is that the data is a sample from a nonnormal distribution.

Null and alternative hypotheses can be described in words, but in statistics texts and journals they are usually described by using a special type of notation. Consider testing to see if the population mean is equal to some number. Suppose you want to know if the average price of hamburger meat has changed from last year's average price of $1.98 per pound. You have sampled prices of hamburger meat at several grocery stores and want to use this sample to test if the population mean is different from $1.98. The null and alternative hypotheses are written as

$$H_o: \mu = 1.98$$

and

$$H_a: \mu \neq 1.98$$

H_o represents the null hypothesis that the population mean (μ) equals $1.98, and H_a represents the alternative hypothesis that the population mean does not equal $1.98.

Once you have established the null and alternative hypotheses, you use the data to calculate a statistic to test the null hypothesis. Next, you compare your calculated value of this *test statistic* to the values of the statistic that would be seen in the situation where the null hypothesis is true. The result of this comparison is a probability value, or *p*-value, that tells you if the null hypothesis should be believed. The *p*-value is the probability that the value of your test statistic could have occurred if the null hypothesis were true. Figure 5.5 depicts this general process that is used in hypothesis testing.

Figure 5.5   **Performing a Hypothesis Test**

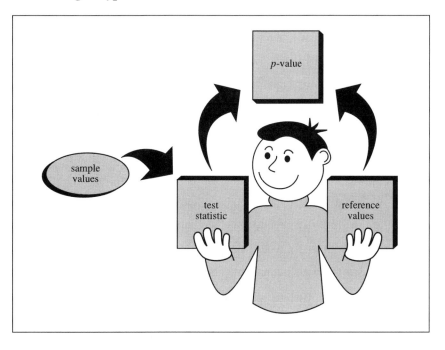

If the *p*-value is close to 0, then it indicates that the value of the test statistic could not reasonably have occurred by chance. Then you *reject the null hypothesis* and conclude that the null hypothesis isn't true. However, if the *p*-value indicates that the value of the test statistic could have occurred by chance, you *do not reject the null hypothesis*. You never accept the null hypothesis; you simply do not have enough evidence to reject it. Unless you measure an entire population, you never have enough evidence to conclude that the population is exactly what you say it is according to the null hypothesis. For example, you could not conclude that the true mean price of hamburger meat is $1.98 per pound unless you obtained prices from every place that sold hamburger meat.

Returning to the example of testing for normality, you test the null hypothesis that the data is from a normal distribution. You calculate a test statistic which summarizes the shape of the distribution. Then, you compare the test statistic with a reference value and get a *p*-value. Based on the result, you may reject the hypothesis that the data is normally distributed. Or, you may fail to reject the hypothesis and proceed with the assumption that the data is normally distributed.

The next section shows how to decide if a *p*-value indicates that a differ-ence is larger than would be expected by chance, and it also discusses the concept of practical significance.

Statistical and Practical Significance

When you conduct a statistical test and get a *p*-value, you usually want to know if the result is significant. In other words, is the value of the test statistic more extreme than you would expect to find by chance? When answering this question, you need to understand statistical significance and practical significance.

Statistical Significance

Statistical significance is based on *p*-values. Typically, you decide in advance what level of significance to use for the test. Choosing the significance level is a way of limiting the risk of being wrong. Specifically, what chance are you willing to take that you are wrong in your conclusions?

For example, a significance level of 5% means that if you collected 100 sam-ples and performed 100 hypothesis tests, you would make the wrong con-clusion about 5 times (5/100=0.05). In the previous sentence, "wrong" has a particular meaning, concluding that the alternative hypothesis is true when it is not. For the hamburger meat example discussed earlier, "wrong" means to conclude that the population mean is different from $1.98 **when, in fact, it is not**. Statisticians call this definition of "wrong" the *Type I* error. By choosing a significance level when you perform a hypothesis test, you control the probability of making a Type I error.

When you choose a significance level, you define the reference prob-ability. For a significance level of 10%, the reference probability is 0.10, which is the significance level expressed in decimal terms. The reference probability is called the α-level (pronounced "alpha-level") for the test.

When you perform a statistical test, if the attained probability (the *p*-value) is less than the reference probability (the α-level), you conclude that the result is statistically significant. Suppose you decide to perform a test at the 10% significance level, which means that the α-level is 0.10. If the *p*-value is less than 0.10, you conclude that the result is statistically signi-ficant at the 10% significance level. If the *p*-value is more than 0.10, you conclude that the result is not statistically significant at the 10% significance level.

As a more concrete example, suppose you perform a test at the 10% significance level and the *p*-value is 0.002. This means you limited the risk of making a Type I error to 10%, giving you an α-level of 0.10. It also means that your test statistic value would occur only about 2 times in 1000 by chance alone if the null hypothesis were true. Because the *p*-value of 0.002 is less than the α-level of 0.10, you reject the null hypothesis. The test is statistically significant at the 10% level.

Choosing a significance level

The choice of the significance level (or α-level) depends on the risk of making a Type I error that you are willing to take. Three levels are commonly used: 0.10, 0.05, and 0.01. These are often referred to as "moderately significant," "significant," and "highly significant," respectively.

The situation you're in should help determine the level of significance you choose. If you are challenging an established principle, then your null hypothesis is that this established principle is true. In this case, you want to be very careful not to reject the null hypothesis if it is true. You choose a very small α-level, say 0.01 (or even 0.001). If, however, you're doing work where the consequences of rejecting the null hypothesis are not so severe, then an α-level of 0.05 or 0.10 may be more appropriate.

More on *p*-values

Hypothesis testing as described in this book involves rejecting or failing to reject a null hypothesis at a predetermined α-level. This means making a decision about the truth of the null hypothesis. But, in some cases, you may only want to use the *p*-value as a summary measure that describes the evidence against the null hypothesis. (This situation occurs most often when people are conducting basic, exploratory research.) The *p*-value serves the purpose of describing the evidence against the null hypothesis. The smaller a *p*-value is, the more you doubt the null hypothesis. A *p*-value of 0.003 provides strong evidence against the null hypothesis, whereas a *p*-value of 0.36 provides less evidence.

Another Type of error

In addition to the Type I error, there is another kind of error, called the *Type II error*. A Type II error occurs when you fail to reject the null hypothesis when it is false. You can generally control this kind of error when you choose the sample size for your study. The Type II error is not discussed in this book because design of experiments is not discussed. If you are planning an experiment, you should consult with a statistician to ensure that the Type II error is controlled.

The table below shows the relationship between the true underlying situation (which you will never know unless you measure the entire population) and your conclusions. When you conclude that there isn't enough evidence to reject the null hypothesis and this matches the unknown underlying situation, you make a correct decision. When you reject the null hypothesis and this matches the unknown underlying situation, you make a correct decision. When you reject the null hypothesis and this doesn't match the unknown underlying situation, you make a Type I error. When you fail to reject the null hypothesis and this does not match the unknown underlying situation, you make a Type II error.

Your Conclusion	**Unknown Underlying Situation**	
	Null Hypothesis True	**Alternative Hypothesis True**
Do Not Reject Null	Correct	Type II error
Reject Null	Type I error	Correct

Practical Significance

Practical significance is based on common sense. Sometimes a p-value indicates statistical significance where the difference is not practically significant. This situation may occur with large data sets or when there is a small amount of variation in the data.

At other times, a p-value indicates nonsignificant differences where the difference is important from a practical standpoint. This situation may occur with small data sets or when there is a large amount of variation in the data.

You need to base your final conclusion both on statistical significance and on common sense.

Example

Suppose you gave a proficiency test to a group of employees who were divided into one of two groups: those who just completed a training program (trainees) and those who have been on the job for a while (experienced employees). Possible scores on the test could range from 0 to 100. You want to find out if the mean scores are different and to use the result to decide whether to change the training program. You perform a hypothesis test at the 5% significance level and obtain a *p*-value of 0.025. From a statistical standpoint, you can conclude that the two groups are significantly different.

What if the averages for the two groups are very similar? If the average score for trainees is 83.5 and the average score for experienced employees is 85.2, is the difference practically significant? Should you go to the time and expense to change the training program based on this small difference? Common sense says no. This situation of finding statistical significance and not finding practical significance is likely to occur with large sample sizes or small variances. If your sample contains several hundred employees in each group or if the variation within each group is small, you are likely to find statistical significance when the difference isn't practically significant.

Continuing the example, suppose your test gives a different outcome. You get a *p*-value of 0.125, which indicates that the two groups are not significantly different from a statistical standpoint (at the 10% level). However, the average score for the trainees is 63.8, and the average score for the experienced employees is 78.4. Common sense says that you need to think about making some changes in the training program. This situation of finding practical significance and not finding statistical significance can occur when the sample sizes are small or the variation in each group is large. Your sample could contain only a few employees in each group, or there could be a lot of variability in each group. In these cases, you are likely to find practically significant differences where a statistical test doesn't indicate significance.

The important thing for you to remember about practical and statistical significance is that you shouldn't take action based on *p*-values alone. Sample sizes, variability in the data, and incorrect assumptions about your data can all produce *p*-values that indicate one action where common sense indicates another. To help avoid this situation, you should consult a statistician when you design your study. A statistician can help you plan a study so that your sample size is large enough to detect a practically significant difference but not so large as to detect a practically insignificant difference. In this way, you control both Type I and Type II errors.

Summaries

Key Ideas

- Populations and samples are both collections of values, but a population contains the entire group of interest, and a sample contains only a subset.

- A sample is a simple random sample if the process used in collecting the sample ensures that any one sample is as likely to be selected as any other sample.

- Summary measures for populations are called parameters, and summary measures for samples are called statistics. Different statistical notation is used for the two.

- The normal distribution is a theoretical distribution with important properties. A normal distribution has a bell-shaped curve that is smooth and symmetric. For a normal distribution, the mean=mode=median.

- The Empirical Rule gives a quick way to summarize data from a normal distribution. This rule says

  - 68% of the values are within one standard deviation of the mean

  - 95% of the values are within two standard deviations of the mean

  - more than 99% of the values are within three standard deviations of the mean.

- A formal statistical test is used to test for normality. Descriptive statistics and normal plots provide additional information.

- Hypothesis testing involves choosing a null and an alternative hypothesis, calculating a test statistic from the data, obtaining the p-value, and comparing the p-value to an α-level.

- By choosing the α-level for the test, you control the probability of making a Type I error, which is the probability of rejecting the null hypothesis when you should not.

Syntax

- To get a formal statistical test for normality, a normal plot, and skewness and kurtosis,

    PROC UNIVARIATE DATA=*data-set-name* **NORMAL PLOT;**
       VAR *variables*;

    where *data-set-name* is the name of a SAS data set, and *variables* is one or more variables that you want to summarize.

- To get a simple vertical bar chart,

    PROC GCHART DATA=*data-set-name*;
       VBAR *variables*;

    where items in italic are defined above. Or, use PROC CHART with the same VBAR statement for a low-resolution chart.

- To get a bar chart and summary statistics with SAS/INSIGHT software,

    PROC INSIGHT;
       OPEN *data-set-name* / **NODISPLAY;**
       DIST *variables*;

    where items in italic are defined above.

    To add a normality test and a normal plot, select `Curves` from the menu bar, then select `Test for Distribution...`, and when the Test for Distribution window appears, select `OK`. The Normal test should be automatically selected in this window.

    To add a curve from a normal distribution with the sample mean and sample standard deviation to the bar chart, select `Curves` from the menu bar, then select `Parametric Density...`, and when the Parametric Density Estimation window appears, select `OK`. The Normal distribution and Sample Estimates should be automatically selected in this window.

Example

The program below produces all the output shown in this chapter:

```
data falcons;
   input aerieht @@;
   label aerieht='Aerie Height in Meters';
   datalines;
15.00 3.50 3.50 7.00 1.00 7.00 5.75 27.00 15.00 8.00
4.75 7.50 4.25 6.25 5.75 5.00 8.50 9.00 6.25 5.50
4.00 7.50 8.75 6.50 4.00 5.25 3.00 12.00 3.75 4.75
6.25 3.25 2.50
;

proc univariate data=falcons normal plot;
   var aerieht;
   title 'Normality Test for Prairie Falcon Data';
run;

proc gchart data=falcons;
   vbar aerieht;
   title 'Bar Chart for Prairie Falcon Data';
run;

proc insight;
   open falcons / nodisplay;
   dist aerieht;
run;
```

Further Reading

For more information about practical experimental design, see

- Bayne, C.K. and Rubin, I.B. (1986), *Practical Experimental Designs and Optimization Methods for Chemists*, New York: VCH Publishers, Inc.

- Box, G.E.P., Hunter, W.G., and Hunter J.S. (1978), *Statistics for Experimenters*, New York: John Wiley & Sons, Inc.

- Cochran, W.G. (1983), *Planning and Analysis of Observational Studies*, New York: John Wiley & Sons, Inc.

- Marks, R.G. (1982), *Designing a Research Project*, Belmont, CA: Lifetime Learning Publications.

For more information about the normal distribution, the Empirical Rule, and hypothesis testing, see the following:

- McClave, J.T. and Dietrich, F.H. (1983), *Statistics*, 7th Edition, Upper Saddle River, NJ: Prentice Hall
- Mendenhall, W. and Beaver, R.J. (1994), *Introduction to Probability and Statistics*, 9th Edition, Belmont, CA: Belmont

For more detail about tests for normality and SAS procedures, see one of these books:

- Moore, D.S. and McCabe, G.P. (1993), *Introduction to the Practice of Statistics*, New York: W.H. Freeman
- *SAS/INSIGHT® User's Guide, Version 6, Third Edition*
- *SAS/GRAPH® Software: Reference, Version 6, First Edition, Volumes 1 and 2*
- *SAS/GRAPH® Syntax, Version 6, First Edition* summarizes syntax for GOPTIONS and the GCHART procedure.
- *SAS® Language and Procedures: Syntax, Version 6, First Edition* gives a syntax summary of procedures in Chapter 10.
- *SAS® Procedures Guide, Version 6, Third Edition* discusses the CHART and UNIVARIATE procedures in Chapters 9 and 42.

Chapter 6 # Estimating the Mean

Like Chapter 5, the focus of this chapter is more on statistical concepts than on using SAS software. The major analysis tool presented is forming a confidence interval for the mean. This tool relies on basic statistical concepts, which are illustrated by using simulated data sets. The SAS programming used to generate the simulated data sets is beyond the scope of this book and is not shown. The SAS statements for forming a confidence interval are shown. Major topics in this chapter are

- estimating the mean when using a single number
- exploring the effect of sample size when estimating the mean
- exploring the effect of population variance when estimating the mean
- understanding the distribution of sample averages
- building confidence intervals for the mean.

Confidence intervals for the mean are appropriate for interval and for ratio variables; however, the general concepts discussed in this chapter apply to all types of data.

Contents

Using One Number to Estimate the Mean

To estimate the mean of a normally distributed population, use the average of a random sample taken from the population. For samples from nonnormal distributions, the average of a random sample is also used to estimate the mean. Although other statistics are better in some instances, a discussion of them is beyond the scope of this book. If your data is not normally distributed, you may want to consult with a statistician before forming an estimate of the mean.

The sample average gives a *point estimate* of the population mean. In other words, the average gives one number, or point, to estimate the mean. The sample size and the population variance both affect the precision of this point estimate. Generally, larger samples give more precise estimates, which means estimates closer to the true unknown population mean. In addition, samples from a population with a small variance generally give more precise estimates. These two qualities interact—large samples from a population with a small variance are likely to give even more precise estimates. The next two sections illustrate these ideas.

Effect of Sample Size

Suppose you want to estimate the average weekly starting salary of recently graduated male engineers in the United States. You can't collect the values for every male engineer in the United States, so you take a random sample of salaries and use the sample values to calculate the average weekly starting salary. This average is an estimate of the population mean. How close do you think the sample average is to the population mean? One way to answer this question would be to take many samples and compute the average for each sample. This collection of sample averages would be clustered around the population mean. You could examine the sample to see how closely most of the averages (for example, 95% of them) are clustered around the mean. Now suppose that the single sample average that you actually obtain is one of the collection of sample averages. Then, intuitively, you would feel "95% sure" that your single observed sample average is close to the population mean.

In the engineer salary example, suppose you could take 200 samples. How would the averages for the different samples vary? The rest of this section explores the effect of different sample sizes on the sample averages.

For the engineer salary example, suppose you know that the true population mean is $670 per week, and that the true population standard deviation is $80. Now suppose you sample 1000 values from the population and find the average for the sample. Then you repeat this process 199 more times, for a total of 200 samples. From each sample, you get a sample average, which estimates the population mean.

To demonstrate what would happen, we simulated this process with some advanced SAS programming. Specifically, the process involves taking 200 samples of size 1000 from the simulated data and calculating the average for each sample. Next, we produce a bar chart of the averages. The results are shown in Output 6.1.

Output 6.1   **Simulation of 200 Samples with n=1000, μ=670, and σ=80**

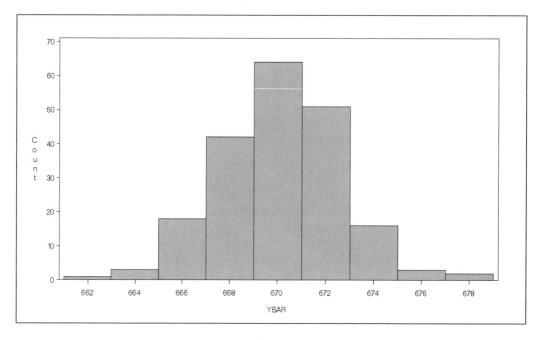

Output 6.1 shows a vertical bar chart of the 200 sample averages, where each sample contains 1000 values. Notice that all of the sample averages are close to the true population mean of 670. In fact, all but 9 of the averages are in the bars labeled 666 through 674. In addition, if we use PROC UNIVARIATE on this data, we can find the 2.5 and 97.5 percentiles to be about 665.5 and 675.0, respectively. Since 2.5% and 97.5% identify 2.5% of the values on each end of the distribution, they combine to identify a total of 5% of the values. This means that about 95% of the averages

differ from the population mean ($670) by no more than about $5. This tells you that any one average has a 95% chance of being within $5 of the population mean, so you are "95% sure" that your observed sample average differs from the mean by no more than about $5.

Reducing the Sample Size

What happens if you reduce the size of the sample to 150? For each sample, you calculate the average of the 150 values. Then you create a bar chart that summarizes the averages from the 200 samples.

What happens if you reduce the size of the sample even further? Suppose you still collect 200 samples, but now each sample contains only 30 values. Again, you calculate the average for each sample and then create a bar chart that summarizes the 200 sample averages.

Output 6.2 shows the results of reducing the sample size to 150 and then further reducing the sample size to 30. The averages for the sample size of 1000 are all close to the true population mean of 670. For the sample size of 150, the averages are not as closely grouped around the population mean. For the sample size of 30, the averages are even less closely grouped around the population mean. For the sample sizes of 150 and 30, some of the sample averages are good estimators of the true population mean, but some are not. Another way to look at this is to consider the range of values required to include 95% of the sample averages. To do so, you can use the 2.5 and 97.5 percentiles (as discussed for Output 6.1 above). The table below shows the values that enclose about 95% of the values for each set of 200 averages.

Sample Size	Range to Include 95% of Averages	"95% Sure" Value
1000	665.5–675.0	$5
150	658.5–681.9	$12
30	645.2–698.6	$29

For the population with the smallest sample size of 30, you are "95% sure" that your single observed average is within $29 of the population mean. For the populations with larger sample sizes, you are "95% sure" that your single observed average is even closer to the population mean.

Output 6.2   Comparison of Sample Sizes of 30, 150, 1000

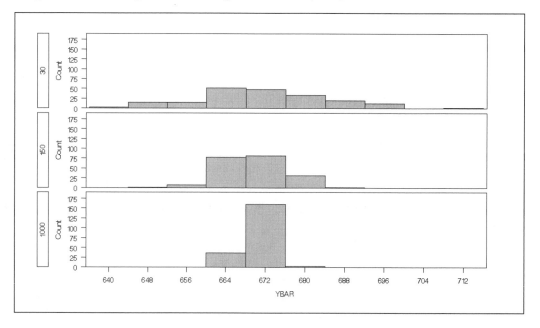

In this example, you have seen how larger sample sizes lead to consistently more precise estimates, that is, a given estimate is more likely to be close to the true population value.

Effect of Population Variability

This section continues with the engineer salary example and explores how population variability affects the estimates from a sample. Recall that one measure of population variability is the standard deviation, σ. As the population standard deviation decreases, the sample average is a more precise estimate of the population mean.

Estimation with a Smaller σ

Suppose that the true population standard deviation is $20 instead of $80, as you assumed earlier. Note that you can't change the population standard deviation the way you can change sample size. The true population standard deviation is fixed, so you are now taking samples from a different population with a true population mean of $670 and a true standard deviation of $20. What happens to the bar chart of sample averages?

What if the true population standard deviation were even smaller, for example, 5? Now the samples are from another distribution with a true population standard deviation of 5. What happens to the bar chart of sample averages?

To demonstrate what would happen, we simulated this process with some advanced SAS programming. As in the previous section, we calculated the sample average for each of 200 samples. Unlike the previous section, the size of each sample was fixed at 1000. For the first group of 200 samples, we used a population standard deviation of 80, and then repeated the process using population standard deviations of 20 and 5. Output 6.3 shows the bar charts of the sample averages.

Output 6.3   **Comparing Standard Deviations of 80, 20, and 5**

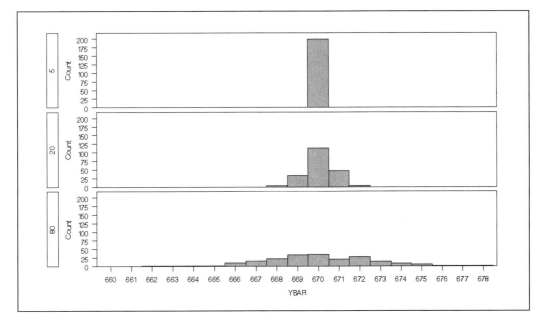

The averages for the populations with smaller standard deviations are closely grouped around the true population mean of 670. For the averages from distribution with a population standard deviation of 5, the averages are very closely grouped around the true population mean of 670. For the averages from the distributions with population standard deviations of 20 and 80, the averages are more widely spaced. However, almost all of the sample averages are good estimators of the true population mean.

Another way to look at this is to consider the range of values required to include 95% of the sample averages (using the percentiles). The table below shows the values that enclose about 95% of the values for each set of 200 averages.

Population σ	Range to Include 95% of Averages	"95% Sure" Value
80	665.5–675.0	$5
20	668.9–671.3	$1.30
5	669.7–670.3	$0.30

For the population with the largest standard deviation of 80, you are "95% sure" that your single observed average is within $5 of the population mean. For the populations with smaller standard deviations, you are "95% sure" that your single observed average is even closer to the population mean.

This example shows how samples from populations with less variability (smaller standard deviations) lead to more precise estimates, that is, the sample averages are consistently closer to the true population mean.

Bound on Error of Estimation

In each of several cases, the simulated averages showed the "95% sure" range as a bound for a large percent (95%) of the possible differences between sample averages and the population mean. Because an average that you observe may be regarded as one of the possible averages, you have a bound on the amount by which it might reasonably differ from the population mean. We call this the *bound on the error of estimation*.

The Distribution of Sample Averages

The last two sections show that the sample size and the population variability can affect the estimate of the population mean. Look again at the bar charts of the sample averages. Just as individual values in a sample have a distribution, so do the sample averages from many samples. This section discusses the distribution of sample averages.

The Central Limit Theorem

Notice that the bar chart in Output 6.1 is generally bell-shaped. Remember that normal distributions are bell-shaped. Combining these two facts, you arrive at the intuitive conclusion that sample averages are nearly normally distributed.

You may think that this intuitive conclusion is correct only because the samples are from a normal distribution (since salaries can conceivably be normally distributed). The fact is that your intuitive conclusion is true even for populations that can't possibly have a normal distribution. As an example, consider another type of distribution, the exponential distribution. One common use for this distribution is to estimate the time to failure. For example, think about notebook computers, which typically have a 3-hour battery. Suppose you measure the time-to-battery failure for 100 notebook computers. We used SAS software to simulate this process and produced Output 6.4.

Output 6.4 **Simulation: Exponential Distribution**

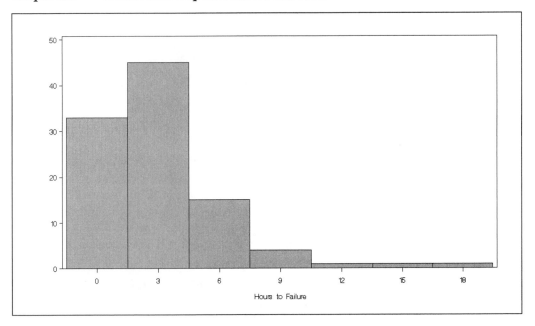

Now suppose you collect 200 samples, each of size 30. Suppose you measure the time-to-battery failure for 30 notebook computers and repeat this process 200 times. (Note that this simplifies the situation; in a real experiment, you would need to control the types of computers,

types of batteries, and so on. However, for the purposes of this example,
assume that the experiment has been run correctly.) If you calculate the
average for each group of 30 notebook computers and plot the sample
averages, you obtain a plot like that shown in Output 6.5. Notice that
the distribution of sample averages is generally bell-shaped.

Output 6.5   Averages for 200 Exponential Distributions

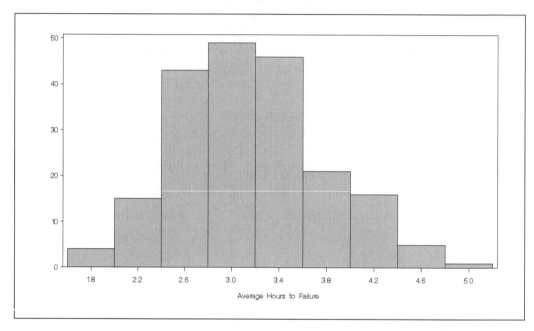

This could lead you to an intuitive conclusion that the sample averages
are nearly normally distributed. This result, that sample averages from
nonnormal distributions are nearly normally distributed, is one of the
most important foundations of statistics. This intuitive conclusion is supported by statistical theory. The *Central Limit Theorem* is a formal mathematical theorem that supports your intuitive conclusion. Essentially, the
Central Limit Theorem says

> **If** you have a simple random sample of n observations from a popu-
> lation with mean μ and standard deviation σ
>
> **and if** n is large,
>
> **then** the sample average $\overline{X}$ is approximately normally distributed
> with mean μ and standard deviation $\sigma/\sqrt{n}$.

Two important practical implications of the Central Limit Theorem are

- Even if the sample values are not normally distributed, the sample average is approximately normally distributed.

- Because the sample average is normally distributed, you can use the Empirical Rule (presented in Chapter 5) to summarize the distribution of sample averages.

Before exploring how you can use these practical implications to summarize data, the Central Limit Theorem is discussed in more detail.

How Big Is "Large"?

The description above says "and if n is large." How big is "large"? The answer depends on how nonnormal the population is. For moderately nonnormal populations, sample averages based on as few as 5 observations (n=5) tend to be nearly normally distributed. But if the population is highly skewed or has "heavy tails" (for example, it contains a lot of extremely large or extremely small values), then a much larger sample size is needed for the sample average to be approximately normally distributed. For practical purposes, samples of larger than 5 are usually collected.

One reason for collecting larger samples was discussed in an earlier section; larger samples lead to more precise estimates of the population mean.

A second reason for collecting larger samples is to increase the chances that the sample is a representative sample. Small samples, even if they are random, are less likely to be representative of the entire population. For example, an opinion poll that is a random sample of 150 people may not be as representative as an opinion poll that is a random sample of 1000 people. (Note that stratified random sampling, mentioned in Chapter 5, can often allow you to take a smaller sample overall. Simply taking larger and larger random samples may not be helpful.)

The Standard Error of the Mean

From the Central Limit Theorem, you know that sample averages are approximately normally distributed. The mean of the normal distribution of sample averages is μ, which is also the mean of the population. The standard deviation of the distribution of sample averages is $\sigma/\sqrt{n}$, where σ is the standard deviation of the population.

The standard deviation of the distribution of sample averages is called the *standard error of the mean*.

The Empirical Rule and the Central Limit Theorem

One of the practical implications of the Central Limit Theorem is that you can use the Empirical Rule to summarize the distribution of sample averages. In other words,

- about 68% of the sample averages are between $\mu - \sigma/\sqrt{n}$, and $\mu + \sigma/\sqrt{n}$
- about 95% of the sample averages are between $\mu - 2\sigma/\sqrt{n}$ and $\mu + 2\sigma/\sqrt{n}$
- more than 99% of the sample averages are between $\mu - 3\sigma/\sqrt{n}$ and $\mu + 3\sigma/\sqrt{n}$.

From now on, this book uses "between $\mu \pm 2\sigma/\sqrt{n}$" to mean between $\mu - 2\sigma/\sqrt{n}$ and $\mu + 2\sigma/\sqrt{n}$. To understand the formulas above, recall that $\sigma/\sqrt{n}$ is the standard deviation of the distribution of sample averages.

The second statement of the Empirical Rule tells you how to compute the 95% bound on the error of estimation; it is equal to $2\sigma/\sqrt{n}$. Recall that in the simulations, we calculated "95% sure" values that enclosed 95% of the sample averages. The table below compares these "95% sure" values, or simulated bounds, with the actual bounds calculated from the Empirical Rule. Notice how closely the simulated and actual bounds agree.

σ	Sample Size(n)	Simulated Bound	Actual Bound
80	1000	5.00	5.06
80	150	12.00	13.06
20	1000	1.30	1.26
5	1000	0.30	0.32

This application of the Empirical Rule also informs you about the distribution of sample averages. For an example, return to the simulation with 200 samples each of size 150. The true population mean is 670 and the true population standard deviation is 80. The standard deviation of the distribution of sample averages is $80/\sqrt{150}$, or 6.53. From the Central Limit Theorem and the Empirical Rule, you can conclude

- about 68% of the sample averages are between 663.47 and 676.53
- about 95% of the sample averages are between 656.94 and 683.06
- more than 99% of the sample averages are between 650.41 and 689.59.

Refer to Output 6.2. Notice that the conclusions are reasonable. All of the sample averages in the chart are between 650 and 690.

You have seen that, with many sample averages, you can get a good estimate of the population mean by looking at the distribution of the sample averages. Also, you can use the distribution of sample averages to tell how close your estimate should be to the true population mean. But what if you have only one sample average? This one sample average gives a point estimate of the population mean, but a point estimate may or may not be close to the true mean (as you have seen in the examples earlier in this chapter). What if you want to get an estimate with some lower and upper limits around it? To do this, you need to form a confidence interval for the mean. The next section shows you how.

Confidence Intervals for the Mean

A *confidence interval* for the mean gives an *interval estimate* for the population mean. This estimate places upper and lower bounds around a point estimate for the mean. The simulations in this chapter show how the sample average estimates the population mean and how the sample size and population variability affect the precision of the estimate. Also, you have seen how the Central Limit Theorem and Empirical Rule can be used to summarize the distribution of sample averages. A confidence interval uses these ideas.

A 95% confidence interval is an interval that is very likely to contain the true population mean μ. Specifically, if you collect a great many samples and calculate a confidence interval for each sample, 95% of the confidence intervals would contain the true population mean μ, and 5% would not. Unfortunately, with only one sample, you don't know whether the confidence interval you calculate is one of the 95% or one of the 5%. However, you can consider your interval to be one of many. And any one of these many intervals has a 95% chance of containing the population mean. Thus, the term "confidence interval" indicates your degree of belief, or confidence, that the interval contains the true population mean μ. The term "confidence interval" is often abbreviated as CI.

Recall the 95% bound on the error of estimation suggested by the Central Limit Theorem and the Empirical Rule. An intuitive bound to use in a 95% CI is $\pm 2\sigma/\sqrt{n}$ since this is the bound that contains 95% of the distribution of sample averages. (Technically, the correct value is 1.96.) However, in most real-life applications, σ is unknown. A natural substitution is to use the sample standard deviation s to replace σ in the formula for the bound. After you do this, the intuitive bound is $\pm 2s/\sqrt{n}$. However, if you use s in the formula instead of σ, the number 2 in the formula is not correct.

Remember, the normal distribution is completely defined by μ and σ. Once you replace σ with s, the use of the normal distribution (and thus the Empirical Rule) is not exactly correct. A t-distribution should be used instead. A t-distribution is very similar to the normal distribution and allows you to adjust for different sample sizes. Thus, the intuitive bound becomes $\pm ts/\sqrt{n}$. The value of t (or the t-value) is based both on the sample size and on the level of confidence you choose. The formula for a confidence interval for the mean is

$$\overline{X} \pm t_{df,\, 1-\alpha/2} \frac{s}{\sqrt{n}}$$

where

$\overline{X}$ is the sample average.

$t_{df,\,1-\alpha/2}$ is the t-value for a given df and α. The df are one less than the sample size ($df=n-1$) and are called the *degrees of freedom* for the t-value. As n gets large, the value of t approaches the value from a normal distribution. The confidence level for the interval is $1-\alpha$. That is, for a 95% confidence level, $\alpha=0.05$. To calculate a 95% confidence interval for a data set with 12 observations, you need to find $t_{11,0.975}$, which is 2.201. Notice that, when finding the t-value, you need to divide α by 2 before you subtract it from 1.

s is the sample standard deviation.

n is the sample size.

Using SAS Software to Find CIs

You can use PROC MEANS to calculate confidence intervals, or CIs. (Recall that this procedure was discussed in Chapter 4.) You simply need to request additional statistics beyond those that the procedure provides by default.

The data below is used as an example. This data consists of interest rates for mortgages from several lenders. It was collected while one of the authors was buying a house. Because mortgage rates differ based on discount points, the size of the loan, the length and type of loan, and whether or not a loan origination fee is charged, the data collected consists of interest rates for the same kind of loan. Specifically, the rates in the data set are for a 30-year fixed-rate loan for $95,000 with no points and a 1% origination fee. Also, because mortgage rates change quickly (sometimes even daily), all data was collected on the same day. The actual bank names are not used in the data below. The following statements produce Output 6.6:

```
data rates;
    input company $ mortrate @@;
    label mortrate='Mortgage Rate';
    datalines;
BANKA 8 BANKB 8.25 BANKC 7.875
BANKD 8 BANKE 8.125 BANKF 8
BANKG 7.875
;

proc means data=rates n mean std clm
    alpha=0.05 maxdec=3;
    var mortrate;
    title 'Summary of Mortgage Rate Data';
run;
```

The PROC MEANS statement contains several options that were not discussed previously. After the DATA= option, the next four options request specific statistics as follows:

Option	Statistic
N	Number of observations
MEAN	Average
STD	Standard Deviation
CLM	Confidence Limits for the Mean

These options are called *statistics keywords* because they request specific statistics.

The ALPHA= option specifies the confidence level for the confidence interval. For a 95% confidence interval, $\alpha=0.05$, so ALPHA=0.05.

The MAXDEC= option is not required but is useful in situations where you want to control the number of decimal points that are displayed in the output. In this case, the mortgage rates are typically calculated to no more than three decimal places, so the procedure uses MAXDEC=3. (Note that you can use this option any time you use PROC MEANS.)

Output 6.6   Confidence Interval for Mortgage Data

```
Summary of Mortgage Rate Data                          1

  Analysis Variable : MORTRATE Mortgage Rate

 N        Mean      Std Dev  Lower 95.0% CLM  Upper 95.0% CLM
 ---------------------------------------------------------------
 7        8.018      0.134          7.894            8.141
 ---------------------------------------------------------------
```

Confidence intervals are often shown enclosed in parenthesis with the lower and upper confidence limits separated by a comma; for example, (7.894, 8.141). For this data, you conclude, with 95% confidence, that the mean mortgage rate is somewhere between 7.894% and 8.141%.

The general form of the statements for obtaining confidence limits with PROC MEANS are:

> **PROC MEANS DATA=***data-set-name* **N MEAN STD CLM**
>   **ALPHA=***value* **MAXDEC=***number* ;
> **VAR** *measurement-variables* ;
>
> where *data-set-name* is the name of a SAS data set, *value* is the α–value, *number* is the number of places to print after the decimal point (typically between 1 and 4), and *measurement-variables* are the variables for which you want confidence intervals.
>
> N, MEAN, STD, and CLM are statistics keywords to print the number of observations, average, standard deviation, and confidence limits, respectively.
>
> ALPHA=0.05 by default.

Summaries

Key Ideas

- Large samples give better estimates of the population mean. That is, a given estimate is more likely to be close to the true mean for a large sample than for a small sample.

- Samples from populations with small variability give better estimates of the population mean than do samples from populations with large variability.

- As a consequence of the Central Limit Theorem, in a large enough sample, the sample average is approximately normally distributed even if the sample values are not normally distributed.

- Confidence intervals for the mean are obtained with the following formula:

$$\overline{X} \pm t_{df,\, 1-\alpha/2} \frac{s}{\sqrt{n}}$$

where $\overline{X}$ is the sample average, n is the sample size, and s is the sample standard deviation. The value of $t_{df, 1-\alpha/2}$ is a t-value that is based on the sample size and the confidence level. The degrees of freedom (df) are one less than the sample size ($df=n-1$), and $1-\alpha$ is the confidence level for the interval. For a 95% confidence interval for a data set with 12 observations, you need to find $t_{11,0.975}$.

Syntax

To calculate a confidence interval,

> **PROC MEANS DATA=**_data-set-name_ **N MEAN STD CLM**
> **ALPHA=**_value_ **MAXDEC=**_number_;
> **VAR** _measurement-variables_;

where _data-set-name_ is the name of a SAS data set, _value_ is the α-value, _number_ is the number of places to print after the decimal point (typically between 1 and 4), and _measurement-variables_ are the variables for which you want confidence intervals. N, MEAN, STD, and CLM are statistics keywords to print the number of observations, average, standard deviation, and confidence limits, respectively.

Example

The program that produced output for the simulations isn't shown. The following program produces the output shown in this chapter for the mortgage rate data:

```
data rates;
    input company $ mortrate @@;
    label mortrate='Mortgage Rate';
    datalines;
BANKA 8 BANKB 8.25 BANKC 7.875
BANKD 8 BANKE 8.125 BANKF 8
BANKG 7.875
;

proc means data=rates n mean std clm
    alpha=0.05 maxdec=3;
    var mortrate;
    title 'Summary of Mortgage Rate Data';
run;
```

Further Reading

For more information about confidence intervals for the mean, see the list of introductory texts in Chapter 5.

For more information about PROC MEANS, see the list of SAS manuals in Chapter 4.

Part 3 **Comparing Groups**

---

7   **Comparing Two Groups**

8   **Comparing More Than Two Groups**

Chapter 7 **Comparing Two Groups**

Do male accountants earn more money than female accountants? Do people who are given a new shampoo use more shampoo than people who are given an old shampoo? Do cows that are fed a grain supplement and hay gain more weight than cows that are only fed hay? Are students' grades on an achievement test higher after they complete a special course on how to take tests? Do employees who follow a regular exercise program for a year have a lower resting pulse rate than they had when they started the program?

All of these questions involve comparing two groups of data. In some instances, the groups are independent (male and female accountants), and in other instances the groups are paired (achievement test results before and after the special course). This chapter discusses the basics of comparing two groups. Analysis methods are given for all types of data. The variable that classifies the data into two groups should be nominal. Specific topics are

- deciding if you have independent or paired groups
- summarizing data from two independent groups
- summarizing data from paired groups
- building a statistical test of hypothesis to compare the two groups
- deciding which statistical test to use
- performing the 2-sample *t*-test and Wilcoxon Rank Sum test for independent groups
- performing the paired-difference *t*-test and Wilcoxon Signed Rank test for paired groups
- comparing two groups when using PROC INSIGHT.

For the various tests, this chapter shows how to use SAS software to do the test and how to interpret the output.

Contents

Deciding between Independent and Paired Groups

When comparing two groups, you usually want to know if the means for the two groups are different. The first step is to decide if you have independent or paired groups.

Independent Groups

Independent groups of data contain measurements that pertain to two unrelated samples of items. Suppose you have random samples of the salaries for male and female accountants. The salary measurements for men and women form two distinct groups, and there is no relation between salaries for any of the women or any of the men. The goal of analysis is to compare the average salaries for the two groups and decide if the averages differ. As another example, suppose a researcher selects a random sample of children, some who use a fluoride toothpaste and some who do not use a fluoride toothpaste. (Again, there is no relationship between the children who use a fluoride toothpaste and those who do not.) A dentist counts the number of cavities for each child. The goal of analysis is to compare the average number of cavities for children who use a fluoride toothpaste and children who do not.

Paired Groups

Paired groups contain measurements for one sample of items, but they contain two measurements for each item. A common example of paired groups is "before-and-after" measurements, where the goal of analysis is to decide if the average change from "before" to "after" is greater than could happen by chance alone. For example, a doctor weighs thirty people before they begin a program to quit smoking and weighs them again six months after they have completed the program. The goal of analysis is to decide if the average weight change is greater than would be expected by chance.

Summarizing Data from Two Independent Groups

This section explains some simple descriptive methods for summarizing two independent groups. These methods are not a substitute for formal statistical analyses. Instead, they can be used to provide additional understanding of the statistical results. The strategy for describing independent groups is to get summary information for each group and use this information to compare the groups. This process is illustrated with an example.

Using PROC MEANS to Compare Groups

Table 7.1 shows the percent of body fat for several men and women. These people participated in unsupervised aerobic exercise or weight training (or both) about three times per week for a year. Then they were measured. (This data was introduced in Chapter 2, where a sample SAS program and output are shown.)

Table 7.1   **Body Fat Data**

Gender	Body Fat (%)	Gender	Body Fat (%)
Male	13.3	Female	22
Male	19	Female	26
Male	20	Female	16
Male	8	Female	12
Male	18	Female	21.7
Male	22	Female	23.2
Male	20	Female	21
Male	31	Female	28
Male	21	Female	30
Male	12	Female	23
Male	16		
Male	12		
Male	24		

* Data is from the Recreation and Fitness Center at SAS Institute Inc.

The SAS statements that follow create a data set that contains the body fat data, print the data set, and calculate the average percent of body fat for men and women. The statements use labels and formats as shown in the "Advanced Topics" section in Chapter 3. These statements produce Output 7.1:

```
proc format;
value $gentext 'm' = 'Male'
               'f' = 'Female';
run;

data bodyfat;
    input gender $ fatpct @@;
    format gender $gentext.;
    label fatpct='Body Fat Percentage';
    datalines;
m 13.3 f 22 m 19 f 26 m 20 f 16 m 8 f 12 m 18 f 21.7
m 22 f 23.2 m 20 f 21 m 31 f 28 m 21 f 30 m 12 f 23
m 16 m 12 m 24
;

proc print data=bodyfat;
    title 'Body Fat for Fitness Program';
run;

proc means data=bodyfat;
    class gender;
    var fatpct;
run;
```

Output 7.1   Comparing Body Fat Data for Men and Women

```
Body Fat for Fitness Program                              1

                    OBS      GENDER      FATPCT

                     1       Male         13.3
                     2       Female       22.0
                     3       Male         19.0
                     4       Female       26.0
                     5       Male         20.0
                     6       Female       16.0
                     7       Male          8.0
                     8       Female       12.0
                     9       Male         18.0
                    10       Female       21.7
                    11       Male         22.0
                    12       Female       23.2
                    13       Male         20.0
                    14       Female       21.0
                    15       Male         31.0
                    16       Female       28.0
                    17       Male         21.0
                    18       Female       30.0
                    19       Male         12.0
                    20       Female       23.0
                    21       Male         16.0
                    22       Male         12.0
                    23       Male         24.0


                 Body Fat for Fitness Program                      2

Analysis Variable : FATPCT Body Fat Percentage


GENDER  N Obs   N       Mean        Std Dev       Minimum       Maximum
-------------------------------------------------------------------------
Female    10    10   22.2900000    5.3196596    12.0000000    30.0000000

Male      13    13   18.1769231    6.0324337     8.0000000    31.0000000
-------------------------------------------------------------------------
```

Output 7.1 shows some simple descriptive statistics for each group. For example, the average percent of body fat for women is approximately 22.29. The average percent of body fat for men is somewhat smaller and is approximately 18.18. From this summary, you intuitively conclude that the averages for the two groups are different, but you don't know whether this difference is greater than that which could have happened by chance.

In the preceding example, the MEANS procedure finds averages for the two groups. The general form of the statements for this process is:

> **PROC MEANS DATA=** *data-set-name* ;
>   **CLASS** *class-variable* ;
>   **VAR** *measurement-variables* ;
>
> where *data-set-name* is the name of a SAS data set, *class-variable* is a variable that classifies the data into groups, and *measurement-variables* are the variables that you want to summarize.

While the VAR statement is not required, you should use it. Otherwise, PROC MEANS gives a summary for every numeric variable in the data set.

Using PROC GCHART to Compare Groups

Another way to summarize data from independent groups is to produce a chart that shows the distribution of values in each group. This section discusses how to produce separate charts for each group and how to produce side-by-side charts.

Producing Separate Charts for Each Group

To produce a separate chart for each group, sort the data into groups and then generate the two charts. First, use PROC SORT with a BY statement to sort the data into groups. Then, use PROC GCHART with the same BY statement.

```
proc sort data=bodyfat;
   by gender;
run;

goptions device=win;
pattern v=solid color=gray;
proc gchart data=bodyfat;
   by gender;
   vbar fatpct;
run;
```

The statements above produce two bar charts; one for females and one for males.

You can produce vertical and horizontal bar charts. You can use the default charts that PROC GCHART produces, or you can use options to customize charts. For more examples of bar charts and a description of how to customize them, see Chapter 4.

If you don't have access to PROC GCHART, you can use the same approach as above. Instead of PROC GCHART, use PROC CHART with the same VBAR statement. Recall that the GOPTIONS and PATTERN statements shown above are used for PROC GCHART; omit them if you use PROC CHART.

The next section discusses the BY statement in more detail and gives a pattern for using the BY statement with other procedures.

Using the BY Statement

In the body-fat example, the BY statement is used with PROC GCHART. This statement can be used with many SAS procedures to provide information on subgroups of data.

The general pattern for using the BY statement follows the pattern shown in the last section. When you use a BY statement with a procedure, you first need to sort the data. Use PROC SORT with a BY statement to sort the data. Use another procedure with the same BY statement. The two BY statements must be identical, but they can contain more than one variable. The procedure then produces output for each combination of levels of the variables listed in the BY statement. Suppose your data contains the variables GENDER, DRUG, and TEMPERAT, where GENDER has two levels, DRUG has three levels, and TEMPERAT is the measured response. If you type,

```
proc sort data=medic;
    by gender drug;
run;

goptions device=win;
pattern v=solid color=gray;
proc gchart data=medic;
    by gender drug;
    var temperat;
run;
```

you get a chart for TEMPERAT for each of the 6 (=2×3) combinations of GENDER and DRUG.

You can use the BY statement with all of the procedures discussed in this book. Simply follow the pattern of first using PROC SORT and then using another procedure with identical BY statements. The summary methods or analyses provided by the procedure are performed for each group created by the levels of the variable (or variables) in the BY statement.

Producing Side-by-Side Charts

Instead of producing separate charts for each group, you may want to produce a side-by-side chart. In this type of chart, the two charts are produced next to each other and share the same vertical axis. To produce a side-by-side chart, use the GROUP= option in the VBAR statement. For the body fat data, type

```
goptions device=win;
pattern v=solid color=gray;
proc gchart data=bodyfat;
    vbar fatpct / group=gender;
    title 'Body Fat for Fitness Program';
run;
```

These statements produce Output 7.2.

Output 7.2   **Producing Side-by-Side Charts Using GROUP=**

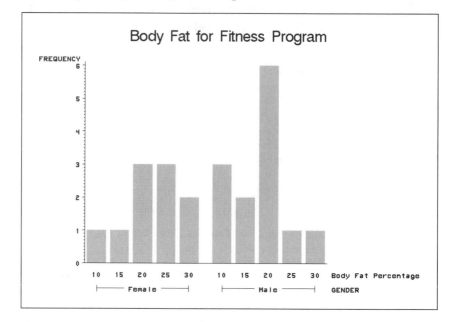

The bar charts in Output 7.2 provide different information than the PROC MEANS summary in Output 7.1. You can now see that the FATPCT values for females fall mostly in the bars with midpoints of 20, 25, and 30, whereas the FATPCT values for males fall mostly in the bars with midpoints of 10, 15, and 20. In fact, almost 85% of the males are in groups with midpoints of 10, 15, or 20, but only 50% of the females are in these three groups.

In Output 7.2, notice that the levels of GENDER are arranged in alphabetical order because the levels of the grouping variable are arranged in alphabetical order in a side-by-side chart. Also, side-by-side charts have the same midpoints for all groups of bars. In contrast, if you produce separate charts for each level of a variable, you need to specify options to get the same midpoints for both charts.

For a side-by-side chart you don't need to sort the data before producing the chart. The general form of the statements for producing this type of chart is:

PROC GCHART DATA=*data-set-name*;
    VBAR *measurement-variables*
      / GROUP=*grouping-variable*;

where *data-set-name* is the name of a SAS data set, *measurement-variables* are the names of the variables to be charted, and *grouping-variable* is the name of the variable that classifies the data into groups. The slash is required.

For side-by-side horizontal bar charts, replace VBAR with HBAR and use the statements above.

You can list only one variable in the GROUP= option. This variable can be either character or numeric, and it should have a limited number of levels. Variables such as height, weight, and temperature are not appropriate because these variables have many levels. Producing a series of side-by-side charts with one observation in each bar does not summarize the data well.

Although you can specify only one grouping variable, you can specify several measurement variables to be charted and produce several side-by-side charts simultaneously. If you list several variables before the slash, you get side-by-side charts for each variable. Suppose you measure the calories, calcium content, and vitamin D content of several cartons of regular and skim milk. The statements

```
proc gchart data=dairy;
    vbar calories calcium vitamind / group=milktype;
run;
```

produce three side-by-side charts; one for each of the three variables listed.

Like other options in PROC GCHART, the GROUP= option appears after a slash. You can use the GROUP= option in combination with the other options in PROC GCHART. For the HBAR or VBAR statement, you can use GROUP= with one of the MIDPOINTS=, LEVELS=, or DISCRETE options. For the HBAR statement, you can also use GROUP= with the NOSTAT option.

Other Ways to Summarize Independent Groups

You can also use PROC UNIVARIATE and PROC FREQ to summarize independent groups. Use these procedures in the same way that you use PROC GCHART. First, sort the data set with PROC SORT, and then use an identical BY statement with the other procedure. PROC UNIVARIATE produces many descriptive statistics and has options to produce a frequency table and descriptive plots. PROC FREQ produces a frequency table. Both of these procedures are described in Chapter 4.

Summarizing Data from Paired Observations

With paired observations, the first step is to find the paired-differences for each observation in the sample. The second step is to summarize the differences.

Finding the Differences between Paired Observations

Sometimes the differences between the two measurements for an observation are already calculated and available for analysis. For example, you may be analyzing data from a cattle feeding program, and the data available to you gives the weight change of each steer. If you already have the differences available, you may want to skip the rest of this section.

At other times only the "before" and "after" data is available. Before you can summarize the data, you need to find the differences. Instead of finding the differences with a calculator, you can find and summarize the differences in one SAS program. To do this, you add *program statements* to the DATA step. There are many kinds of program statements in SAS software. The simplest program statement creates new variables as described in Table 7.2.

Table 7.2   **Creating New Variables with Program Statements**

To create a new variable in the DATA step, follow these steps:

1. Type the DATA and INPUT statements for the data set.

2. Choose the name of the new variable. (Follow the rules for SAS names in Table 3.3.) Write the name of the variable and follow the name with an equal sign. For example, if the name of the new variable is DIFF, type

   ```
   diff =
   ```

3. Decide what combination of other variables will be used to create the new variable. Express this combination of variables after the equal sign. For paired groups, you are usually interested in the difference between two variables. Suppose the variable DIFF is to be the difference between AFTER and BEFORE, type

   ```
   diff = after - before
   ```

4. End the program statement with a semicolon. For this example, the completed program statement is

   ```
   diff = after - before;
   ```

5. Follow the program statement with the DATALINES statement and then with the lines of data to complete the DATA step. Or, if including data from an ASCII text file, use the INFILE statement.

The spacing that was used for the program statement in the above example was chosen for readability. None of the spaces are required. The statement

```
diff=after-before;
```

produces the sames results as the statment in the example.

The SAS statements that follow create a data set and use a program statement to create a new variable. The data consists of the actual scores on two exams for an introductory statistics class. Both exams covered the same material, and twenty students took both exams. Thus, each student has a pair of scores, one for each test. The professor wants to find out if the exams appear to be equally difficult; if they are, the average difference in scores should be small.

```
data sta6207;
    input student exam1 exam2 @@;
    scordiff=exam2-exam1;
    label scordiff='Differences in Exam Scores';
    datalines;
1 93 98 2 88 74 3 89 67 4 88 92 5 67 83 6 89 90
7 83 74 8 94 97 9 89 96 10 55 81 11 88 83 12 91 94
13 85 89 14 70 78 15 90 96 16 90 93 17 94 81
18 67 81 19 87 93 20 83 91
;
```

The next section discusses how to describe the differences between paired observations.

Technical Details

You can create several new variables in the same DATA step by including a program statement for each new variable. In addition, many combinations of variables can be used to create new variables. Some examples are:

```
totcav = begcav + newcav;
```
Total cavities are the sum of cavities at the beginning and new cavities.

```
newvar = oldvar + 5;
```
The new variable is the old variable plus 5.

```
dollars = numsold*unitcost;
```
Dollars earned is the product of the number sold and the cost for each one.

```
yldacre = totyield/numacres;
```
Yield per acre is the total yield divided by the number of acres.

```
credlimt = checkamt ** 2;
```
Credit limit is the square of the amount in the checking account.

In general, use a plus sign (+) to indicate addition, a minus sign (–) for subtraction, an asterisk (*) for multiplication, a slash (/) for division, and two asterisks and a number (**n) to raise a variable to the n-th power.

Describing the Differences between Paired Observations

After the first step of finding differences, the next step is to describe the differences. For the test-scores data, type

```
proc means data=sta6207;
   var scordiff;
   title 'Summary of Differences in Test Scores';
run;

goptions device=win;
pattern v=solid color=gray;
proc gchart data=sta6207;
   vbar scordiff;
   title 'Chart of Differences in Test Scores';
run;
```

Output 7.3 shows the output from PROC MEANS, and Output 7.4 shows the output from PROC GCHART.

Output 7.3   PROC MEANS Output for Test Scores Data

```
Summary of Differences in Test Scores                         1

        Analysis Variable : SCORDIFF Differences in Exam Scores


    N         Mean        Std Dev       Minimum       Maximum
 ------------------------------------------------------------------
   20      2.5500000    10.9711344    -22.0000000    26.0000000
 ------------------------------------------------------------------
```

The average difference between exam scores is 2.55. Note that there are 20 differences, one for each pair in the data set.

Output 7.4   Bar Chart of Test Score Differences

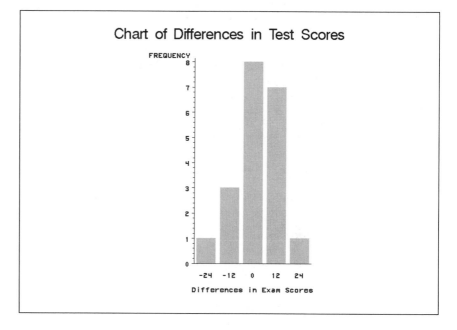

This bar chart shows the distribution of values for SCORDIFF. Notice that the highest frequency occurs for the values that are between -6 and 6. This bar encloses 0, so you might think that the average change in test scores is not statistically significant. However, there are some large positive and negative changes.

You summarize a difference variable from paired observations in the same way that you summarize a single variable. The general form of the statements for summarizing a difference variable is the same as that for summarizing a single variable and is shown in Chapter 4. For more detailed descriptions of the MEANS and GCHART procedures and for information about how to customize bar charts, see Chapter 4.

Other Ways to Summarize Paired Observations

For more extensive descriptive statistics, a frequency table, and simple summary plots, use PROC UNIVARIATE. To get only a frequency table, use PROC FREQ. To use these procedures to summarize a difference variable from paired observations, use the same statements that you would use to summarize a single variable. For complete information, see Chapter 4.

Building Hypothesis Tests to Compare Two Groups

So far, this chapter has presented how to describe differences between groups. But when you start a study, you usually want to do more than just describe differences. You want to know how important the differences are and if they are large enough to be "significant". You want to test the ideas you had about differences before you conducted the study and collected the data. In statistical terms, you want to perform a hypothesis test. This section discusses hypothesis testing in the framework of comparing two groups. The general idea of hypothesis testing is introduced in Chapter 5, where the statistical concepts are summarized.

In building a test of hypothesis, you work with two hypotheses. In the case of comparing two independent groups, the null hypothesis is usually that the two means are the same, and the alternative hypothesis is that the two means are different. For this case, the notation used in most statistics texts and journal articles is

$$H_o: \mu_A = \mu_B$$

and

$$H_a: \mu_A \neq \mu_B$$

where H_o indicates the null hypothesis, H_a indicates the alternative hypothesis, and μ_A and μ_B are the population means for groups A and B.

When comparing paired groups, the null hypothesis is usually that the mean difference is 0, and the alternative hypothesis is that the mean difference is different from 0. In this case, the notation is

$$H_o: \mu_D = 0$$

and

$$H_a: \mu_D \neq 0$$

where H_o indicates the null hypothesis, H_a indicates the alternative hypothesis, and μ_D indicates the mean of the differences.

In statistical tests to compare two groups, the hypotheses above are tested by calculating a test statistic from the data and comparing its value to a reference value that would be seen in the situation where the null hypothesis is true. The test statistic is compared to different reference values based on the sample size. This is partially because smaller differences can be detected with a large sample size. As a result, if you used the same set of reference values for large and small sample sizes, you would be more likely to make incorrect decisions. This is similar to the confidence intervals discussed in Chapter 6, where different t-statistics were used. In that situation, the t-statistic was based on the degrees of freedom, which were determined by the sample size. Similarly, when comparing two groups, the degrees of freedom for a reference value are based on the sample sizes of the two groups. Specifically, the degrees of freedom are equal to $N-2$, where N is the total sample size for the two groups.

Deciding Which Statistical Test to Use

Because you test different hypotheses for independent and paired samples, you use different tests. In addition, there are parametric and nonparametric tests for each case. In deciding which statistical test to use, first decide if you have independent or paired groups and then decide if you should use a parametric or a nonparametric test. This second decision is based on whether the assumptions for the parametric test seem reasonable. The next four sections describe the different tests to use in each of the four situations. These tests are summarized in Table 7.3.

Table 7.3   **Statistical Tests for Comparing Two Groups**

Type of Test	Type of Groups	
	Independent	**Paired**
Parametric	Two-sample t-test	Paired-difference t-test
Nonparametric	Wilcoxon Rank Sum test	Wilcoxon Signed Rank Test

Understanding Results

For any of the four tests in Table 7.3, there are two possible outcomes: the p-value is lower than the predetermined reference probability, or it is not.

Groups Significantly Different

If the p-value is less than the reference probability, the result is statistically significant, and you reject the null hypothesis. For independent groups, you conclude that averages for the two groups are significantly different. For paired groups, you conclude that the average difference is significantly different from 0.

Groups Not Significantly Different

If the p-value is greater than the reference probability, the result is not statistically significant, and you fail to reject the null hypothesis. For independent groups you conclude that averages for the two groups are not significantly different. For paired groups, you conclude that the average difference is not significantly different from 0.

Do not conclude that the means for two groups are the same or that the mean difference is 0. You do not have enough evidence to make these conclusions. You don't know that the averages are identical; the results of the test only tell you that the averages are not significantly different from one another. Also, you don't have evidence to conclude that the difference is 0; the results of the test only tell you that the average difference is not significantly different from 0.

Remember that you don't accept the null hypothesis; instead, you either reject or fail to reject the null hypothesis. For a more detailed discussion of hypothesis testing, see Chapter 5.

Performing the Two-Sample *t*-test

The two-sample *t*-test is a parametric test to compare two independent samples.

Assumptions and Hypothesis Test

Usually, the null hypothesis is that the means for the two groups are equal and the alternative hypothesis is that they are not. There are three assumptions for this test:

- observations are independent
- observations for each group are a random sample from a population with a normal distribution
- variances for the two independent groups are equal.

As a consequence of the second assumption, the two-sample *t*-test should be used only for interval or ratio variables.

The steps in performing the analysis are:

1. Create a SAS data set.
2. Check the data set for errors.
3. Decide the significance level for the test.
4. Check the assumptions for the test.
5. Perform the test.
6. Make conclusions from the test results.

For the body fat data, suppose you want to use a 5% significance level. The assumption of independent observations is met because each person's body fat measurement is unrelated to every other person's measurement. For the assumption of normality, you can test for normality for each group (see Chapter 5) and find that this assumption is reasonable. The assumption of equal variances seems reasonable based on the similarity of the standard deviations (s =5.32 for females and 6.03 for males). This assumption can be tested with PROC TTEST.

Using PROC TTEST

PROC TTEST first provides a test to check the assumption of equal variances for the two independent groups. Then, PROC TTEST provides both the exact two-sample *t*-test, which assumes equal variances, and an approximate test that can be used if the assumption of equal variances isn't met. For the body fat data, type

```
proc ttest data=bodyfat;
    class gender;
    var fatpct;
    title 'Body Fat for Fitness Program';
run;
```

The PROC TTEST statement requests a two-sample *t*-test for the BODYFAT data set. The CLASS statement names the variable that classifies the data set into two groups. The VAR statement names the measurement variable to be analyzed. The preceding statements produce Output 7.5.

Output 7.5   Comparing Two Independent Groups with PROC TTEST

```
Body Fat for Fitness Program                              1

                           TTEST PROCEDURE

Variable: FATPCT         Body Fat Percentage

GENERATE    N        Mean        Std Dev     Std Error     Minimum      Maximum
------------------------------------------------------------------------------
Female     10    22.29000000   5.31965955   1.68222406   12.00000000   30.00000000
Male       13    18.17692308   6.03243371   1.67309608    8.00000000   31.00000000


Variances        T        DF     Prob>|T|
-----------------------------------------
Unequal       1.7336     20.5     0.0980
Equal         1.7042     21.0     0.1031

For H0: Variances are equal, F' = 1.29     DF = (12,9)     Prob>F' = 0.7182
```

Performing Hypothesis Tests

To compare two independent groups, first look at the last line of the output, labeled *For H0: Variances are equal*. This line gives the results of a test for equal variances. Find the number to the right of *Prob>F' =*. This is the *p*-value for the test of equal variances. For the body fat data, the *p*-value is 0.7182. This indicates that it is reasonable to assume equal variances. In general, if this *p*-value is larger than 0.10, you can use the two-sample *t*-test for equal variances. The *p*-value of 0.10 corresponds to a 10% significance level for the test for equal variances.

Now that you know the results of the test for equal variances, you can test to find out if the means for the groups are different. Beginning with the column labeled *Variances*, the results of two statistical tests are shown. The row labeled *Equal* gives the results of an exact two-sample *t*-test. Use these results if you can assume equal variances for the two groups. The row labeled *Unequal* gives the results of an approximate two-sample *t*-test. Use these results if you can't assume equal variances for the two groups.

Since you can assume equal variances for the body fat data, look at the row labeled *Equal*. The *p*-value for the exact two-sample *t*-test is 0.1031, which is greater than 0.05. This indicates that the body fat averages for men and women in the fitness program are not significantly different at the 5% significance level.

Yet other data in this area indicate that the body fat averages are significantly different for men and women. Why don't you find significance with this set of data? One possible reason is the small sample size. Only a few people were measured, and perhaps a larger data set would have given a more accurate picture of the populations. Another possible reason is uncontrolled factors affecting the data. Although these people were participants in a fitness program, their activities were not monitored nor were their diets. Perhaps these or other factors had enough influence on the data to obscure differences that exist.

Notice that the two groups would be significantly different at the 15% significance level. Now you see why you **always choose the significance level first:** your criterion for statistical significance shouldn't be based on the results of the test.

The list below identifies the portions of output discussed so far and summarizes the purpose of each portion.

T, DF, $Prob>|T|$

give the value of the *t*-statistic, the associated degrees of freedom, and the *p*-value for both the exact and approximate tests. The *t*-statistic for the approximate test is an approximate *t*-statistic. Large values of *t*-statistics indicate significant differences. For the exact test, *DF* is calculated by adding the sample sizes for each group and then subtracting 2 (21=10+13-2). For the approximate test, *DF* is calculated differently.

$F' =$, $DF =$, $Prob>F' =$

give the value of the test statistic, the degrees of freedom, and the *p*-value associated with the test for equal variances.

In the preceding example, you saw how to interpret output from PROC TTEST for the body fat data. Table 7.4 gives a general method to use for interpreting output from PROC TTEST.

Table 7.4   **Interpreting Results from PROC TTEST**

---

1. Look at the line labeled *For H0: Variances are equal.* At the end of this line, look at the probability after *Prob>F' =*. If this probability is greater than 0.10, proceed with the assumption of equal variances. Otherwise, use the approximate *t*-test, which is labeled as the test for unequal variances.

2. Look at the appropriate row based on the results of the test for equal variances. The column labeled *T* gives the value of the test statistic, the column labeled *DF* gives the degrees of freedom, and the column labeled *Prob>|T|* gives the *p*-value.

3. From the appropriate row of the column labeled *Prob>|T|*, make conclusions about the differences between the two groups. To perform the test at the 5% significance level, you conclude the two groups are significantly different if the probability is less than 0.05. To perform the test at the 10% significance level, you conclude that the two groups are significantly different if the probability is less than 0.10. Conclusions for tests at other significance levels are made in a similar manner.

Explaining Other Items in the Output

In addition to the information needed to make conclusions about the differences between groups, PROC TTEST gives some summary statistics and details about the hypothesis tests. These are described in the list below:

Variable: FATPCT

    names the variable to be analyzed.

GENDER

    gives the name of the variable in the CLASS statement and lists the values of the variable.

N, Mean, Std Dev, Std Error

give the number of observations in each group, the average for each group, the standard deviation for each group, and the standard error of the mean for each group.

Minimum, Maximum

give the minimum and maximum observation in each group. For some line sizes, these two items do not appear. See Chapter 2 for a discussion of the LINESIZE= option.

Summarizing PROC TTEST

The general form of the statements for using PROC TTEST to perform a two-sample *t*-test is:

PROC TTEST DATA= *data-set-name* ;
    CLASS *class-variable* ;
    VAR *measurement-variables* ;

where *data-set-name* is the name of a SAS data set, *class-variable* is a variable that classifies the data into groups, and *measurement-variables* are the variables you want to summarize.

The CLASS statement is required, and *class-variable* can have only two levels. While the VAR statement is not required, you should use it. Otherwise, *t*-tests are performed for every numeric variable in the data set.

You can use the BY statement to perform several *t*-tests corresponding to the several levels of another variable. However, another statistical analysis may be more appropriate, and you should consult a statistical text or a statistician before you do this analysis.

Performing the Wilcoxon Rank Sum Test

The Wilcoxon Rank Sum test is a nonparametric test for comparing two independent groups. It provides a nonparametric analogue to the two-sample *t*-test and is sometimes referred to as the Mann-Whitney *U* test. The null hypothesis is that the two populations are the same. The only other assumption for this test is that the observations are independent. In practice, this test is used with measurement variables that are ordinal, interval, and ratio.

Using PROC NPAR1WAY

To illustrate the Wilcoxon Rank Sum test, consider an experiment to investigate the content of gastric juices of two groups of patients.*

The patients are divided into two groups: patients with peptic ulcers and "normal" or control patients without peptic ulcers. The goal of the analysis is to determine if the average lysozyme levels for the two groups are significantly different at the 5% significance level. (Lysozyme is an enzyme that can destroy the cell walls of some kinds of bacteria.) The SAS program to create and analyze this data is shown below. The WILCOXON option in the PROC NPAR1WAY statement requests the Wilcoxon Rank Sum test. The CLASS statement identifies the variable that classifies the observations into two groups. The VAR statement identifies the variable to use to compare the two groups. These statements produce Output 7.6:

```
data gastric;
   input group $ lysolevl @@;
   datalines;
U 0.2 U 10.4 U 0.3 U 10.9 U 0.4 U 11.3 U 1.1 U 12.4 U 2.0
U 16.2 U 2.1 U 17.6 U 3.3 U 18.9 U 3.8 U 20.7 U 4.5
U 24.0 U 4.8 U 25.4 U 4.9 U 40.0 U 5.0 U 42.2 U 5.3
U 50.0 U 7.5 U 60.0 U 9.8
N 0.2 N 5.4 N 0.3 N 5.7 N 0.4 N 5.8 N 0.7 N 7.5 N 1.2 N 8.7
N 1.5 N 8.8 N 1.5 N 9.1 N 1.9 N 10.3 N 2.0 N 15.6 N 2.4
N 16.1 N 2.5 N 16.5 N 2.8 N 16.7 N 3.6 N 20.0
N 4.8 N 20.7 N 4.8 N 33.0
;

proc nparlway data=gastric wilcoxon;
   class group;
   var lysolevl;
   title 'Comparison of Ulcer and Control Patients';
run;
```

*"Data is from Tables II and III in Myer, K., Pridden, J.F., Lehman, W.L., et al. (1948), "Lysozyme activity in ulcerative alimentary disease," *American Journal of Medicine*, 5, 482-495. Used with permission of Cahners Publishing Company. Copyright © 1948.

Output 7.6   Performing the Wilcoxon Rank Sum Test with PROC NPAR1WAY

```
Comparison of Ulcer and Control Patients                    1

                    N P A R 1 W A Y   P R O C E D U R E

          Wilcoxon Scores (Rank Sums) for Variable LYSOLEVL
                    Classified by Variable GROUP


                      Sum of      Expected      Std Dev         Mean
      GROUP      N     Scores     Under H0      Under H0        Score

        U       29     976.0       870.0      65.9439284    33.6551724
        N       30     794.0       900.0      65.9439284    26.4666667
                    Average Scores Were Used for Ties



          Wilcoxon 2-Sample Test (Normal Approximation)
          (with Continuity Correction of .5)

          S =  976.000     Z =  1.59984     Prob > |Z| = 0.1096


          T-Test Approx. Significance = 0.1151


          Kruskal-Wallis Test (Chi-Square Approximation)
          CHISQ =  2.5838     DF =  1     Prob > CHISQ = 0.1080
```

The one assumption for the Wilcoxon Rank Sum test (that the observations are independent) is met, so you can proceed with interpreting the output.

Finding the *p*-value

To find the *p*-value, look at the number to the right of *Prob* > |*Z*|. For the ulcer data, this value is 0.1096, which is greater than the significance level of 0.05. Therefore, you conclude that average lysozyme levels for the control patients and patients with ulcers are not significantly different at the 5% significance level.

In general, to interpret output from a Wilcoxon Rank Sum test, check the *p*-value that appears just after *Prob* > |*Z*|. If this *p*-value is less than the value associated with the predetermined significance level, conclude that the averages for the two groups are significantly different. If the *p*-value is greater than the reference probability, conclude that the averages are not significantly different. Again, in the case of nonsignificance, don't conclude that the means are identical. (See the discussion about interpreting results, earlier in this chapter.)

Understanding Other Items in the Output

In addition to the results of the Wilcoxon Rank Sum test, PROC NPAR1WAY prints results of some other tests. Some of these results appear on the same line as the *p*-value and some appear below the *p*-value. These additional tests are not explained in this book. The list below gives an explanation of the descriptive information printed by PROC NPAR1WAY.

Wilcoxon Scores (Rank Sums) for Variable LYSOLEVL

identify the test that is performed and the variable that is analyzed. Wilcoxon Scores are explained below.

Classified by Variable GROUP

names the variable that classifies the data into groups.

GROUP

lists the levels of the variable that defines the groups. The title and content of this column depend on the variable listed in the CLASS statement. In this example, the variable that defines the groups is called GROUP, and the levels of GROUP are U (ulcer) and N (normal).

N

lists the number of observations in each group.

Sum of Scores

lists the sum of the Wilcoxon scores associated with each group. To get these scores, all values of the measurement variable are arranged from highest to lowest and are assigned ranks. The lowest value receives a 1. The scores for each group are then summed to get the number in this column.

Expected Under H0

lists the Wilcoxon scores expected under the null hypothesis of no difference between the groups. If sample sizes for the two groups are the same, these values will also be the same.

Std Dev Under H0

gives the standard deviation of the sum of scores under the null hypothesis.

Mean Score

> gives the average score for each group. This is calculated as *(Sum of Scores)/N.*

Average Scores Were Used for Ties

> describes how ties were handled by the procedure. Ties occur when you arrange the data from highest to lowest and two values are the same. Suppose the observations that would be ranked as 7 and 8 have the same value for the measurement variable. Then, these observations are both assigned a rank of 7.5 (=15/2). This message is for information; there isn't an option to control how ties are handled.

Wilcoxon 2-Sample Test (Normal Approximation) (with Continuity Correction of .5)

> provides details about the Wilcoxon Rank Sum test that is performed by PROC NPAR1WAY. These two lines always appear.

Summarizing PROC NPAR1WAY

The general form of the statements for using PROC NPAR1WAY to perform a Wilcoxon Rank Sum test is:

> **PROC NPAR1WAY DATA=** *data-set-name* ;
>   **CLASS** *class-variable* ;
>   **VAR** *measurement-variable* ;
>
> where *data-set-name* is the name of a SAS data set, *class-variable* is a variable that classifies the data into groups, and *measurement-variable* is the variable you want to analyze.
>
> **The CLASS statement is required**, and *class-variable* can have only two levels. While the VAR statement is not required, you should use it. Otherwise, tests are performed for every numeric variable in the data set.

You can use the BY statement to perform several tests that correspond to the several levels of another variable. However, another statistical analysis may be more appropriate, and you should consult a statistical text or a statistician before you do this analysis.

Performing the Paired-Difference *t*-test

The paired difference *t*-test is a parametric test for comparing paired groups.

Assumptions and Hypothesis Test

The paired-difference *t*-test has assumptions that are similar to those of the two-sample *t*-test. The two assumptions for this test are

- each pair of measurements is independent of other pairs
- differences are from a normal distribution.

Because the test analyzes the differences between paired observations, it is appropriate for use with interval or ratio variables.

For the hypotheses that are described earlier in "Building Hypothesis Tests to Compare Two Groups," the paired-difference *t*-test is automatically performed by PROC UNIVARIATE. Although the procedure always performs this test, it is most useful for paired differences where the goal is to test if the average is significantly different from 0.

Using PROC UNIVARIATE

To illustrate this test, data from a liquid chromatography experiment is used.[*]

In this experiment, a chemist was investigating synthetic fuels produced from coal and wanted to measure the naphthalene values by using two different liquid chromatography methods. Each of the 10 fuel samples was divided into two units: one unit was measured using standard liquid chromatography (STD), and the other unit was measured using high pressure liquid chromatography (HP). The goal of analysis is to test if the mean difference between the two methods is different from 0 at the 5% significance level. In other words, the chemist is willing to accept a 1 in 20 chance of saying that the average difference is significantly different from 0 when in fact it is not.

First, create a data set and check it for errors. Then, the steps in analysis are to choose a significance level, to decide if assumptions are met, to perform the test, and to interpret the results.

---

[*] Data is from Table 2.1 in Bayne, C.K. and Rubin, I.B. (1986), *Practical Experimental Designs and Optimization Methods for Chemists.* New York: VCH Publishers. Used with permission. Copyright © 1986.

The statements that follow produce Output 7.7, which is abbreviated to show only a portion of the PROC UNIVARIATE output.

```
data chromat;
   input hp std @@;
   methdiff=hp-std;
   datalines;
12.1 14.7 10.9 14.0 13.1 12.9 14.5 16.2 9.6 10.2 11.2 12.4
 9.8 12.0 13.7 14.8 12.0 11.8 9.1 9.7
;

proc print data=chromat;
   title 'Difference between Chromatography Methods';
proc univariate data=chromat;
   var methdiff;
run;
```

Output 7.7   Comparing Paired Groups for Chromatography Data

```
Difference between Chromatography Methods                    1

                 OBS      HP     STD     METHDIFF

                   1    12.1    14.7      -2.6
                   2    10.9    14.0      -3.1
                   3    13.1    12.9       0.2
                   4    14.5    16.2      -1.7
                   5     9.6    10.2      -0.6
                   6    11.2    12.4      -1.2
                   7     9.8    12.0      -2.2
                   8    13.7    14.8      -1.1
                   9    12.0    11.8       0.2
                  10     9.1     9.7      -0.6
          Difference between Chromatography Methods          2

                      Univariate Procedure

Variable=METHDIFF

                             Moments

             N                10   Sum Wgts          10
             Mean          -1.27   Sum            -12.7
             Std Dev    1.126499   Variance       1.269
             Skewness   -0.23368   Kurtosis    -0.96873
             USS           27.55   CSS           11.421
             CV         -88.7007   Std Mean     0.35623
             T:Mean=0   -3.56511   Pr>|T|        0.0061
             Num ^= 0         10   Num > 0            2
             M(Sign)          -3   Pr>=|M|       0.1094
             Sgn Rank      -24.5   Pr>=|S|       0.0078
```

Check for Data Errors

Look at the printed data set, and examine it for errors in the data. For a longer data set, you could use some of the data verifying techniques that are discussed in Chapter 4.

Decide if Assumptions Are Reasonable

Next, consider the two assumptions for the paired-difference *t*-test. The first assumption (that each pair of measurements is independent of other pairs) is met because there are 10 different samples that are then divided into paired units. The second assumption (that the differences are from a normal distribution) is also met. You can perform a test for normality or use one of the other summary methods discussed in Chapter 5.

What if this second assumption had not been met? With only 10 observations, you don't have a very complete picture of the distribution. Think of weighing 10 people and then deciding whether weights are normally distributed based only on the weights of those 10 people. Sometimes you have additional knowledge about the population that permits you to use tests that require a normally distributed population. For example, you may know that the weights are generally normally distributed and use that information. However, this approach should be used with caution. You should use it only when you have substantial information about the population. Otherwise, if you are concerned about the assumption of normality or if your test for normality indicates that your data is not a sample from a normally distributed population, consider performing a Wilcoxon Signed Rank test, which is discussed in the next section.

Perform Test and Interpret Results

Now that you have examined the data for errors and decided that the assumptions for the paired-difference *t*-test are reasonable, look at the PROC UNIVARIATE output. (Only part of the output is shown in Output 7.7). Look at the row labeled *T:Mean=0*. This row gives the value of the *t*-statistic and the associated probability. The *t*-statistic is -3.565, and the associated probability is 0.0061. Because the *p*-value is less than 0.05 (which is associated with a 5% significance level), the chemist concludes that the average difference in naphthalene values from the two methods is significantly different from 0.

In general, to interpret output from a paired difference *t*-test, check the value given for *Prob>|T|*. If this *p*-value is less than the predetermined significance level, conclude that the average difference is significantly different from 0. If the *p*-value is larger, conclude that the average difference is not significantly different from 0.

Summarizing the Paired-Difference *t*-test

The general form of the statements for using PROC UNIVARIATE to perform a paired-difference *t*-test is:

> **PROC UNIVARIATE=** *data-set-name* ;
>   **VAR** *measurement-variable* ;
>
> where *data-set-name* is the name of a SAS data set, and *measurement-variable* is the variable that you want to analyze.
>
> While the VAR statement is not required, you should use it. Otherwise, tests are performed for every numeric variable in the data set.

You can use the BY statement to perform several paired-difference *t*-tests that correspond to the several levels of another variable. However, another statistical analysis may be more appropriate, and you should consult a statistical text or a statistician before you do this.

Performing the Wilcoxon Signed Rank Test

The Wilcoxon Signed Rank test is a nonparametric analogue to the paired-difference *t*-test. The Wilcoxon Signed Rank test assumes that each pair of observations is independent of other pairs. This test can be used with ordinal, interval, and ratio variables.

As usual, before doing the analysis, create a data set and look for errors. Then, choose a significance level, decide if the assumption is met, perform the test, and interpret the output.

Using the chromatography data as an example, suppose that the chemist still wants to run the test at the 5% significance level. The assumption of independent pairs of observations is met. As with the paired-difference *t*-test, the Wilcoxon Signed Rank test is automatically performed by PROC UNIVARIATE.

In Output 7.7, look at the row labeled *Sgn Rank*. This row gives the value of the signed rank statistic and its associated probability. The value of the test statistic is –24.5 and the associated probability is 0.0078. Because this *p*-value is less than 0.05 (which is associated with a 5% significance level), the chemist concludes that the average difference in naphthalene values from the two methods is significantly different from 0.

In general, to interpret output from a Wilcoxon Signed Rank test, look at the value given for *Prob>|S|*. If this *p*-value is less than the predetermined significance level, conclude that the average difference is significantly different from 0. If the *p*-value is greater, conclude that the average difference is not significantly different from 0. Again, in the case of nonsignificance, do not conclude that the mean difference is 0.

Summarizing the Wilcoxon Signed Rank Test

The general form of the statements for using PROC UNIVARIATE to perform a Wilcoxon Signed Rank test is identical to that shown for "Summarizing the Paired-Difference *t*-test" earlier in this chapter.

You can use the BY statement to perform several Wilcoxon Signed Rank tests corresponding to the several levels of another variable. However, another statistical analysis may be more appropriate, and you should consult a statistical text or a statistician before you do this.

Comparing Two Groups by Using PROC INSIGHT

This section shows how to compare *paired groups* by using PROC INSIGHT. The section shows both summary methods and statistical tests for paired groups.

This section also shows how you can summarize two *independent groups* by using PROC INSIGHT. You can perform statistical tests to compare two independent groups by using PROC INSIGHT, as a special case of comparing more than two groups. To do this, you can use the same approach discussed in the next chapter under "Comparing Groups by Using PROC INSIGHT."

Comparing Test Scores Data

Remember that comparing paired groups involves comparing the difference between the "before" and "after" measurements for each observation. Both the descriptive analyses and the statistical tests involve investigating whether the distribution of differences includes 0.

To obtain descriptive summaries of the differences for the test scores data, type:

```
proc insight;
   open sta6207 / nodisplay;
   dist scordiff;
run;
```

The preceding statements create Output 7.9 and Output 7.10.

Output 7.9   **PROC INSIGHT Plots for Test Scores Differences**

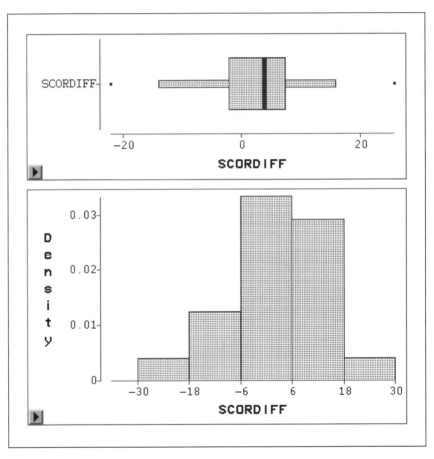

Output 7.10   **PROC INSIGHT Statistics for Test Scores Data**

```
                        Moments
 N              20.0000  Sum Wgts         20.0000
 Mean            2.5500  Sum              51.0000
 Std Dev        10.9711  Variance        120.3658
 Skewness       -0.3419  Kurtosis          0.8116
 USS          2417.0000  CSS            2286.9500
 CV            430.2406  Std Mean          2.4532

                       Quantiles
 100% Max       26.0000      99.0%       26.0000
  75% Q3         7.5000      97.5%       26.0000
  50% Med        4.0000      95.0%       21.0000
  25% Q1        -2.0000      90.0%       15.0000
   0% Min      -22.0000      10.0%      -13.5000
      Range     48.0000       5.0%      -18.0000
      Q3-Q1      9.5000       2.5%      -22.0000
      Mode       3.0000       1.0%      -22.0000
```

Outputs 7.9 and Output 7.10 show summary statistics and graphs similar to those shown previously for the test scores data.

Comparing Chromatography Data

To obtain descriptive summaries for the chromatography data using PROC INSIGHT, type

```
proc insight;
   open chromat / nodisplay;
   dist methdiff;
run;
```

The preceding statements produce Output 7.11 and Output 7.12.

Output 7.11   PROC INSIGHT Plots for Chromatography Data

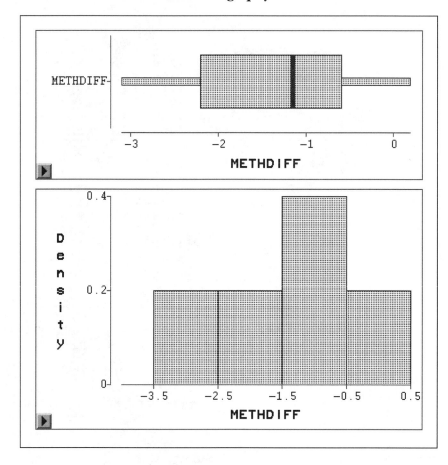

Output 7.12 **PROC INSIGHT Statistics for Chromatography Data**

```
┌─────────────────────────────────────────────────┐
│ ▶              Moments                            │
│ N              10.0000  Sum Wgts      10.0000     │
│ Mean           -1.2700  Sum          -12.7000     │
│ Std Dev         1.1265  Variance       1.2690     │
│ Skewness       -0.2337  Kurtosis      -0.9687     │
│ USS            27.5500  CSS           11.4210     │
│ CV            -88.7007  Std Mean       0.3562     │
├─────────────────────────────────────────────────┤
│ ▶              Quantiles                          │
│ 100% Max        0.2000   99.0%         0.2000     │
│  75% Q3        -0.6000   97.5%         0.2000     │
│  50% Med       -1.1500   95.0%         0.2000     │
│  25% Q1        -2.2000   90.0%         0.2000     │
│   0% Min       -3.1000   10.0%        -2.8500     │
│      Range      3.3000    5.0%        -3.1000     │
│      Q3-Q1      1.6000    2.5%        -3.1000     │
│      Mode      -0.6000    1.0%        -3.1000     │
└─────────────────────────────────────────────────┘
```

To perform a paired-difference t-test and a Wilcoxon Signed Rank test for the chromatography data, follow the steps shown in Table 7.5 below.

Table 7.5 **Obtaining Statistical Tests for Paired Groups**

Obtaining Statistical Tests for Paired Groups when Using PROC INSIGHT

After submitting statements to obtain descriptive summaries of the difference variable,

1. Select `Tables` from the menu bar.

2. Select `Location tests...` in the list that displays.

3. Select `Student's t-test` and `Signed Rank` in the window that displays.

4. Select OK.

This adds the two tables shown in Output 7.13 to the PROC INSIGHT window that contains information about the test scores.

Output 7.13   **PROC INSIGHT Tests for Chromatography Data**

Student's T Test for Mean		
Parameter (Mu)	Statistic	P-Value
0	-3.5651	0.0061

Signed Rank Test for Location				
Parameter (Mu)	N ^= Mu	N > Mu	Statistic	P-Value
0	10	2	-24.5000	0.0078

Note that these results are the same as the paired-difference *t*-test and Wilcoxon Signed Rank test results shown in Output 7.8.

Summarizing Body Fat Data

This section shows how to use PROC INSIGHT to summarize data from two independent groups. For the body fat data, type

```
proc insight;
    open bodyfat / nodisplay;
    by gender;
    dist fatpct;
run;
```

The preceding statements generate Output 7.14 and Output 7.15.

Output 7.14   **PROC INSIGHT Plots for Body Fat Data for Women**

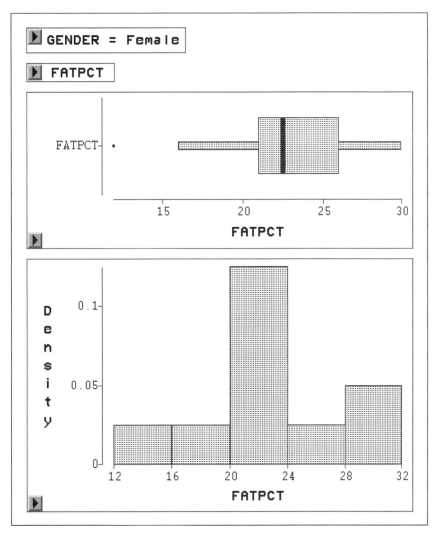

Output 7.15   PROC INSIGHT Plots for Body Fat Data for Men

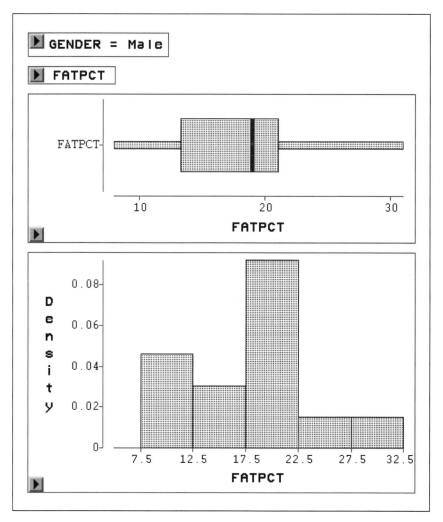

The statements also generate summary statistics similar to Output 7.14. The statistics are generated separately for females and males. Note that the bar charts are similar to those generated earlier in the chapter.

Summarizing PROC INSIGHT

The general form of the statements to summarize data from paired groups and from independent groups is shown below. Table 7.5 shows the general form for getting a paired-difference *t*-test and a Wilcoxon Signed Rank test by using PROC INSIGHT.

> **PROC INSIGHT**;
>   **OPEN** *data-set-name* / **NODISPLAY** ;
>   **BY** *grouping-variable*;
>   **DIST** *measurement-variable* ;
>
> where *data-set-name* is the name of a SAS data set, *grouping-variable* is the variable that classifies the data into two independent groups, and *measurement-variable* is the variable that contains paired-differences.
>
> For independent groups, use the BY statement for summarizing the two groups.
>
> For paired groups, do not use the BY statement.

Summaries

Key Ideas

- Independent groups contain observations for two different groups in the population, and paired groups contain paired measurements for each observation.

- The same SAS procedures that summarize a single group can be used to summarize independent and paired groups. For paired groups, summarize the difference variable just as you would a single variable. For independent groups, first sort the data using a BY statement in PROC SORT, and then use the identical BY statement in a procedure that summarizes the data.

- Program statements can be used in the DATA step to create new variables.

- To choose a statistical test, first decide if the data is from independent or paired groups, and then decide whether to use a parametric or a nonparametric test. This second decision is often based on whether the assumptions for a parametric test can be met. Tests for the four cases are summarized in the following:

Type of Test	Type of Groups	
	Independent	Paired
Parametric	Two-sample *t*-test	Paired-difference *t*-test
Nonparametric	Wilcoxon Rank Sum test	Wilcoxon Signed Rank Test

The steps for performing these tests are to choose a significance level, to use SAS software to perform the test, and to interpret the output.

Syntax

- To summarize data from independent groups:

  PROC MEANS DATA=*data-set-name* ;
  CLASS *class-variable* ;
  VAR *measurement-variables* ;

  where *data-set-name* is the name of a SAS data set, *class-variable* is the variable that classifies the data into groups, and *measurement-variables* are the variables to be summarized.

- To obtain a bar chart for each independent group:

  PROC SORT DATA=*data-set-name* ;
     BY *grouping-variable*;
  PROC GCHART DATA=*data-set-name*;
     BY *grouping-variable;*
  VBAR *measurement-variables*;

  where items in italic are as defined previously. Note that *grouping-variable* performs the same role here as *class-variable* does for PROC MEANS above.

  The UNIVARIATE and FREQ procedures can also be used in place of the GCHART procedure in this pattern. First, sort the data by using a BY statement in PROC SORT, and then use the identical BY statement with the other procedure. If PROC GCHART is not available, PROC CHART can be used instead. The same BY and VBAR statements can be used.

- To produce side-by-side charts for data from independent groups,

  PROC GCHART DATA=*data-set-name*;
      VBAR *measurement-variables* / **GROUP=***grouping-variable*;

  where items in italic are as defined previously. For horizontal side-by-side charts, replace VBAR with HBAR in the statements above.

- To summarize paired groups, summarize the difference variable by using the MEANS, UNIVARIATE, FREQ, and CHART procedures as you would for a single variable.

- To perform a two-sample *t*-test,

  PROC TTEST DATA=*data-set-name* ;
      CLASS *class-variable* ;
      VAR *measurement-variables* ;

  where items in italic are as defined previously.

- To perform a Wilcoxon Rank Sum test,

  PROC NPAR1WAY DATA=*data-set-name* **WILCOXON**;
      CLASS *class-variable* ;
      VAR *measurement-variables* ;

  where items in italic are as defined previously.

- To perform a paired-difference *t*-test or a Wilcoxon Signed Rank test,

  PROC UNIVARIATE DATA=*data-set-name* ;
      VAR *measurement-variables* ;

  where items in italic are as defined previously.

- To summarize data using PROC INSIGHT,

  PROC INSIGHT;
      OPEN *data-set-name* / **NODISPLAY** ;
      BY *grouping-variable* ;
      DIST *measurement-variable* ;

  where *data-set-name* is the name of a SAS data set, *grouping-variable* is the variable that classifies data into two independent groups, and *measurement-variable* is the variable that contains paired-differences.

  For independent groups, use the BY statement for summarizing the two groups. For paired groups, do not use the BY statement. To obtain statistical tests for paired groups, submit the statements needed to summarize your data using PROC INSIGHT and then follow the steps in Table 7.5.

Example

The following program produces all of the output shown in this chapter:

```
proc format;
value $gentext 'm' = 'Male'
               'f' = 'Female';
run;

data bodyfat;
   input gender $ fatpct @@;
   format gender $gentext.;
   label fatpct='Body Fat Percentage';
   datalines;
m 13.3 f 22 m 19 f 26 m 20 f 16 m 8 f 12 m 18 f 21.7
m 22 f 23.2 m 20 f 21 m 31 f 28 m 21 f 30 m 12 f 23
m 16 m 12 m 24
;

proc print data=bodyfat;
   title 'Body Fat for Fitness Program';
run;

proc means data=bodyfat;
   class gender;
   var fatpct;
run;

proc gchart data=bodyfat;
vbar fatpct / group=gender;
run;

proc ttest data=bodyfat;
   class gender;
   var fatpct;
   title 'Body Fat for Fitness Program';
run;

data sta6207;
   input student exam1 exam2 @@;
   label scordiff='Differences in Exam Scores';
   scordiff=exam2-exam1;
   datalines;
1 93 98 2 88 74 3 89 67 4 88 92 5 67 83 6 89 90
7 83 74 8 94 97 9 89 96 10 55 81 11 88 83 12 91 94
13 85 89 14 70 78 15 90 96 16 90 93 17 94 81
18 67 81 19 87 93 20 83 91
;
```

```
proc means data=sta6207;
   var scordiff;
   title 'Summary of Differences in Test Scores';
run;

proc gchart data=sta6207;
   vbar scordiff;
   title 'Chart of Differences in Test Scores';
run;

data gastric;
   input group $ lysolevl @@;
   datalines;
U 0.2 U 10.4 U 0.3 U 10.9 U 0.4 U 11.3 U 1.1 U 12.4 U 2.0
U 16.2 U 2.1 U 17.6 U 3.3 U 18.9 U 3.8 U 20.7 U 4.5
U 24.0 U 4.8 U 25.4 U 4.9 U 40.0 U 5.0 U 42.2 U 5.3
U 50.0 U 7.5 U 60.0 U 9.8
N 0.2 N 5.4 N 0.3 N 5.7 N 0.4 N 5.8 N 0.7 N 7.5 N 1.2 N 8.7
N 1.5 N 8.8 N 1.5 N 9.1 N 1.9 N 10.3 N 2.0 N 15.6 N 2.4 N 16.1
N 2.5 N 16.5 N 2.8 N 16.7 N 3.6 N 20.0
N 4.8 N 20.7 N 4.8 N 33.0
;

proc nparlway data=gastric wilcoxon;
   class group;
   var lysolevl;
   title 'Comparison of Ulcer and Control Patients';
run;

data chromat;
   input hp std @@;
   methdiff=hp-std;
   datalines;
12.1 14.7 10.9 14.0 13.1 12.9 14.5 16.2 9.6 10.2 11.2 12.4
9.8 12.0 13.7 14.8 12.0 11.8 9.1 9.7
;

proc print data=chromat;
   title 'Difference between Chromatography Methods';
proc univariate data=chromat;
   var methdiff;
run;
```

```
proc insight;
   open sta6207 / nodisplay;
   dist scordiff;
run;

proc insight;
   open chromat / nodisplay;
   dist methdiff;
run;

proc insight;
   open bodyfat / nodisplay;
   by gender;
   dist fatpct;
run;
```

To obtain the statistical tests for the chromatography data (shown in Output 7.13), submit the preceding PROC INSIGHT statements and then follow the steps in Table 7.5.

Further Reading

For more information about nonparametric methods, see the following:

- Conover, W.J. (1980), *Practical Nonparametric Statistics*, 2nd Edition, New York: John Wiley & Sons, Inc.

- Hollander, M. and Wolfe, D.A. (1973), *Nonparametric Statistical Methods*, New York: John Wiley & Sons, Inc.

- Siegel, S. (1956), *Nonparametric Statistics for the Behavioral Sciences*, New York: McGraw-Hill Book Company.

For more information about *t*-tests, see the introductory statistics texts listed at the end of Chapter 5. See also the following book:

- Steel, R.G.D. and Torrie, J.H. (1980), *Principles and Procedures of Statistics,* 2nd Edition, New York: McGraw-Hill Book Company.

For more information about the TTEST and NPAR1WAY procedures, see one of these manuals:

- *SAS/STAT® Software: Syntax, Version 6, First Edition*

- *SAS/STAT® Software: Reference, Version 6, Fourth Edition, Volumes 1 and 2*

Chapter 8 **Comparing More Than Two Groups**

Suppose you ran an experiment to compare the effects of 6 fertilizers on the growth of geraniums. You had 30 plants, and you randomly assigned 5 plants to each of the 6 fertilizer groups. You carefully controlled other factors: you used the same type of soil for all 30 plants, you made sure they all received the same number of hours of light each day, and you applied the fertilizers on the same day and in the same amounts to all 30 plants. At the end of this designed experiment, you measured the height of each plant. Now you want to compare the 6 fertilizer groups in terms of plant height. This chapter discusses this type of problem. Specific topics are

- summarizing data from more than two groups
- building a test of hypothesis for data in several groups
- performing a one-way analysis of variance with PROC ANOVA
- performing a Kruskal-Wallis test with PROC NPAR1WAY
- exploring differences with multiple comparison procedures
- comparing more than two groups using PROC INSIGHT.

The methods discussed in this chapter are appropriate for situations where each group consists of measurements of different items. The methods are not appropriate when "groups" are simply measurements of the same item at different times, for example, if you were to measure the same 15 plants 2, 4, and 6 weeks after applying fertilizer. (These are repeated measures designs. They are not discussed here. See "Further Reading" for references.)

The analysis method that you choose determines whether ordinal, interval, or ratio variables can be analyzed by using the methods shown here. The variable that classifies the data into groups should be a nominal variable.

Contents

Summarizing Data from More Than Two Groups

This section discusses the methods used to summarize data in several groups. These methods are not a replacement for formal statistical tests, but they give you an intuitive understanding of the data and may make the results from a statistical test easier to understand.

Before you can summarize data, you need to create a SAS data set. Then examine the data set for errors before you make any decisions. For a small data set, print the data and verify the printout against the data that you collected. For a larger data set, you probably want to use some of the methods discussed in Chapter 4. Because you can use the same SAS procedures to look for errors and to summarize the data, this process isn't very difficult.

To illustrate these summary methods, data from an investigation of teachers' salaries for different subject areas is used. This data contains variables for the subject area and for the annual salaries earned by the teachers. The goal of analysis is to determine if the teachers' salaries depend on the subject area they are teaching.

Using the SORT and MEANS Procedures

One way to summarize data in several groups is to find the average for each group. The following statements create a SAS data set for the teacher salary data. This program uses labels and formats as discussed in the "Advanced Topics" section of Chapter 3. The statements also print the data and summarize the data. Output 8.1 shows the PROC MEANS results.

```
options ls=90;
proc format;
   value $subtxt
     'speced' = 'Special Ed'
     'mathem' = 'Mathematics'
     'langua' = 'Language'
     'music'  = 'Music'
     'scienc' = 'Science'
     'socsci' = 'Social Science';
data tchsal;
   input subjarea $ annsal @@;
   label subjarea='Subject Area'
         annsal='Annual Salary';
```

```
format subjarea $subtxt.;
  datalines;
speced 35584 mathem 27814 langua 26162 mathem 25470
speced 41400 mathem 34432 music 21827 music 35787
music 30043 mathem 45480 mathem 25358 speced 42360
langua 23963 langua 27403 mathem 29610 music 27847
mathem 25000 mathem 29363 mathem 25091 speced 31319
music 24150 langua 30180 socsci 42210 mathem 55600
langua 32134 speced 57880 mathem 47770 langua 33472
music 21635 mathem 31908 speced 43128 mathem 33000
music 46691 langua 28535 langua 34609 music 24895
speced 42222 speced 39676 music 22515 speced 41899
music 27827 scienc 44324 scienc 43075 langua 49100
langua 44207 music 46001 music 25666 scienc 30000
mathem 26355 mathem 39201 mathem 32000 langua 26705
mathem 37120 langua 44888 mathem 62655 scienc 24532
mathem 36733 langua 29969 mathem 28521 langua 27599
music 27178 mathem 26674 langua 28662 music 41161
mathem 48836 mathem 25096 langua 27664 music 23092
speced 45773 mathem 27038 mathem 27197 music 44444
speced 51096 mathem 25125 scienc 34930 speced 44625
mathem 27829 mathem 28935 mathem 31124 socsci 36133
music 28004 mathem 37323 music 32040 scienc 39784
mathem 26428 mathem 39908 mathem 34692 music 26417
mathem 23663 speced 35762 langua 29612 scienc 32576
mathem 32188 mathem 33957 speced 35083 langua 47316
mathem 34055 langua 27556 langua 35465 socsci 49683
langua 38250 langua 30171 mathem 53282 langua 32022
socsci 31993 speced 52616 langua 33884 music 41220
mathem 43890 scienc 40330 langua 36980 scienc 59910
mathem 26000 langua 29594 socsci 38728 langua 47902
langua 38948 langua 33042 mathem 29360 socsci 46969
speced 39697 mathem 31624 langua 30230 music 29954
mathem 45733 music 24712 langua 33618 langua 29485
mathem 28709 music 24720 mathem 51655 mathem 32960
mathem 45268 langua 31006 langua 48411 socsci 59704
music 22148 mathem 27107 scienc 47475 langua 33058
speced 53813 music 38914 langua 49881 langua 42485
langua 26966 mathem 31615 mathem 24032 langua 27878
mathem 56070 mathem 24530 mathem 40174 langua 27607
speced 31114 langua 30665 scienc 25276 speced 36844
mathem 24305 mathem 35560 music 28770 langua 34001
mathem 35955
  ;
```

```
proc print data=tchsal;
    title 'Teacher Salary Data';
run;

proc means data=tchsal;
    title 'Summary of Teacher Salary Data';
    class subjarea;
    var annsal;
run;
```

The output from PROC PRINT (not shown in Output 8.1) shows the data so that you can look for errors. The output from PROC MEANS gives simple summary statistics for each subject area. Note that music teachers have the lowest average value of ANNSAL, and social science teachers have the highest average value of ANNSAL. From these results, you would intuitively expect to find some overall differences among average teachers' salaries based on the subjects that they teach. However, you don't know if the differences in the average value of ANNSAL are greater than would be expected by chance only or not. To find this out, you need to use a statistical test, as shown later in this chapter.

Output 8.1   **PROC MEANS Summary of Teacher Salary Data**

```
                    Summary of Teacher Salary Data                      1

Analysis Variable : ANNSAL Annual Salary

SUBJAREA        N Obs    N       Mean      Std Dev     Minimum      Maximum
-------------------------------------------------------------------------
Language           42    42    33840.12    7194.69    23963.00    49881.00

Mathematics        56    56    34221.04    9517.30    23663.00    62655.00

Music              26    26    30294.54    7953.11    21635.00    46691.00

Science            11    11    38382.91   10434.09    24532.00    59910.00

Social Science      7     7    43631.43    9343.73    31993.00    59704.00

Special Ed         19    19    42204.79    7480.01    31114.00    57880.00
-------------------------------------------------------------------------
```

In the previous example, PROC MEANS summarizes the data. The general form of the statements for using the MEANS procedure to summarize data from several groups is:

PROC MEANS DATA=_data-set-name_ ;
  CLASS _class-variable_ ;
  VAR _measurement-variable_ ;

where _data-set-name_ is the name of a SAS data set, _class-variable_ is the variable that classifies the data into groups, and _measurement-variable_ is the variable that is to be summarized.

While the VAR statement is not required, you should use one. Otherwise, all numeric variables in the data set are summarized.

By using the MEANS procedure, you obtain several simple statistics. The next section discusses how to get more complex summary statistics.

Using the SORT and UNIVARIATE Procedures

For a more extensive summary, use the SORT and UNIVARIATE procedures in combination. First, use the SORT procedure with a BY statement, and then use the UNIVARIATE procedure and the identical BY statement. This is most useful when you have many observations in each group. For example, you may want to use a stem-and-leaf plot to summarize the data.

The BY statement in PROC SORT names the variable to sort by, and the BY statement in PROC UNIVARIATE produces a separate summary for each level of that variable. Use the same BY statement with both procedures. This example provides a pattern for you to follow with your own data. The statements to produce a PROC UNIVARIATE summary for each subject area for the teacher salary data are:

```
proc sort data=tchsal;
   by subjarea;
run;

options linesize=100;
proc univariate data=tchsal plot;
   by subjarea;
var annsal;
run;
```

If you forget the BY statement with PROC SORT, you receive an error message (in the SAS log) that the data is not sorted. Because the data isn't sorted, PROC UNIVARIATE does not run. If you remember the BY statement with PROC SORT but not with PROC UNIVARIATE, you do not get any error messages, but you get only one summary for the entire data set instead of a summary for each level of the grouping variable.

When used with a BY statement and the PLOT option, PROC UNIVARIATE produces side-by-side box plots for the different groups. While the procedure also prints the usual box plot for each group, the side-by-side box plots can be helpful in visualizing the potential differences between groups. Output 8.2 shows the side-by-side box plots for the teacher salary data.

Output 8.2   Side-by-Side Box Plots from PROC UNIVARIATE

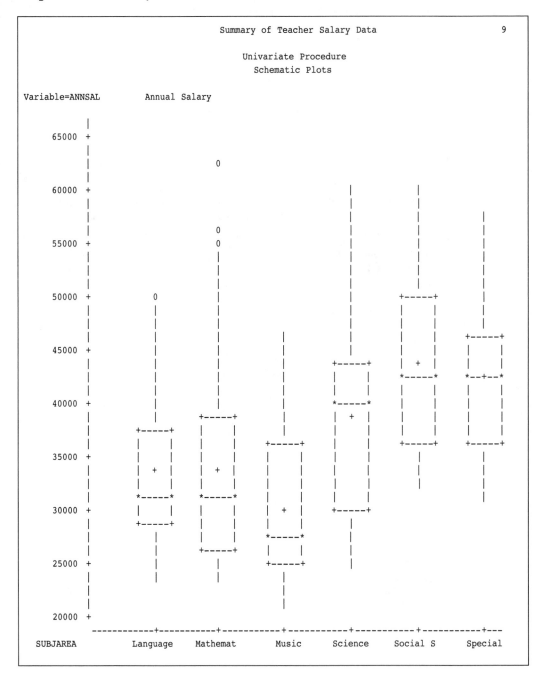

The box plots help visualize the differences between the means for the six subject areas. Music has the lowest average, and social science has the highest average. You can also see that mathematics has more outliers than the other groups. As with the PROC MEANS results, you would intuitively expect to find some overall differences among the average teachers' salaries based on the subjects they teach. To find out if the differences in average annual salary are greater than would be expected by chance requires using statistical tests that are discussed later in this chapter.

Notice that PROC UNIVARIATE truncates the formatted values of SUBJAREA to 8 characters for the side-by-side box plots. The SAS log contains a note explaining this. Also notice that the LINESIZE= option is set to 100 for this plot. With the line size of 80 (used for almost all other output in this book), the last two side-by-side plots print on a different page. Increasing the line size to 100 allows all plots to print on the same page, which makes it much easier to compare the plots.

For more detailed information about PROC UNIVARIATE, see Chapter 4.

Using the GCHART Procedure to Compare Groups

Another way to summarize data from several groups is to produce a chart that shows the distribution of values in each group. This section summarizes how to produce separate charts for each group and how to produce side-by-side charts. Bar charts are most useful for data that has many observations in each group.

Producing Separate Charts for Each Group

To produce a separate chart for each group, follow the pattern for using the BY statement. First use PROC SORT with a BY statement to identify the variable that classifies the data into groups. Then use PROC GCHART and the identical BY statement. You can produce vertical and horizontal bar charts. Also, you can use the default charts produced by PROC GCHART or customize the charts by using options. For a complete description of PROC GCHART, see Chapter 4.

Producing Side-by-Side Charts

Instead of producing separate charts for each group, you may want to produce a side-by-side chart. In this type of chart, the charts for each group are produced next to each other and share the same vertical axis. To produce a side-by-side chart, use the GROUP= option in PROC GCHART. For an example of this type of chart, see Chapter 7.

Building a Hypothesis Test to Compare More Than Two Groups

So far this chapter has discussed how to describe differences between groups. When you start a study, you usually want to do more than simply describe differences. You want to know how important the differences are and if they are large enough to be statistically significant. You want to test the ideas that you had about differences before you conducted the study and collected the data. In statistical terms, you want to perform a hypothesis test. This section discusses hypothesis testing in the framework of comparing several groups. (The general idea of hypothesis testing is introduced in Chapter 5, where the statistical concepts are summarized.)

In building a hypothesis test, you use two hypotheses. When you compare several groups, the null hypothesis is usually that the means for the different groups are the same, and the alternative hypothesis is that the means for the different groups are different. The teacher salary example has six groups. In this case, the notation used in most statistics texts and journal articles to show these two hypotheses is

$$H_o: \mu_A = \mu_B = \mu_C = \mu_D = \mu_E = \mu_F$$

and

$$H_a : \text{at least two means are different}$$

where H_o is the null hypothesis that the population means for all groups are the same, H_a is the alternative hypothesis that not all population means are equal, and $\mu_A, \mu_B, \mu_C, \mu_D, \mu_E,$ and μ_F are the population means for the six groups of teachers. Notice that the general alternative hypothesis doesn't specify which means are different from one another but only that some differences exist. The preceding example shows the hypotheses for comparing six groups. For fewer groups or more groups, simply delete or add the appropriate number of means to indicate the correct hypotheses.

In a statistical test to compare several groups, the preceding hypotheses are tested by partitioning the total variation in the data into variation due to differences between groups and variation due to "error." The "error" variation doesn't refer to mistakes in the data but to the natural variation within a group and possibly to variation due to other factors that weren't considered in the experiment. Because this test consists of analyzing the variation in the data, it is referred to as an *analysis of variance* and is abbreviated as *ANOVA*. The specific case of considering only the variation between groups and the variation due to error is called a *one-way ANOVA*. Figure 8.1 depicts how the total variation is partitioned into variation between groups and variation due to error.

Figure 8.1   **One-Way Analysis of Variance**

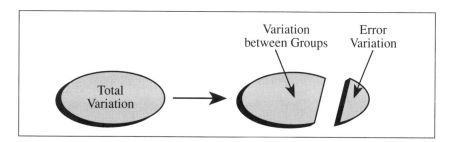

An *ANOVA* involves deciding if the variation due to differences between groups is larger than would be expected by chance. This is done by comparing the variation between groups to the error variation. The idea is that the error variation represents the natural variation that would be expected by chance, and if the variation between groups is large relative to the error variation, the group means are likely to be different.

ANOVA and Kruskal-Wallis Tests

In this book, the term *ANOVA* refers specifically to a parametric analysis of variance, which can be used if some assumptions about the data are met. If these assumptions aren't met, a nonparametric analogue to an analysis of variance, the Kruskal-Wallis test, can be used. Although there are also some assumptions for this test, they are less restrictive than the assumptions for an *ANOVA*. Both analyses are available with SAS software; the parametric analysis of variance is performed by PROC ANOVA, and the Kruskal-Wallis test is performed by PROC NPAR1WAY.

To decide which test is appropriate, look to see if the assumptions for an *ANOVA* are met. If they are, use PROC ANOVA. If they aren't, use the Kruskal-Wallis test in PROC NPAR1WAY.

Balanced and Unbalanced Data

If all groups have the same sample size, the data is *balanced*. If the sample sizes differ among groups, the data is *unbalanced*.

This distinction can be important for follow-up tests to an *ANOVA* or for other types of experimental designs. However, for a one-way analysis of variance or a Kruskal-Wallis test, you don't need to worry about whether the data is balanced. PROC ANOVA and PROC NPAR1WAY automatically handle balanced and unbalanced data correctly in this situation.

Understanding Results

In either an *ANOVA* or a Kruskal-Wallis test, there are two possible outcomes: the attained significance level is less than the predetermined significance level, or it is not.

Groups Significantly Different

If the *p*-value is less than the reference probability, you reject the null hypothesis and conclude that averages for the groups are significantly different. Note that you don't know which averages are different from one another, only that some significant differences exist.

Your next step may be to use a *multiple comparison procedure* to further investigate the differences between groups. Two parametric multiple comparison procedures are discussed later in this chapter. (Nonparametric multiple comparison procedures aren't discussed in this book.)

An alternative to multiple comparison procedures is to perform some preplanned comparisons that you decided to make before you ran the study and examined the data. For example, in medical studies, new drugs are compared with a placebo. You can use SAS software to define and test your own comparisons. Because this topic is more advanced, it's not explained in this book. (See the list of references in "Further Reading.") If you have certain comparisons you know you want to make, you should consult a statistician for help in designing your study.

Groups Not Significantly Different

If the *p*-value is greater than the reference probability, you fail to reject the null hypothesis and conclude that the averages for the groups are not significantly different. **Do not "accept the null hypothesis" and conclude that the groups are the same.** This distinction is very important. When testing for differences between groups, you never have enough evidence to conclude that the groups are identical. A bigger sample may have led to the conclusion that the groups are different. Perhaps there are other factors that weren't controlled, and they influenced the experiment enough to obscure differences between groups. For more information, see the general discussion about building hypothesis tests in Chapter 5.

Performing a One-Way Analysis of Variance

This section discusses the assumptions for a one-way analysis of variance, how to test them, how to use PROC ANOVA, and how to interpret the output.

Assumptions

The assumptions for an analysis of variance are

- observations are independent. The measurement for one item cannot affect the measurement for another item.

- observations are sampled from a normal distribution. If there are differences between groups, there may be a different normal distribution for each group.

- groups have equal variances.

Because the data needs to be observations from a normal distribution, the measurement variable needs to be either interval or ratio. If your measurement variable is ordinal, turn to the section on the Kruskal-Wallis test later in this chapter.

Testing Assumptions

Because you have already created a data set and examined it for errors, the first step in analysis is to decide if the assumptions for an *ANOVA* are reasonable.

The assumption of independent observations is met because the value of ANNSAL for one observation is unrelated to the value of ANNSAL for another observation.

The assumption of equal variances seems reasonable: look at the similarity of the standard deviations in Output 8.1 and the relatively similar heights of the box plots in Output 8.2. The standard deviations do vary, but it is difficult to tell whether the variability is due to true changes in the variance or due to sample size. Look at the differences in sample size for the different subject areas. There are 7 observations for social sciences and 56 observations for mathematics. And, the standard deviations for these groups are fairly similar. However, compare the standard deviations for social sciences and special education. It's more difficult to decide if the difference in standard deviations (which is larger) is due to a true underlying difference in the variances or due to the less precise estimate of variance as a result of the smaller sample sizes. For the purposes of this book, we assume equal variances and perform an analysis of variance. Starting with Release 6.12, the ANOVA procedure provides a test for equal variances. This is discussed in "Using PROC ANOVA to Test for Equal Variances."

The assumption of normality is difficult to verify. To truly test this assumption, you need to perform a test of normality for each group. For the groups that have a larger number of observations, this could be meaningful. But, for the groups with only a few observations, you don't have enough data to perform an adequate test. And, because you need to make the assumption about all groups, this is difficult. For the purposes of this book, we will assume normality and perform the analysis of variance.

In general, if you have additional information (such as other data sets) that indicates that the populations are normally distributed, and if this data set is a representative sample of the population, you can probably proceed on the basis of the idea that the assumption of normality seems reasonable. In addition, the analysis of variance F-statistic for comparing groups works well even for data that contains samples from nonnormal populations. However, if you are uncomfortable with this process, don't have any other data or information about the distribution of measurements, or have large groups that don't seem to be samples from normally distributed populations, you should use the Kruskal-Wallis test.

Using PROC ANOVA

To perform an analysis of variance with SAS software, use PROC ANOVA. For the special case of a one-way analysis of variance, you can use PROC ANOVA for both balanced and unbalanced data. In general, however, you should use PROC GLM for unbalanced data.

First, decide on the significance level for your test. For the teacher salary data, suppose you want to compare groups at the 10% significance level, so the reference probability value is 0.10. To perform a one-way analysis of variance for the teacher salary data, type

```
proc anova data=tchsal;
   class subjarea;
   model annsal=subjarea;
   title 'ANOVA for Teacher Salary Data';
run;
```

The CLASS statement lists the variable that classifies the data into groups. The MODEL statement describes the relationship you want to investigate. In this case, you want to find out how much of the variation in the salaries (ANNSAL) is due to differences among the subject areas (SUBJAREA). The preceding statements produce Output 8.3.

Output 8.3   **Analysis of Variance for Teacher Salary Data**

```
                           ANOVA for Teacher Salary Data                    1

                           Analysis of Variance Procedure
                               Class Level Information

Class      Levels    Values

SUBJAREA     6       Language Mathematics Music Science Social Science
                     Special Ed


                    Number of observations in data set = 161
                           ANOVA for Teacher Salary Data                    2

                           Analysis of Variance Procedure

Dependent Variable: ANNSAL    Annual Salary
                                   Sum of            Mean
Source                     DF      Squares           Square     F Value    Pr > F

Model                       5    2297379854.0    459475970.8     6.30      0.0001

Error                     155   11305093092.6     72936084.5

Corrected Total           160   13602472946.6

                  R-Square           C.V.         Root MSE           ANNSAL Mean

                  0.168894         24.31512       8540.2626           35123.255


Source                     DF      Anova SS     Mean Square    F Value    Pr > F

SUBJAREA                    5    2297379854.0    459475970.8     6.30      0.0001
```

Interpreting the First Page of Output

The first page of output tells you the name of the variable that classifies the data into groups, the number of levels of the variable, the values of the variable, and the number of observations in the data set. If some of your observations have missing values for the measurement variable, you receive a note that tells you how many observations were used in analysis.

Interpreting the Second Page of Output

Although the second page may look complicated, for a one-way analysis of variance you only need to look at one number to compare groups and decide if the averages are significantly different.

To find the *p*-value, find the row of output labeled *SUBJAREA* and look at the column labeled *Pr>F.* The number in this column gives you the *p*-value for comparing groups. For this example, the *p*-value is 0.0001. When you compare it to the reference probability value of 0.10, you conclude that the mean annual salary is significantly different among the different subject areas.

In general, to find the *p*-value, find the row of output labeled with the name of the variable in the CLASS statement. The *p*-value under the *Pr > F* column gives you the results of the hypothesis test for comparing group means.

Understanding Other Parts of the Output

This page of output gives additional information that may help you. The list below describes the rest of the output:

Dependent Variable:ANNSAL

names the measurement variable that is used in analysis. You can specify analysis for several variables; PROC ANOVA prints a separate analysis for each variable.

Source

lists the sources of variation in the data. For a one-way analysis of variance, the first list summarizes all sources of variation and the second list summarizes only the variation between groups. For a one-way analysis of variance, the line for *Model* in the first list matches the line for the variable (*SUBJAREA*, in this example) in the second list. This is because the model has only one source of variation.

DF

contains the degrees of freedom. For a one-way analysis of variance, the *DF* for *Corrected Total* should be one less than the number of observations used in the analysis (160=161-1). The *DF* for *Model* should be one less than the number of groups (5=6-1). The *DF* for *Error* is the difference between the first two (155=160-5). The *DF* for the variable that defines groups (*SUBJAREA* in this example) should be the same as the *DF* for *Model* because the only source of variation in the MODEL statement is this variable.

Sum of Squares, Anova SS

measures the amount of variation attributed to a given source. Sums of Squares are often abbreviated as SS, hence *Anova SS*. Note that the *Model SS* and *Error SS* sum to the *Corrected Total SS*. Note also that the *Model SS* and the *SUBJAREA SS* are the same. This would not be true for more complicated models.

Mean Square (MS)

is the sum of squares divided by degrees of freedom *(MS=SS/DF)*. The mean squares are used to construct the statistical test for differences between groups.

F Value

is the value of the test statistic. For a one-way analysis of variance, both *F Values* are the same because the MODEL statement contains only the variable that defines groups. *F* is calculated by dividing the *MS* for *Model* by the *MS* for *Error*. (Remember that an analysis of variance involves partitioning the variation and testing to find out how much variation is due to differences between groups. This partitioning is done by the *F*-test, which involves calculating an *F*-value from the mean squares.)

Pr > F

gives the *p*-value for the test. This value should be compared with the reference probability value you selected before you ran the test.

ANNSAL Mean

gives the overall average for the measurement variable.

Root MSE

gives an estimate of the standard deviation after accounting for differences between groups. This is the square root of the *Mean Square* for *Error.*

C.V.

gives the coefficient of variation, which is calculated by multiplying the standard deviation by 100 and then dividing by the average.

R-Square

for a one-way analysis of variance, describes how much of the variation in the data is due to differences between groups. This number ranges from 0 to 1; the closer it is to 1, the more variation in the data is due to differences between groups.

Using PROC ANOVA to Test for Equal Variances

One of the assumptions for an ANOVA is that the groups have equal variances. When all the groups are about the same size, the analysis of variance may be used even though the variances are somewhat different. In cases where the groups are of very different sizes, you may want to test the assumption by using PROC ANOVA. For the teacher salary data, the group sample sizes vary from 7 to 56. Suppose you want to test for equal variances at the 10% significance level. The reference probability for a test is then 0.10. For the teacher salary data, type

```
proc anova data=tchsal;
   class subjarea;
   model annsal=subjarea;
   means subjarea / hovtest;
run;
```

The preceding statements produce Output 8.3, which was discussed earlier. The MEANS statement is new and produces Output 8.4. The HOVTEST option tests for "Homogeneity Of Variances," which is another way of saying "equal variances."

Output 8.4   **Testing for Equal Variances in PROC ANOVA**

```
                     ANOVA for Teacher Salary Data                    1

                     Analysis of Variance Procedure

            Levene's Test for Equality of ANNSAL Variance
            ANOVA of Squared Deviations from Group Means

                          Sum of        Mean
     Source        DF     Squares       Square      F Value    Pr > F

     SUBJAREA        5     5.312E16      1.062E16     0.9278    0.4647
     Error         155     1.775E18      1.145E16
```

As with the analysis of variance results, this page of output may look complicated, but you only need to look at one number to find the p-value and decide if the variances are significantly different.

To find the p-value, find the row of output labeled *SUBJAREA* and look at the column labeled *Pr>F*. The number in this column gives you the p-value for testing the assumption of equal variances. Because

0.4647 > 0.10, the *p*-value is greater than the reference probability value. You conclude that there is not enough evidence to declare the variances in annual salary for the six subject areas significantly different.

The rest of the output is similar to the analysis of variance output seen earlier. Explaining this test in more detail is beyond the scope of this book; see "Further Reading" for more detail.

Summarizing PROC ANOVA

The general form of the statements for performing a one-way analysis of variance with PROC ANOVA is:

> **PROC ANOVA DATA=***data-set-name* ;
>   **CLASS** *class-variable* ;
>   **MODEL** *measurement-variable* = *class-variable*;
>   **MEANS** *measurement-variable* / **HOVTEST** ;
>
> where *data-set-name* is the name of a SAS data set, *class-variable* is the variable that classifies the data into groups, and *measurement-variable* is the variable to be summarized. The HOVTEST option performs a test for equal variances among the groups. If HOVTEST is used, the slash is required.
>
> **The PROC ANOVA, the CLASS, and the MODEL statements are required.**

You can use a BY statement in PROC ANOVA and get several one-way *ANOVAs* for several levels of another variable. However, other analyses may be appropriate in this case, so you should check with a statistician before you do this.

Performing a Kruskal-Wallis Test

The Kruskal-Wallis test is a nonparametric analogue to the one-way analysis of variance, and it is performed using PROC NPAR1WAY.

Assumptions

If the assumption of normality for an *ANOVA* is not met, you can use a nonparametric analogue, the Kruskal-Wallis test. In practice, the Kruskal-Wallis test is used for ordinal, interval, and ratio variables. The null hypothesis is that the populations for the groups are the same. The only other assumption for this test is that the observations are independent.

Using PROC NPAR1WAY

To perform a Kruskal-Wallis test with SAS software, use PROC NPAR1WAY. First, choose the significance level for your test. For the teacher salary data, suppose you want to compare groups at the 10% significance level, so the reference probability value is 0.10. To perform a Kruskal-Wallis test on the teacher salary data, type

```
proc npar1way data=tchsal wilcoxon;
    class subjarea;
    var annsal;
    title 'Nonparametric Tests for Teacher Salary Data';
run;
```

The CLASS statement lists the variable that classifies the data into groups. The VAR statement lists the variable that you want to analyze. These statements produce Output 8.5.

Output 8.5   Performing a Kruskal-Wallis Test with PROC NPAR1WAY

```
          Nonparametric Tests for Teacher Salary Data          1

               N P A R 1 W A Y   P R O C E D U R E

      Wilcoxon Scores (Rank Sums) for Variable ANNSAL
                Classified by Variable SUBJAREA
```

SUBJAREA	N	Sum of Scores	Expected Under H0	Std Dev Under H0	Mean Score
Language	42	3280.0	3402.0	259.755654	78.095238
Mathemat	56	4183.0	4536.0	281.744565	74.696429
Music	26	1391.0	2106.0	217.680959	53.500000
Science	11	1061.0	891.0	149.248116	96.454545
Social S	7	857.0	567.0	120.635816	122.428571
Special	19	2269.0	1539.0	190.848107	119.421053

```
        Kruskal-Wallis Test (Chi-Square Approximation)
        CHISQ =  29.874    DF =  5     Prob > CHISQ = 0.0001
```

Interpreting the Output

As with the output for an analysis of variance, you only need to look at one number to decide the results of the test. To find the *p*-value for the Kruskal-Wallis test, look at the number to the right of *Prob > CHISQ=*. For the teacher salary example, this value is 0.0001, which is less than the reference probability value of 0.10. You conclude average annual salary for the six subject areas is significantly different at the 10% significance level.

On the same line as the *p*-value, *CHISQ=* gives the value of the test statistic. *DF=* gives the degrees of freedom associated with this statistic. This number should be one less than the number of groups in the data (5=6-1).

In addition to the results of the Kruskal-Wallis test, PROC NPAR1WAY gives you more information about the data and prints some of the information used in the hypothesis test. The rest of the output is discussed in the list below:

Wilcoxon Scores (Rank Sums) for Variable ANNSAL

tells you what type of test is being performed and the name of the variable that is being analyzed. Wilcoxon scores are explained below.

Classified by Variable SUBJAREA

names the variable that classifies the data into groups.

SUBJAREA

lists the levels of the variable that define groups. The title and content of this column are based on the variable listed in the CLASS statement.

N

lists the number of observations in each group.

Sum of Scores

lists the sum of the Wilcoxon scores associated with each group. To get these scores, all values of the measurement variable are arranged from highest to lowest and assigned ranks with the lowest value receiving a 1. The scores for each group are then summed to get the number in this column.

Expected Under H0

lists the Wilcoxon scores expected under the null hypothesis of no differences between groups. Note that these values differ. For the case where all groups have the same sample size, the values in this column are all the same.

Std Dev Under H0

gives the standard deviation of the sum of scores under the null hypothesis.

Mean Score

gives the average score for each group. This is calculated as *(Sum of Scores)/N*. For example, the mean score for Science is about 96.45 (=1061/11).

Average Scores were used for Ties

describes how ties were handled by the procedure. Ties occur when you arrange the data from highest to lowest and two values are the same. Suppose that the observations that would be ranked as 7 and 8 have the same value for the measurement variable. Then, these observations are both assigned a rank of 7.5 (=15/2). This message is for information; there isn't an option to control how ties are handled.

Summarizing PROC NPAR1WAY

The general form of the statements for performing a Kruskal-Wallis test with PROC NPAR1WAY is:

> **PROC NPAR1WAY DATA=***data-set-name* **WILCOXON** ;
>   **CLASS** *class-variable* ;
>   **VAR** *measurement-variable* ;
>
> where *data-set-name* is the name of a SAS data set, *class-variable* is the variable that classifies the data into groups, and *measurement-variable* is the variable to be analyzed.
>
> **The CLASS statement is required.** While the VAR statement is not required, you should use it. Otherwise, an analysis is performed for every numeric variable in the data set.

You can use a BY statement with PROC NPAR1WAY and get a Kruskal-Wallis test for several levels of another variable. However, other analyses may be appropriate in this case, so you should check with a statistician before you do this.

Multiple Comparison Procedures

If you perform an analysis of variance and find out that groups are significantly different, you know only that some means are different from others. You don't know which means differ from one another. The rest of this section shows how to find this out when you use an analysis of variance. Although you can do this type of analysis when you use nonparametric methods, a discussion of this is beyond the scope of this book.

Defining Some Statistical Terms

To help you decide which multiple comparison procedure is appropriate, we first need to define some statistical terms. There is a lack of agreement among statisticians about these definitions (and about which tests are best). For a consistent explanation, we use the same definitions found in manuals for SAS software. You may find different definitions and different recommendations in various statistics texts.

What we call a *multiple comparison* procedure is any test that makes two or more comparisons among three or more means. This book does not cover all the multiple comparison procedures available with SAS software; if you are looking for a particular procedure and don't see it discussed here, don't assume it isn't available. See "Further Reading" for more information.

When the concept of hypothesis testing was first introduced in Chapter 5, we related choosing an α-level to the level of risk of making a wrong decision. To understand multiple comparison procedures, you need to make another decision about risk. Specifically, you need to decide if you want to control the chances of making a wrong decision (deciding that means are different when they aren't) for all comparisons overall or if you want to control the chances of making an error for each individual comparison.

To make this decision process a little clearer, think about the TCHSAL data. There are six subject areas, so there are 15 combinations of two means to compare. Do you want to control the chance of making a wrong decision (deciding that two means are different when they aren't) for all 15 comparisons at once? If you do, you are controlling the *experimentwise error rate*, or the chance of making an error for the experiment overall. On the other hand, do you want to control the chance of making a wrong decision for each of the 15 comparisons? If you do, you are controlling the *comparisonwise error rate*, or the chance of making an error for each comparison. We abbreviate the comparisonwise error rate as *CER* and the experimentwise error rate as *MEER*. You will also see the abbreviation *MEER* used for *maximum experimentwise error rate* in SAS manuals.

The next several sections show how to perform several multiple comparison procedures; some that control the CER and some that control the MEER. In each case, you use a MEANS statement with PROC ANOVA and specify a test. Before you run any programs, you should read all of these sections. The final section, "More about Multiple Comparison Procedures," shows you how to perform these tests without re-doing the analysis of variance.

Controlling the CER with Repeated *t*-tests

You already know one way to control the comparisonwise error rate when comparing pairs of means: simply use the two-sample *t*-test at the appropriate α-level. To control the CER when comparing several pairs of means, simply perform repeated two-sample *t*-tests, one for each pair, and control the CER by controlling the error rate for each test.

> ### Technical Details
>
> In the special case of equal sample sizes for all groups, the process of performing multiple *t*-tests is the same as using a test known as Fisher's Least Significant Difference test, usually referred to as Fisher's LSD test. You don't need to worry about whether your sample sizes are equal or not. If you request multiple *t*-tests, SAS software picks Fisher's LSD test if it can be used.

To perform multiple comparison procedures in an analysis of variance, use the MEANS statement in PROC ANOVA and add an option to specify the test you want performed. To perform multiple *t*-tests, use the T option. For the TCHSAL data, type

```
proc anova data=tchsal;
   class subjarea;
   model annsal=subjarea;
   means subjarea / t;
   title 'ANOVA for Teacher Salary Data';
run;
```

This program is the same one used for the analysis of variance, except that the MEANS statement has been added. These statements produce Output 8.3 (shown earlier) and Output 8.6.

Output 8.6   Multiple *t*-test in PROC ANOVA

```
                        ANOVA for Teacher Salary Data                    2
                       Analysis of Variance Procedure
                      T tests (LSD) for variable: ANNSAL


        NOTE: This test controls the type I comparisonwise error rate not the
              experimentwise error rate.

             Alpha= 0.05  Confidence= 0.95  df= 155  MSE= 72936084
                         Critical Value of T= 1.97539

         Comparisons significant at the 0.05 level are indicated by '***'.

                                        Lower    Difference    Upper
                         SUBJAREA     Confidence   Between   Confidence
                        Comparison      Limit       Means      Limit

    Social Science - Special Ed          -6032        1427       8886
    Social Science - Science             -2908        5249      13405
    Social Science - Mathematics          2647        9410      16174    ***
    Social Science - Language             2904        9791      16679    ***
    Social Science - Music                6153       13337      20521    ***

    Special Ed     - Social Science      -8886       -1427       6032
    Special Ed     - Science             -2570        3822      10214
    Special Ed     - Mathematics          3505        7984      12463    ***
    Special Ed     - Language             3700        8365      13029    ***
    Special Ed     - Music                6819       11910      17002    ***

    Science        - Social Science     -13405       -5249       2908
    Science        - Special Ed        -10214       -3822       2570
    Science        - Mathematics         -1402        4162       9726
    Science        - Language            -1171        4543      10257
    Science        - Music                2020        8088      14156    ***

    Mathematics    - Social Science     -16174       -9410      -2647    ***
    Mathematics    - Special Ed        -12463       -7984      -3505    ***
    Mathematics    - Science             -9726       -4162       1402
    Mathematics    - Language            -3063         381       3825
    Mathematics    - Music                 -77        3926       7930

    Language       - Social Science     -16679       -9791      -2904    ***
    Language       - Special Ed        -13029       -8365      -3700    ***
    Language       - Science            -10257       -4543       1171
    Language       - Mathematics         -3825        -381       3063
    Language       - Music                -664        3546       7755

    Music          - Social Science     -20521      -13337      -6153    ***
    Music          - Special Ed        -17002      -11910      -6819    ***
    Music          - Science            -14156       -8088      -2020    ***
    Music          - Mathematics         -7930       -3926         77
    Music          - Language            -7755       -3546        664
```

Output 8.6 shows a confidence interval for the difference between each pair of means for the different subject areas. When the confidence interval for the difference encloses 0, the difference between the two means is not significant. A confidence limit that contains 0 says that the difference in means for the two groups might be 0, so there cannot be a significant difference between the two groups. A confidence limit that doesn't enclose 0 says that the difference in means for the two groups is not 0, so there is a significant difference between the two groups.

Under the heading *SUBJAREA Comparison*, the output lists each pair of subject areas. For each pair of subject areas, the output gives confidence limits and the difference between the two averages. In the far right column (without a heading), the output indicates significant differences with three asterisks. From these results, you can conclude:

- The average annual salary for social science teachers is significantly different from the average annual salary for mathematics, language, and music teachers.

- The average annual salary for special education teachers is significantly different from the average annual salary for mathematics, language, and music teachers.

- The average annual salary for science teachers is significantly different from that for music teachers.

- The average annual salaries for other pairs of subject areas is not significantly different.

Notice that the output shows the SUBJAREA comparisons twice, so that the table of confidence limits essentially repeats. As an example, the comparison between social science and special education appears both as *Social Science - Special Ed* and as *Special Ed - Social Science.* The statistical significance is the same for both.

Output 8.6 contains a note reminding you that this test controls the comparisonwise error rate. The output gives you some additional information about the tests that were performed. This information is discussed in the list below:

Alpha=

gives the α-level for the test. In this example, the default error rate of 5 chances in 100 is used. You can specify other α- levels as discussed later in "More About Multiple Comparison Procedures."

Confidence=

gives the confidence level for the test. This is 1-α, so the confidence level is 0.95 in this example.

df=

gives the degrees of freedom for the test. For balanced sample sizes, the degrees of freedom should be the number of groups multiplied by the sample size minus 1. These degrees of freedom are the same as those for the *Mean Square* for *Error* in the analysis of variance.

MSE=, Critical Value of T=

lists the variance that is used and the critical value for the tests. If the test statistic for a given test is greater than the critical value, the difference between groups is significant at the level given by *Alpha=*.

Controlling the MEER with Bonferroni *t*-tests

To control the comparisonwise error rate (CER), you have used multiple *t*-tests. To control the experimentwise error rate (MEER), you can use multiple *t*-tests with a smaller α-level for each test. This is exactly what is done with Bonferroni *t*-tests. You choose an α-level for the overall experiment and then divide this by the number of tests. For example, if you want to control the MEER at 0.05 and you have 15 tests, then each test is performed with an α-level of 0.0033 (0.05/15=0.0033). To control the overall experimentwise error at a low level, each *t*-test is performed using a very low α-level. If you have a large number of means, this process can be very conservative and fail to detect significant differences between groups.

To request Bonferroni *t*-tests for the teacher salary data, type

```
proc anova data=tchsal;
   class subjarea;
   model annsal=subjarea;
   means subjarea / bon;
   title 'ANOVA for Teacher Salary Data';
run;
```

The only difference between this program and the one for multiple *t*-tests is that the BON option is used instead of the T option. This program produces Output 8.3 (shown earlier) and Output 8.7.

Output 8.7   Performing Bonferroni *t*-tests to Compare Means

```
                        ANOVA for Teacher Salary Data                       3

                        Analysis of Variance Procedure

                  Bonferroni (Dunn) t tests for variable: ANNSAL

         NOTE: This test controls the Type I experimentwise error rate but
               generally has a higher Type II error rate than Tukey's for all
               pairwise comparisons.

           Alpha= 0.05  Confidence= 0.95  df= 155  MSE= 72936084
                       Critical Value of T= 2.98138

     Comparisons significant at the 0.05 level are indicated by '***'.
```

		Simultaneous Lower Confidence Limit	Difference Between Means	Simultaneous Upper Confidence Limit	
SUBJAREA Comparison					
Social Science	- Special Ed	-9831	1427	12684	
Social Science	- Science	-7062	5249	17559	
Social Science	- Mathematics	-797	9410	19618	
Social Science	- Language	-603	9791	20186	
Social Science	- Music	2495	13337	24179	***
Special Ed	- Social Science	-12684	-1427	9831	
Special Ed	- Science	-5825	3822	13469	
Special Ed	- Mathematics	1224	7984	14744	***
Special Ed	- Language	1325	8365	15404	***
Special Ed	- Music	4225	11910	19595	***
Science	- Social Science	-17559	-5249	7062	
Science	- Special Ed	-13469	-3822	5825	
Science	- Mathematics	-4235	4162	12559	
Science	- Language	-4081	4543	13167	
Science	- Music	-1070	8088	17246	
Mathematics	- Social Science	-19618	-9410	797	
Mathematics	- Special Ed	-14744	-7984	-1224	***
Mathematics	- Science	-12559	-4162	4235	
Mathematics	- Language	-4816	381	5578	
Mathematics	- Music	-2116	3926	9969	
Language	- Social Science	-20186	-9791	603	
Language	- Special Ed	-15404	-8365	-1325	***
Language	- Science	-13167	-4543	4081	
Language	- Mathematics	-5578	-381	4816	
Language	- Music	-2808	3546	9899	
Music	- Social Science	-24179	-13337	-2495	***
Music	- Special Ed	-19595	-11910	-4225	***
Music	- Science	-17246	-8088	1070	
Music	- Mathematics	-9969	-3926	2116	
Music	- Language	-9899	-3546	2808	

Output 8.7 is very similar to Output 8.6, which showed the results of repeated *t*-tests. For each pair of subject areas, the output shows a confidence interval for the difference between means. From these results, you can conclude:

- The average annual salary for social science teachers is significantly different from the average annual salary for music teachers.
- The average annual salary for special education teachers is significantly different from the average annual salary for mathematics, language, and music teachers.
- The average annual salaries for other pairs of subject areas are not significantly different.

Compare the conclusions above with the conclusions that were made for multiple *t*-tests. The differences point out a basic fact about controlling the CER and controlling the MEER: you find fewer significant differences between groups when you control the MEER. However, you are also at a lower risk of making at least one wrong decision in the whole experiment because the MEER is lower.

Most of the rest of Output 8.7 is quite similar to Output 8.6. The note near the top of the output reminds you that this test controls the experiment-wise error rate. This note refers to Tukey's test, which also controls the MEER. Tukey's test isn't discussed in this book; see the list of references in "Further Reading" for more detail.

Comparing Results for the TCHSAL Data

To gain a better understanding of what happens when you control the CER and the MEER, compare the results obtained for the different multiple comparison procedures for the TCHSAL data. The results of pairwise comparisons for the T and BON multiple comparison procedures are summarized in Table 8.2. For simplicity, the comparisons where differences are significant are indicated with YES; other comparisons (the NO's) are left blank.

Table 8.2   **Multiple Comparisons using T and BON for the TCHSAL Data**

SUBJAREA Comparison	T Significant	BON Significant
Social Science - Special Ed		
Social Science - Science		
Social Science - Mathematics	YES	
Social Science - Language	YES	
Social Science - Music	YES	YES
Special Ed - Social Science		
Special Ed - Science		
Special Ed - Mathematics	YES	YES
Special Ed - Language	YES	YES
Special Ed - Music	YES	YES
Science - Social Science		
Science - Special Ed		
Science - Mathematics		
Science - Language		
Science - Music	YES	

The results from multiple t-tests detect more significant differences between groups. However, these results correspond to an increased overall risk of making incorrect decisions. Although you know that each comparison has an α-level of 0.05 (because you controlled the CER), you don't know the α-level for the overall experiment. With the Bonferroni tests, you do know the overall α-level for the experiment because it corresponds to a known risk of making incorrect decisions. However, you find fewer significant differences between the groups.

Balanced Data with the *t* and BON Tests

The teacher salary data is unbalanced because the number of teachers in each subject area differs. For unbalanced data, performing multiple comparisons is usually simplest to understand with confidence intervals as shown above. This section discussed another approach that is typically used for balanced data.

To illustrate multiple comparisons with balanced data, results from an experiment that compares muzzle velocities for different types of gunpowder are used. The muzzle velocity is measured for eight cartridges from each of three types of gunpowder. The SAS statements that follow create and print the data set, summarize the data using PROC UNIVARIATE, and perform an analysis of variance using PROC ANOVA. These statements produce the output that is shown in Output 8.8 through 8.11. (These statements also produce additional output, which is not shown.)

```
data bullets;
    input powder $ velocity @@;
    datalines;
BLASTO 27.3 BLASTO 28.1 BLASTO 27.4 BLASTO 27.7
BLASTO 28.0 BLASTO 28.1 BLASTO 27.4 BLASTO 27.1
ZOOM 28.3 ZOOM 27.9 ZOOM 28.1 ZOOM 28.3 ZOOM 27.9
ZOOM 27.6 ZOOM 28.5 ZOOM 27.9 KINGPOW 28.4 KINGPOW 28.9
KINGPOW 28.3 KINGPOW 27.9 KINGPOW 28.2 KINGPOW 28.9
KINGPOW 28.8 KINGPOW 27.7
;

proc print data=bullets;
    title 'Bullets Data';
run;

proc sort data=bullets;
    by powder;
run;

proc univariate data=bullets normal plot;
    by powder;
    var velocity;
run;

proc anova data=bullets;
    class powder;
    model velocity=powder;
    means powder / t ;
    means powder / bon ;
run;
```

Output 8.8 shows the side-by-side box plots for the three types of gunpowder. From the plots, you intuitively conclude that KINGPOW has a higher average velocity than the other two types of gunpowder, but you don't know if the difference is statistically significant.

In considering the assumptions for an analysis of variance, the observations are independent. The standard deviations for the three groups are similar, as indicated by the similar sizes in the box heights. With only eight observations, it is difficult to test for normality. For the purposes of this book, we consider the assumptions for an *ANOVA* to be met. We will test for differences between the three groups of gunpowder using the 5% significance level, so the reference value is 0.05.

Output 8.8   **Side-by-Side Box Plots for Gunpowder Data**

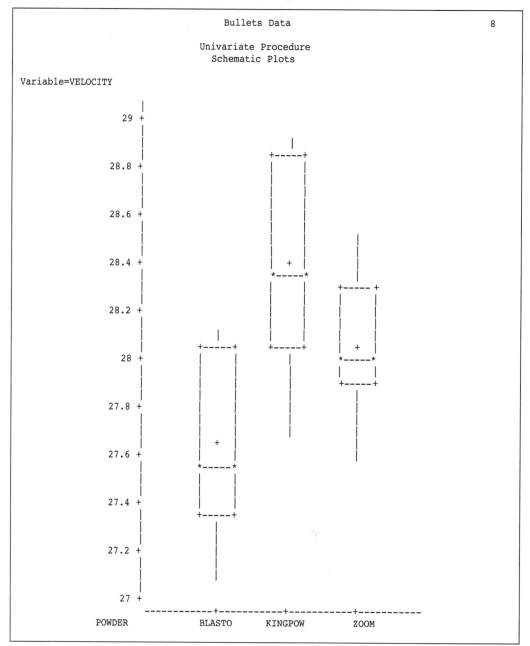

Output 8.9 shows the results of the analysis of variance.

Output 8.9   **PROC ANOVA Results for Gunpowder Data**

```
                                Bullets Data                              1

                         Analysis of Variance Procedure
                           Class Level Information

                Class     Levels     Values

                POWDER        3       BLASTO KINGPOW ZOOM


            Number of observations in data set = 24


                                Bullets Data                              2

                         Analysis of Variance Procedure

Dependent Variable: VELOCITY
                                  Sum of          Mean
Source                  DF        Squares        Square    F Value    Pr > F

Model                    2     2.26333333    1.13166667      7.60     0.0033

Error                   21     3.12625000    0.14886905

Corrected Total         23     5.38958333


             R-Square              C.V.       Root MSE       VELOCITY Mean

             0.419946           1.376550      0.3858355         28.029167


Source                  DF        Anova SS   Mean Square    F Value    Pr > F

POWDER                   2     2.26333333    1.13166667      7.60     0.0033
```

The *p*-value for comparing groups is 0.0033, which is less than the reference probability value of 0.05. You conclude that the average velocity is significantly different among the three types of gunpowder.

Output 8.10 shows the results of the MEANS statement using the T option. This performs multiple *t*-tests to compare the means. Because the sample sizes are all equal, this is Fisher's LSD test. Output 8.10 shows the results of the multiple comparison test using a different approach than seen earlier for the unbalanced data. A column headed *T Grouping* tells you which means are different from one another. From these tests, you conclude the following:

- The average muzzle velocities for KINGPOW and ZOOM gunpowder are not significantly different. (These two averages are assigned the letter A.)

- Both KINGPOW and ZOOM have significantly higher average muzzle velocity than BLASTO. (The average for BLASTO is assigned the letter B.)

These differences should make sense at an intuitive level because they are the ones shown in the side-by-side box plots from PROC UNIVARIATE. However, now you know that the differences are greater than could be expected by chance. Without the statistical test, you only knew that they seemed different, but you didn't know how likely the observed differences were.

Output 8.10   Multiple *t*-test for Gunpowder Data

```
                        Bullets Data                          4

                  Analysis of Variance Procedure

              T tests (LSD) for variable: VELOCITY

    NOTE: This test controls the Type I comparisonwise error rate not the
          experimentwise error rate.

                 Alpha= 0.05   df= 21   MSE= 0.148869
                      Critical Value of T= 2.08
                 Least Significant Difference= 0.4012

    Means with the same letter are not significantly different.


            T Grouping           Mean      N  POWDER

                     A          28.3875     8  KINGPOW
                     A
                     A          28.0625     8  ZOOM

                     B          27.6375     8  BLASTO
```

Output 8.10 contains a note that reminds you that this test controls the comparisonwise error rate. Most of the rest of Output 8.10 contains information similar to the information in Output 8.6. Output 8.10 gives some additional information that is discussed below.

Least Significant Difference=

gives the smallest difference between two means that will be significantly different at the level given by Alpha=. For the BULLET data, this is 0.4012.

Output 8.11 shows the results of performing the Bonferroni tests. Once again, the output shows the brand names of the gunpowders, the average velocity for each type of powder, and the sample sizes. The groupings of gunpowders are different than they were when the CER was controlled. From the Bonferonni *t*-tests, you conclude the following:

- The average muzzle velocities for KINGPOW and ZOOM are not significantly different. (These two averages are assigned the letter A.)

- The average muzzle velocities for ZOOM and BLASTO are not significantly different. (These two averages are assigned the letter B.)

- The average muzzle velocities for KINGPOW and BLASTO are significantly different. (These two averages do not have an overlap between the "A" group and the "B" group.)

Output 8.11   Bonferroni *t*-tests for Gunpowder Data

```
        Bullets Data                              12

                  Analysis of Variance Procedure

          Bonferroni (Dunn) T tests for variable: VELOCITY

    NOTE: This test controls the Type I experimentwise error rate, but
          generally has a higher Type II error rate than REGWQ.

              Alpha= 0.05  df= 21  MSE= 0.148869
                   Critical Value of T= 2.60
              Minimum Significant Difference= 0.5018

    Means with the same letter are not significantly different.

        Bon Grouping          Mean     N  POWDER

                       A       28.3875  8  KINGPOW
                       A
                  B    A       28.0625  8  ZOOM
                  B
                  B            27.6375  8  BLASTO
```

Most of the rest of Output 8.11 is quite similar to Output 8.10. A note tells you that this test controls the experimentwise error rate. (The REGWQ test mentioned in Output 8.11 isn't discussed in this book. See the "Further Reading" section at the end of the chapter for references.) Once again, the α-level, degrees of freedom, MSE, and critical value for the test are shown. The *Minimum Significant Difference* gives the smallest difference between group averages that will be significant. For the BULLET data, this difference is 0.5018.

As with the teacher salary data, the Bonferroni *t*-tests declared fewer significant differences between groups than did the repeated *t*-tests. However, with the Bonferroni tests, you control the overall α-level for the experiment, which corresponds to a known risk of making incorrect decisions.

For balanced data, PROC ANOVA prints the multiple comparison tests as shown in this section. For unbalanced data, PROC ANOVA prints the T and BON multiple comparison tests using confidence intervals. It is possible to obtain confidence intervals for balanced data, as discussed in the next section. It is also possible to obtain the LINES style of output for unbalanced data. However, you should consult with a statistician before doing this because differences in group sizes can mean that the approach is not appropriate.

More about Multiple Comparison Procedures

For each multiple comparison procedure, you used a MEANS statement and an option. This section gives some shortcuts, and it shows how to perform tests at significance levels other than 0.05.

Using Other Significance Levels

You can change the default 5% significance level for multiple comparison procedures with the ALPHA= option in the MEANS statement. For a 5% significance level, ALPHA=0.05, which is the default. You can specify values between 0.0001 and 0.9999. To perform the BON test at the 15% significance level for the TCHSAL data, use this statement:

```
means subjarea / bon alpha=0.15;
```

In practice, significance levels above 15% are not often used.

Obtaining Confidence Intervals for Balanced Data

For balanced data, you can obtain the confidence intervals that are shown for unbalanced data. Balanced data automatically uses the LINES style of output. The statements below show use of the LINES and the CLDIFF options to control the appearance of the output.

```
means powder / t lines;
means powder / t cldiff;
```

The first statement generates the results that are shown in Output 8.10. The second statement generates results for the BULLET data in the style that is shown earlier for the TCHSAL data (Output 8.6).

Obtaining Only the Means

You can also use a MEANS statement without any options. In this case, the output gives the sample size and average for each group.

Running Tests in Sequence

PROC ANOVA is an interactive procedure. If you use line mode or display manager mode, you can perform an analysis of variance and then perform multiple comparison procedures without rerunning the *ANOVA*. Enter the PROC ANOVA, CLASS, and MODEL statements; add a RUN statement to see the analysis of variance; and then add a MEANS statement and a second RUN statement to perform multiple comparison procedures. The following program produces the output that is seen in Output 8.3 and Output 8.6.

```
proc anova data=tchsal;
    class subjarea;
    model annsal=subjarea;
    title 'ANOVA for Teacher Salary Data';
run;
    means subjarea / t;
run;
```

When you use the preceding statements, a final RUN statement does not end the ANOVA procedure, which is waiting to receive additional statements. You can end the procedure in several ways: you can start another DATA or PROC step; you can end the SAS session by submitting the ENDSAS statement; or you can use the QUIT statement. The QUIT statement "quits" whatever interactive procedure is in progress. The form of the statement is simply the word QUIT followed by a semicolon:

```
quit;
```

The QUIT statement is needed if you are using SAS in display manager mode. If you are using SAS in another mode, the QUIT statement isn't needed.

Summarizing Multiple Comparison Procedures

The general form of the statements for performing multiple comparison procedures for an analysis of variance is:

> PROC ANOVA statement
>   CLASS statement
>   MODEL statement
>   **MEANS** *class-variable* / *options*;
>
> where *class-variable* is the variable that classifies the data into groups, and options are either omitted or are one or more of the following:
>
> **T**   for multiple *t*-tests
>
> **BON**   for Bonferroni *t*-tests
>
> **ALPHA=***level*   to control the significance level. Choose a level between 0.0001 and 0.9999; the default is 0.05.
>
> **CLDIFF**   to show differences with confidence intervals. This is the default for unequal sample sizes.
>
> **LINES**   to show differences with lines. This is the default for equal sample sizes.
>
> If you use an option, the slash is required.

Once again, note that many other multiple comparison procedures are available with PROC ANOVA. This book discusses only these two. See the "Further Reading" section for references.

Comparing More Than Two Groups Using PROC INSIGHT

This section shows how to summarize more than two groups and how to obtain an analysis of variance for more than two groups.

Summaries for More Than Two Groups

For PROC INSIGHT, the statements to summarize more than two groups are the same as those used to summarize two groups. For the teacher salary data, type

```
proc insight;
    open tchsal / nodisplay;
    by subjarea;
    dist annsal;
run;
```

The preceding statements produce summary information for each subject area. The two plots produced for the language teachers' salaries are shown in Output 8.12 and the summary statistics for the language teachers' salaries are shown in Output 8.13.

Output 8.12   PROC INSIGHT Plots for Teacher Salary Data

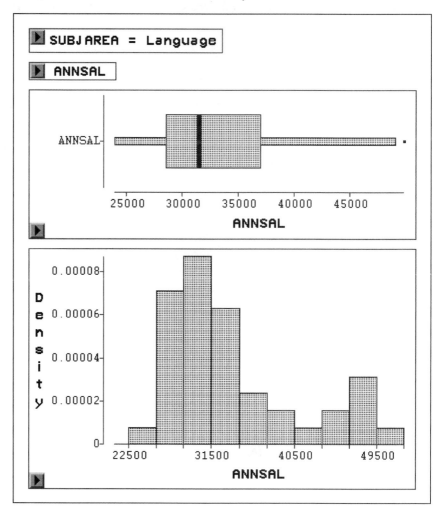

Output 8.13   **INSIGHT Summary for Teacher Salary Data**

```
┌────────────────────────────────────────────────────────────┐
│                                                              │
│  ▶ SUBJAREA = Language                                       │
│                                                              │
│  ▶ ANNSAL                                                    │
│                                                              │
│  ┌────────────────────────────────────────────────────┐     │
│  │ ▶                   Moments                          │     │
│  │ N              42.0000  Sum Wgts       42.0000       │     │
│  │ Mean       33840.1190   Sum          1421285.00      │     │
│  │ Std Dev     7194.6884   Variance    51763541.7       │     │
│  │ Skewness       1.0329   Kurtosis       -0.0599       │     │
│  │ USS          5.022E+10  CSS           2.122E+09       │     │
│  │ CV             21.2608  Std Mean      1110.1645       │     │
│  └────────────────────────────────────────────────────┘     │
│                                                              │
│  ┌────────────────────────────────────────────────────┐     │
│  │ ▶                  Quantiles                         │     │
│  │ 100% Max     49881.0000    99.0%  49881.0000         │     │
│  │  75% Q3      36980.0000    97.5%  49100.0000         │     │
│  │  50% Med     31514.0000    95.0%  48411.0000         │     │
│  │  25% Q1      28535.0000    90.0%  47316.0000         │     │
│  │   0% Min     23963.0000    10.0%  27403.0000         │     │
│  │      Range   25918.0000     5.0%  26705.0000         │     │
│  │      Q3-Q1    8445.0000     2.5%  26162.0000         │     │
│  │      Mode    23963.0000     1.0%  23963.0000         │     │
│  └────────────────────────────────────────────────────┘     │
│                                                              │
└────────────────────────────────────────────────────────────┘
```

The information shown in Output 8.12 and Output 8.13 provides similar
information to output shown earlier in the chapter.

Performing an Analysis of Variance

PROC INSIGHT uses a *general linear models* approach for analyzing
data. This provides much information that is outside the scope of this
book. However, for the case of a one-way analysis of variance, you can
simply look at a portion of the PROC INSIGHT output and obtain the
results you need.

To perform an analysis of variance for the teacher salary data using PROC INSIGHT, type

```
proc insight;
   open tchsal / nodisplay;
      fit annsal=subjarea;
run;
```

The preceding statements generate results, which include those shown in Output 8.14.

Output 8.14   PROC INSIGHT Analysis of Variance

```
┌───────────────────────────────────────────────────────────────────────┐
│  ┌──────────────────────────────────────┐                              │
│  │ ▶ ANNSAL      =      SUBJAREA         │                              │
│  │ Response Distribution:  Normal        │                              │
│  │ Link Function:      Identity          │                              │
│  └──────────────────────────────────────┘                              │
│  ┌──────────────────────────────────────┐                              │
│  │ ▶ Nominal Variable Information        │                              │
│  │    Level         SUBJAREA             │                              │
│  │        1 │ Language                   │                              │
│  │        2 │ Mathematics                │                              │
│  │        3 │ Music                      │                              │
│  │        4 │ Science                    │                              │
│  │        5 │ Social Science             │                              │
│  │        6 │ Special Ed                 │                              │
│  └──────────────────────────────────────┘                              │
│  ┌───────────────────────────────────────────────────────────────────┐│
│  │ ▶              Analysis of Variance                                 ││
│  │ Source   DF    Sum of Squares   Mean Square   F Stat    Prob > F    ││
│  │ Model     5        2.297E+09      459475971    6.2997     0.0001     ││
│  │ Error   155        1.131E+10     72936084.5                          ││
│  │ C Total 160        1.360E+10                                         ││
│  └───────────────────────────────────────────────────────────────────┘│
└───────────────────────────────────────────────────────────────────────┘
```

To interpret these results, look for the *Pr>F* column at the far right of the *Analysis of Variance* table. This contains the *p*-value for testing if the mean salaries for the different subject areas differ. The value is 0.0001, which is the same as the value you received from PROC ANOVA. You can conclude that the mean salaries differ based on the subject area.

However, using PROC INSIGHT you cannot perform the nonparametric tests or the multiple comparison tests.

Summarizing PROC INSIGHT

The general form of the statements to summarize data from multiple groups and to perform an analysis of variance when using PROC INSIGHT is:

> **PROC INSIGHT**;
>   **OPEN** *data-set-name* / **NODISPLAY** ;
>   **BY** *grouping-variable* ;
>   **DIST** *measurement-variable* ;
>   **FIT** *measurement-variable* = *class-variable* ;
>
> where *data-set-name* is the name of a SAS data set, *grouping-variable* and *class-variable* are the variables that classify the data into multiple groups, and *measurement-variable* is the variable to be analyzed.

Summary

Key Ideas

- To summarize data from more than two groups, separate the data into groups and get summary information for each group.

- An analysis of variance (*ANOVA*) is a test for comparing several groups. This test assumes that the data are independent samples from normally distributed populations and that the groups have equal variances.

- If the assumptions for an *ANOVA* aren't met, the Kruskal-Wallis test provides a nonparametric analogue.

- Multiple comparison procedures are tests that show which means are different from one another. You need to decide if you want to control the error rate for each comparison (CER) or the error rate for the entire experiment (MEER).

Syntax

- To summarize data from several groups,

    PROC MEANS DATA= *data-set-name* ;
      CLASS *grouping-variable* ;
      VAR *measurement-variable* ;

  where *data-set-name* is the name of a SAS data set, *grouping-variable* is the variable that classifies the data into groups, and *measurement-variable* is the variable to be summarized.

- To obtain a more detailed summary of data from several groups,

    PROC SORT DATA= *data-set-name* ;
      BY *grouping-variable* ;
    PROC UNIVARIATE DATA= *data-set-name* **PLOT** ;
    BY *grouping-variable* ;
    VAR *measurement-variable* ;

  where items in italic are as defined previously. The PLOT option with a BY statement produces side-by-side box plots in addition to the box plots for each level of the grouping-variable.

  The GCHART and FREQ procedures can be used in place of the UNIVARIATE procedure in the pattern above. In addition, PROC CHART can be used to generate low-resolution charts.

- To perform an analysis of variance and perform multiple comparison procedures,

    PROC ANOVA DATA= *data-set-name* ;
      CLASS *class-variable* ;
      MODEL *measurement-variable* = *class-variable* ;
      MEANS *class-variable* / *options* ;

  where *options* are either omitted or are one or more of the following: **HOVTEST, T, BON, CLDIFF, LINES** and **ALPHA=***level*. Choose a *level* between 0.0001 and 0.9999; the default is 0.05. If you specify an option, the slash is required. Other items in italic are as defined previously.

- To perform a Kruskal-Wallis test,

  PROC NPAR1WAY DATA= *data-set-name* **WILCOXON**;
  CLASS *class-variable* ;
  VAR *measurement-variable* ;

  where items in italic are as defined previously.

- To summarize data by using PROC INSIGHT,

  PROC INSIGHT ;
  OPEN *data-set-name* / **NODISPLAY** ;
  BY *grouping-variable* ;
  DIST *measurement-variable* ;

  where items in italic are as defined previously.

- To perform an analysis of variance by using PROC INSIGHT,

  PROC INSIGHT ;
  OPEN *data-set-name* / **NODISPLAY** ;
  FIT *measurement-variable* = *class-variable* ;

  where items in italic are as defined previously.

Example

The program below produces all the output shown in this chapter:

```
options ls=90;
proc format;
   value $subtxt
   'speced' = 'Special Ed'
   'mathem' = 'Mathematics'
   'langua' = 'Language'
   'music'  = 'Music'
   'scienc' = 'Science'
   'socsci' = 'Social Science';
data tchsal;
   input subjarea $ annsal @@;
   label subjarea='Subject Area'
         annsal='Annual Salary';
   format subjarea $subtxt.;
   datalines;
speced 35584 mathem 27814 langua 26162 mathem 25470
speced 41400 mathem 34432 music 21827 music 35787
music 30043 mathem 45480 mathem 25358 speced 42360
langua 23963 langua 27403 mathem 29610 music 27847
mathem 25000 mathem 29363 mathem 25091 speced 31319
```

```
music 24150 langua 30180 socsci 42210 mathem 55600
langua 32134 speced 57880 mathem 47770 langua 33472
music 21635 mathem 31908 speced 43128 mathem 33000
music 46691 langua 28535 langua 34609 music 24895
speced 42222 speced 39676 music 22515 speced 41899
music 27827 scienc 44324 scienc 43075 langua 49100
langua 44207 music 46001 music 25666 scienc 30000
mathem 26355 mathem 39201 mathem 32000 langua 26705
mathem 37120 langua 44888 mathem 62655 scienc 24532
mathem 36733 langua 29969 mathem 28521 langua 27599
music 27178 mathem 26674 langua 28662 music 41161
mathem 48836 mathem 25096 langua 27664 music 23092
speced 45773 mathem 27038 mathem 27197 music 44444
speced 51096 mathem 25125 scienc 34930 speced 44625
mathem 27829 mathem 28935 mathem 31124 socsci 36133
music 28004 mathem 37323 music 32040 scienc 39784
mathem 26428 mathem 39908 mathem 34692 music 26417
mathem 23663 speced 35762 langua 29612 scienc 32576
mathem 32188 mathem 33957 speced 35083 langua 47316
mathem 34055 langua 27556 langua 35465 socsci 49683
langua 38250 langua 30171 mathem 53282 langua 32022
socsci 31993 speced 52616 langua 33884 music 41220
mathem 43890 scienc 40330 langua 36980 scienc 59910
mathem 26000 langua 29594 socsci 38728 langua 47902
langua 38948 langua 33042 mathem 29360 socsci 46969
speced 39697 mathem 31624 langua 30230 music 29954
mathem 45733 music 24712 langua 33618 langua 29485
mathem 28709 music 24720 mathem 51655 mathem 32960
mathem 45268 langua 31006 langua 48411 socsci 59704
music 22148 mathem 27107 scienc 47475 langua 33058
speced 53813 music 38914 langua 49881 langua 42485
langua 26966 mathem 31615 mathem 24032 langua 27878
mathem 56070 mathem 24530 mathem 40174 langua 27607
speced 31114 langua 30665 scienc 25276 speced 36844
mathem 24305 mathem 35560 music 28770 langua 34001
mathem 35955
;

proc print data=tchsal;
title 'Teacher Salary Data';
run;

proc means data=tchsal;
   title 'Summary of Teacher Salary Data';
   class subjarea;
   var annsal;
run;
```

```
proc sort data=tchsal;
   by subjarea;
run;

options linesize=100;
proc univariate data=tchsal plot;
   by subjarea;
   var annsal;
run;

proc npar1way data=tchsal wilcoxon;
   class subjarea;
   var annsal;
   title 'Nonparametric Tests for Teacher Salary Data';
run;

proc anova data=tchsal;
   class subjarea;
   model annsal=subjarea;
   means subjarea / hovtest;
   means subjarea / t;
   means subjarea / bon;
title 'ANOVA for Teacher Salary Data';
run;
quit;

proc insight;
   open tchsal / nodisplay;
   by subjarea;
   dist annsal;
run;

proc insight;
   open tchsal / nodisplay;
   fit annsal=subjarea;
run;

data bullets;
   input powder $ velocity @@;
   datalines;
BLASTO 27.3 BLASTO 28.1 BLASTO 27.4 BLASTO 27.7
BLASTO 28.0 BLASTO 28.1 BLASTO 27.4 BLASTO 27.1
ZOOM 28.3 ZOOM 27.9 ZOOM 28.1 ZOOM 28.3 ZOOM 27.9
ZOOM 27.6 ZOOM 28.5 ZOOM 27.9 KINGPOW 28.4 KINGPOW 28.9
KINGPOW 28.3 KINGPOW 27.9 KINGPOW 28.2 KINGPOW 28.9
KINGPOW 28.8 KINGPOW 27.7
;
```

```
proc print data=bullets;
   title 'Bullets Data';

proc sort data=bullets;
   by powder;
run;

proc univariate data=bullets normal plot;
   by powder;
   var velocity;
run;

proc anova data=bullets;
   class powder;
   model velocity=powder;
   means powder / t ;
   means powder / bon ;
run;
quit;
```

Further Reading

For more information about the Kruskal-Wallis test and other nonparametric analyses, see the following:

- Conover, W.J. (1980), *Practical Nonparametric Statistics*, 2nd Edition, New York: John Wiley & Sons, Inc.

- Hollander, M. and Wolfe, D.A. (1973), *Nonparametric Statistical Methods*, New York: John Wiley & Sons, Inc.

- Siegel, S. (1956), *Nonparametric Statistics for the Behavorial Sciences*, New York: McGraw Hill Book Company.

For more information about *ANOVA* and about multiple comparison procedures, see the following:

- Box, G.E.P, Hunter, W.G., and Hunter, J.S. (1978), *Statistics for Experimenters*, New York: John Wiley & Sons, Inc.

- Littell, R.C., Freund, R.J., and Spector, P.C. (1991), *SAS System for Linear Models*, Third Edition, Cary, NC: SAS Institute Inc.

- Hochberg, Y. and Tamhane, A.C. (1987), *Multiple Comparison Procedures*, New York: John Wiley & Sons, Inc.

- Hsu, J.C. (1996), *Multiple Comparisons Theory and Methods*, New York: Chapman and Hall.

- Milliken, G.A. and Johnson, D.E. (1984), *Analysis of Messy Data Volume I: Designed Experiments*, Belmont, CA: Lifetime Learning Publications.

- Ott, R.L. (1993), *An Introduction to Statistical Methods and Data Analysis*, Belmont, CA: Duxbury Press.

- Snedecor, G.W. and Cochran, W.G. (1967), *Statistical Methods, 6th Edition,* Ames, IA: Iowa State University Press.

- Steel, R.G.D. and Torrie, J.H. (1980), *Principles and Procedures of Statistics*, New York: McGraw-Hill Book Company.

For more about PROC ANOVA, PROC NPAR1WAY, and other SAS procedures that perform an analysis of variance, see the chapter "Introduction to Analysis of Variance Procedures" in the manuals listed below. For more specific details about the ANOVA, NPAR1WAY and INSIGHT procedures, see the chapters about these procedures. For more information about multiple comparison procedures, see the "Comparison of Means" section in the chapter about the GLM procedure.

- *SAS/STAT® Software: Syntax, Version 6, First Edition*

- *SAS/STAT® Software: Reference, Version 6, Fourth Edition, Volumes 1 and 2*

- *SAS/INSIGHT® Users' Guide, Version 6, Third Edition.*

For more about the procedures that are used to summarize data from multiple groups (MEANS, SORT, UNIVARIATE, CHART, and GCHART), see the references listed at the end of Chapter 4.

Although there may also be technical reports with updated information for various releases, the best source of the most recent information is the online help and online documentation. These are most appropriate in display manager mode.

Part 4   # Fitting Lines to Data

Chapter 9 # Correlation and Regression

Can SAT scores be used to predict college grade-point averages? How does the age of a house affect its selling price? Is heart rate affected by the amount of blood cholesterol? How much of an increase in sales results from a specific increase in advertising expenditures? These are questions about the relationships between pairs of variables: SAT scores and college GPA, age and price of houses, heart rate and blood cholesterol, and sales and advertising expenses. As one variable increases, the other variable increases or decreases. Correlation and regression analyses are statistical methods used to answer questions about relations between variables. The correlation coefficient is a number that measures the strength of the relation between variables. Regression analysis uses equations to describe how one variable is related to another variable or to a group of variables.

This chapter shows how to use SAS software for basic correlation and regression analyses. Major topics include

- computing the correlation coefficient and testing its significance

- computing a regression equation

- using a regression equation to predict one variable from another

- computing prediction limits and confidence limits for values from a regression equation

- plotting regression equations through the data

- plotting prediction and confidence limits.

The methods discussed in this chapter are appropriate for either interval or ratio variables. Although there are regression methods for other types of data, these methods are outside the scope of this book.

Contents

Creating a Data Set

A homeowner was interested in the effect his air conditioner had on his electric bill, so he recorded the number of hours he used his air conditioner for each of 21 days. He also monitored his electric meter for these days and computed the amount of electricity used in kilowatt-hours. Finally, he recorded the number of times the dryer was used each day. The statements that follow create a SAS data set named KILOWATT with variables KWH, AC, and DRYER, and produce Output 9.1:

```
data kilowatt;
   input kwh ac dryer @@;
   datalines;
35 1.5 1 63 4.5 2 66 5.0 2 17 2.0 0 94 8.5 3 79 6.0 3
93 13.5 1 66 8.0 1 94 12.5 1 82 7.5 2 78 6.5 3 65 8.0 1
77 7.5 2 75 8.0 2 62 7.5 1 85 12.0 1 43 6.0 0 57 2.5 3
33 5.0 0 65 7.5 1 33 6.0 0
;

proc print data=kilowatt;
   var kwh ac;
   title 'Kilowatt-Hours and Air Conditioner Hours';
run;
```

Output 9.1   **List of Kilowatt-Hours and Air Conditioner Hours**

```
           Kilowatt-Hours and Air Conditioner Hours

                  OBS    KWH     AC
                   1      35     1.5
                   2      63     4.5
                   3      66     5.0
                   4      17     2.0
                   5      94     8.5
                   6      79     6.0
                   7      93    13.5
                   8      66     8.0
                   9      94    12.5
                  10      82     7.5
                  11      78     6.5
                  12      65     8.0
                  13      77     7.5
                  14      75     8.0
                  15      62     7.5
                  16      85    12.0
                  17      43     6.0
                  18      57     2.5
                  19      33     5.0
                  20      65     7.5
                  21      33     6.0
```

Plotting Two Variables

It is usually informative to plot the data before computing any statistical measures. In this case, the homeowner is interested in the effect that using the air conditioner (AC) has on kilowatt-hours (KWH), so KWH is plotted on a vertical axis against AC on a horizontal axis. To plot the KILOWATT data, use the GPLOT procedure.

```
symbol1 v=x h=.6 c=black;
symbol2 v=dot h=.4 c=black;
symbol3 v=plus h=.5 c=black;
symbol4 v=plus h=.5 c=black;
proc gplot data=kilowatt;
    plot kwh*ac;
    title 'Plot of KWH against AC: KILOWATT Data Set';
run;
```

Output 9.2 shows that larger values of KWH tend to occur with larger values of AC. However, the relationship is not "perfect" because some days have larger AC values than other days, but they have smaller KWH values. This is because there are other factors (such as use of kitchen appliances) that affect the amount of electricity used.

Technical note:
Plots in Chapters 9 and 10 were obtained using high-resolution graphics facilities in SAS Software and a laser printer. If you have SAS/GRAPH on your system and are running SAS Release 6.12 or higher, then you have these capabilities. If you do not have these capabilities, you can obtain similar plots in a line-printer mode. Statements are included at the end of Chapter 9 that produce the line-printer plots.

Output 9.2   Plot of Kilowatt-Hours versus Air Conditioner Hours

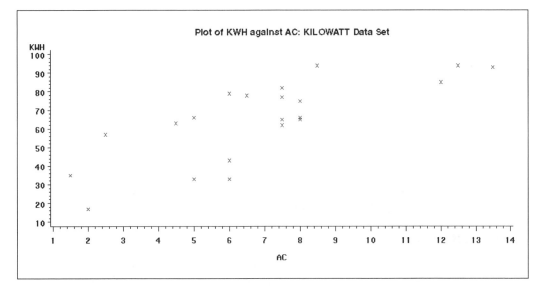

For plots like the one above, use PROC GPLOT. The PLOT statement tells the GPLOT procedure what variables to plot. Specify the variable for the vertical axis, then type an asterisk (*), and then specify the variable for the horizontal axis. SAS software automatically scales the plot so that it fits on a page. The SYMBOL statements are used to customize the plot. The general form of the statements for producing a simple plot is:

PROC GPLOT DATA = *data-set-name* ;
    PLOT *y-variable*x-variable* ;

where *data-set-name* is the name of a SAS data set, *y-variable* is the variable for the vertical axis, and *x-variable* is the variable for the horizontal axis.

Calculating the Correlation Coefficient

A number called the *correlation coefficient* measures the strength of the relation between two variables. The letter *r* represents the correlation coefficient. Values of *r* range from –1.0 to +1.0. An *r* equal to +1 corresponds to a plot of points that fall exactly on an upward-sloping straight line, and an *r* that is equal to –1 corresponds to a plot of points that fall exactly on a downward-sloping straight line. Values of +1 or –1 usually don't occur in real situations because plots of real data don't fall exactly on straight lines. In reality, you get values of *r* between –1 and +1. Relatively large positive values of *r*, such as 0.7, correspond to plots that have a clear upward trend, and large negative values of *r* correspond to plots that have a downward trend. An *r* equal to 0 corresponds to a scattering of points that shows neither an upward nor a downward trend.

Using PROC CORR

Use the CORR procedure to compute correlation coefficients. To get the correlation coefficient that measures the strength of the relation between KWH and AC, type

```
proc corr data=kilowatt;
    var kwh ac;
    title 'Correlation between KWH and AC: KILOWATT Data Set';
run;
```

Output 9.3 contains the value of *r* and other statistics.

Output 9.3   **PROC CORR Output for KILOWATT Data**

```
                Correlation between KWH and AC: KILOWATT Data Set

                             Correlation Analysis

                      2 'VAR' Variables:   KWH      AC

                             Simple Statistics

Variable          N        Mean      Std Dev        Sum      Minimum      Maximum

KWH              21    64.857143    21.884437   1362.000000   17.000000    94.000000
AC               21     6.928571     3.135625    145.500000    1.500000    13.500000


        Pearson Correlation Coefficients / Prob > |R| under Ho: Rho=0 / N = 21

                                        KWH             AC

                       KWH           1.00000         0.76528
                                       0.0            0.0001


                       AC            0.76528         1.00000
                                      0.0001           0.0
```

The first section of the output labeled *Simple Statistics* contains summary statistics similar to those given by PROC MEANS.

The second section of the output contains rows and columns headed by each variable name, in this case KWH and AC. Each cell contains two numbers: the correlation coefficient (r) and a p-value. The p-value is the significance probability for testing the null hypothesis that the true correlation in the population is 0. The value of r, which measures the relation between KWH and AC, is 0.765. It reflects the clear upward trend in the plot of KWH against AC (shown in Output 9.2). The p-value of 0.0001 gives very strong evidence that the true population correlation is not 0. (This true correlation is usually called *Rho*, which is what the heading on the output refers to.)

The relation between KWH and AC is summarized in two cells: the cell in the KWH column and AC row, and the cell in the AC column and KWH row. The table also shows the relations between KWH and KWH, and AC and AC. The correlations for these cases are 1 because the correlation of a variable with itself is always 1.

The heading above the correlation table gives one additional piece of information, the sample size for each correlation. This example has only two variables, so the sample size for all cells of the table is the same and is given in the heading. For tables with several variables and different sample sizes for each variable, the sample size is printed as a third row in each cell of the table. For example, you compute the correlation coefficients for KWH, AC, and OVEN (where OVEN is the number of hours that the oven was used), and there are only 15 values for OVEN. In this case, the cells that involve KWH and AC would use $n=21$, but the cells involving KWH and OVEN, or AC and OVEN would use $n=15$.

You can use PROC CORR to find correlations between two or more variables. The general form of the statements for PROC CORR is:

> **PROC CORR DATA** = *data-set-name* ;
>   **VAR** *variables* ;
>
> where *data-set-name* is the name of a SAS data set, and *variables* are the names of the variables that you want to find correlations for.
>
> Note that you must specify at least two variables so the output is meaningful. The correlation of a variable with itself is always 1.

Cautions about Correlations

There are two important cautions to remember when you interpret correlations. First, correlation isn't the same as causation. Second, "shopping for significance" among a large group of correlations is not a good idea.

When two variables are highly correlated, it doesn't necessarily mean that one causes the other. In some cases, there may be an underlying causal relation, but you don't know this from the correlation coefficient. Proving cause-and-effect relations is much more difficult than just showing a high correlation.

The second caution follows from the first. Researchers often make the mistake of measuring many variables, finding the correlations between all possible pairs, and choosing the "significant" correlations to draw conclusions. Recall the interpretation of a significance level and you'll see their mistake: If a researcher performs 100 correlations and tests their significance at the .05 level, then about 5 significant correlations will be found by chance alone.

Questions Not Answered by Correlation

From the value of r in Output 9.3, you can conclude that as use of the air conditioner increases, so does the number of kilowatt-hours consumed. This isn't a surprise. Some more important questions are:

- How many kilowatt-hours would be consumed for each hour's use of the air conditioner?
- What is a prediction of the kilowatt-hour consumption in a day when the air conditioner is used for a specified number of hours?
- What is an estimate of the average kilowatt-hour consumption on days when the air conditioner is used for a specified number of hours?
- What are the confidence limits for the predicted kilowatt-hour consumption?

You can answer these types of questions with a regression analysis of the data. This is the subject of the next several sections.

Performing Straight-Line Regression

A correlation coefficient tells you that some sort of relation exists, but it doesn't tell you much more than that. For example, Figure 9.1 shows two plots between variables. In each plot, the correlation coefficient is 1.0; however, the relations depicted in the two plots are quite different. A correlation of 1.0 means that all the points fall exactly on a straight line, but it doesn't fully describe the relation between the variables.

To investigate the form of the relation between the variables, you use a *regression analysis*. One way to use regression is to fit a straight line through a set of points. For the two plots in Figure 9.1, you would get two very different straight lines, even though the correlation is 1.0 for both plots.

Figure 9.1   **Two Plots with _r_=1.0**

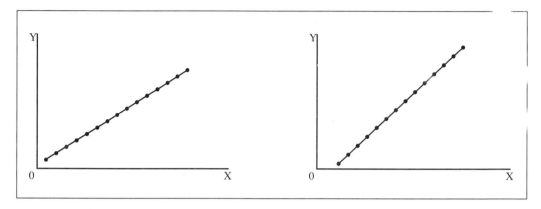

Answering Some Questions with Regression

For the KILOWATT data set, some questions couldn't be answered by using only the correlation coefficient. Without going into detail about regression analysis, this section shows how some of those questions can be answered. The next section gives some statistical background about regression.

The plot of KWH against AC in Output 9.2 shows that the points are scattered in a pattern that increases from lower left to upper right. This increasing trend can be shown by drawing a straight line through the pattern. Output 9.4 repeats Output 9.2 and shows a straight line drawn through the data points. The line is called a *regression line*. SAS statements to produce Output 9.4 are shown in the "Example" section.

The slope of the regression line in Output 9.4 is the amount of vertical increase for each unit of horizontal increase (the "rise" over the "run"). Therefore, the slope represents the average number of kilowatt-hours that are consumed by using the air conditioner for one hour. This would answer the first question that was asked in the preceding section about correlation.

Output 9.4   Plot of KWH and AC with Straight Line

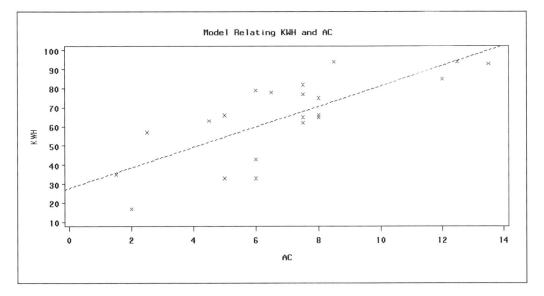

Now consider the second question about predicting the kilowatt-hour consumption for a particular day when the air conditioner is used for a specified number of hours. Suppose you want to predict the kilowatt-hour consumption for a day when the air conditioner is used for eight hours (AC=8). The KILOWATT data set contains three observations with AC=8. They have three different values for KWH: 66, 65, and 75. This tells you there is a range of possible values for KWH for a given value of AC. When you look at the plot in Output 9.4, you see that on another day when AC=8, KWH could reasonably range from around 50 to 90. The best guess would be somewhere in the middle of the range. Or, you could use the line sketched through the scattering of points to predict the kilowatt-hour consumption. Simply read upward from AC=8 to the line, and then read the predicted value for KWH from the vertical axis. You can see that such a value would be around 70.

To answer these two questions, you use a line drawn through the data. The lines that several people might draw for this data set would probably be similar because the plot has a fairly definite pattern. However, the lines would not be identical so the predicted value for KWH would differ as well. For data sets without an obvious pattern in the plot, different people could draw very different lines through the data and get widely differing predicted values. Using regression analysis, as described in the next section, everyone would get the same straight line. This process is called *fitting a regression line*. The method that is used most often for fitting a line uses a principle called *least squares*.

Understanding Least Squares Regression

Look at Figure 9.2. The principle of least squares involves fitting a line through the points so that the vertical differences between all the points and the line are minimized. For each point, the difference between the point and the line is calculated. Then, this difference is squared to give points above and below the line the same importance (squared differences are all positive). The squared differences are then summed. The "best" line is the line that minimizes this sum of squared differences, hence the name least squares.

Figure 9.2   Process of Least Squares

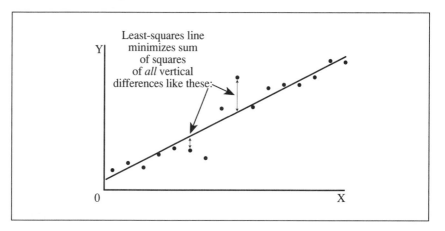

Regression Equations

A straight-line relation between two variables can be summarized with the equation:

$$y = \beta_0 + \beta_1 x + \varepsilon$$

This equation is called the *regression model*. It says that the measurement variable y is a straight line function of x, with an intercept β_0 and a slope β_1. Finally, there is some random variation in the data, which is called error. Error is represented by ε in the model equation and it accounts for the fact that the same x value doesn't always give the same y value. This equation represents the entire population of values for x and y. In reality, you measure a sample and use the sample to estimate the straight line. The estimated line produced by least squares regression is

$$y = b_0 + b_1 x$$

where b_0 and b_1 are the estimates of β_0 and β_1, respectively. The value b_0 gives the predicted value of y when x is 0. This is the *intercept* of the line because it is the place where the line intercepts the vertical axis. The value b_1 gives the increase in y that results from a one-unit increase in x and is called the *slope* of the line.

Assumptions for Least Squares Regression

For least squares regression, all variables must be either interval or ratio. In addition, the values of x-variables should be known without error. For the KILOWATT data, the homeowner knows how long the air conditioner was working each day. But there are other things in the house that consume electricity in varying amounts from day to day. This variation is the so-called error in the model equation. The errors are assumed to be independent. A final assumption is that the errors in the data are normally distributed with a mean of 0 and a variance of σ^2. However, the regression equation has meaning even if the assumption is not met. The assumption is needed for tests of hypothesis and confidence intervals.

To help distinguish between the x-variables and the y-variables, different names are used. The y-variable is called the *dependent variable*, and the x-variable (or variables) are called the *independent variable(s)*. One way to remember the distinction is to remember that the x-variables are known, so they are independent of the measuring technique used for the y-variables.

Using PROC REG to Fit a Straight Line

The REG procedure is the most general SAS procedure for regression analysis. The rest of this chapter discusses various parts of the REG procedure. The general form of the REG procedure is summarized in the "Syntax" summary at the end of this chapter. If you use SAS software in interactive line mode or display manager mode, you can use the basic statements to fit a line, look at the output, and then add more statements without restarting PROC REG. The statements shown in this chapter use PROC REG interactively. Once PROC REG is started in a section, all statements in that section continue the procedure.

To use PROC REG to fit the least squares straight line through the AC and KWH data points, type the following statements, which produce Output 9.5. (Actually, only the PROC REG, MODEL, and RUN statements are needed. The purpose of the other statements is explained later.)

```
proc reg data=kilowatt graphics;
    model kwh=ac;
    id ac;
    var dryer;
    plot kwh*ac pred.*ac 195m.*ac u95m.*ac/overlay;
    title 'Model Relating KWH and AC';
run;
```

A MODEL statement is required when you use PROC REG to fit a line to data. In this case, the MODEL statement tells PROC REG to fit a straight line to the data points. The ID statement identifies the observations in some parts of the output (shown later). The equation for the fitted straight line is

$$KWH = b_0 + b_1 AC$$

The number b_0 is the predicted value for KWH if you substitute 0 for AC in the right-hand side of the equation. This is the value for KWH at the point where the fitted line intercepts the vertical axis. In this example, the intercept gives an estimate of the kilowatt-hours consumed when the air conditioner isn't used. The number b_1 is the slope of the line. It is the amount of increase in predicted KWH that would result from a one-unit increase in AC. In other words, b_1 is the amount of electricity consumed by using the AC for 1 hour.

Output 9.5   **PROC REG Output for KILOWATT Data**

```
                        Model Relating KWH and AC


Model: MODEL1
Dependent Variable: KWH


                         Analysis of Variance

                            Sum of         Mean
        Source      DF      Squares       Square     F Value      Prob>F

        Model        1    5609.66260   5609.66260     26.855      0.0001
        Error       19    3968.90883    208.88994
        C Total     20    9578.57143


           Root MSE      14.45303     R-square      0.5856
           Dep Mean      64.85714     Adj R-sq      0.5638
           C.V.          22.28440


                        Parameter Estimates

                     Parameter      Standard    T for H0:
        Variable  DF   Estimate        Error    Parameter=0    Prob > |T|

        INTERCEP   1   27.851072    7.80653827       3.568       0.0021
        AC         1    5.341082    1.03067009       5.182       0.0001
```

Output 9.5 contains several statistics, but not all of them will be discussed.
The output is divided into three general parts, which are described in the
sections that follow.

Model Information

The top left corner of the printout contains two lines labeled *Model* and
Dependent Variable. The dependent variable is the measurement variable
on the left-hand side of the equation in the MODEL statement. *Model*
shows a label assigned to each MODEL statement. Default labels are
MODEL1 for the model in the first MODEL statement, MODEL2 for the
model in the second MODEL statement, and so on. This book uses the
default labels.

Parameter Estimates

This section of Output 9.5 presents the coefficients for the regression line, b_0 and b_1, with standard errors. It also provides tests to determine if the coefficients are significantly different from 0.

Variable, Parameter Estimate

The column labeled *Variable* identifies where the coefficients should go in the equation for the fitted line. The column labeled *Parameter Estimate* gives the values for the coefficients. The intercept, b_0, is identified in the *Variable* column by the keyword *INTERCEP*. The slope, b_1, is identified by the name of the variable in the MODEL statement, which is AC in this example. The value of b_0 is 27.85, and the value of b_1 is 5.34. The equation of the fitted line is then

$$KWH = 27.85 + 5.34(AC)$$

Therefore, the predicted kilowatt-hour consumption when the air conditioner is not used (AC=0) is 27.85. Also, the estimated amount of electricity consumption for one hour's use of the air conditioner is 5.34 kilowatt hours. (Since a kilowatt is 1000 watts, the air conditioner consumes 5340 watts per hour. This is more than would be consumed by fifty-three 100-watt light bulbs.)

It's always a good idea to examine the computations to see if they make sense with the data. Look at Output 9.4 and you see that a fitted straight line should intersect the vertical axis around KWH=30. So KWH=27.85 is a reasonable value for the intercept. As another verification, substitute AC=12 into the fitted equation to get KWH=27.85+(5.34 ×12)=91.93. Look again at Output 9.4 and you see that 91.93 is about where the line should be when AC=12.

DF

gives the degrees of freedom for a parameter estimate. This should equal 1 for each parameter.

Standard Error

measures how much the parameter estimates would vary from one collection of data to the next. Standard errors can be used to construct confidence intervals about the parameter estimates. This is discussed later in "Confidence Limits for the Parameter Estimates."

T for HO: Parameter=0

gives *t*-values for testing the null hypothesis that the parameter equals 0. These *t*-values are equal to the parameter estimates divided by their standard errors (for example, 5.182 = 5.341/1.031 for the AC parameter). They are used to test if the parameter estimates differ significantly from 0.

Prob > |T|

gives the *p*-value (significance probability) for the *t*-value. For the AC parameter, the *p*-value is 0.0001, which gives overwhelming evidence that the slope is not 0. In other words, increasing AC does produce a measurable increase in KWH. (If you pay an electric bill and have an air conditioner, then you are already aware of this fact.) The intercept also is clearly not 0, which shouldn't be a surprise either. Even if you don't use an air conditioner, you use some electricity.

Analysis of Variance

This section of output gives information about how well a straight line fits the data. If you have read Chapter 8, you see similarities in the output. In both Chapter 8 and this chapter, the term "Analysis of Variance" refers to a table of computations which enable you to analyze the variation in the data.

Source, DF

identify the sources of variation in the data and the degrees of freedom for each source. For the total variation, identified as *C Total, DF* should be one less than the sample size (for example, 21-1 for the KILOWATT data). For the variation explained by the model, identified as *Model*, the degrees of freedom should be 1 for a straight-line model. The degrees of freedom for *Error* is the difference (19=20-1).

Sum of Squares (SS)

separates the variation in the data into portions that can be attributed to the model and to error. Part of the total variation in kilowatt-hour consumption is due to variation in amounts of air conditioner use, and part is due either to random error or to factors other than air conditioner use. Notice that

$$9578.57 = 5609.66 + 3968.91$$

or, in general,

$$Total\ SS = Model\ SS + Error\ SS$$

The second equation is a basic and important one in regression analysis. Total variation is partitioned into variation due to the variables in the model and variation due to error. If this reminds you of what happens in an analysis of variance in Chapter 8, you're right. It's the same idea. Recall the three observations with AC=8 and with KWH values of 65, 6(and 75. Because these three different KWH values occurred on days wi the same value of AC, the variation among them must be due to error (or factors other than the use of the air conditioner).

Mean Square (MS)

equals the sum of squares divided by the degrees of freedom. *Error MS* =208.89 estimates the variance of a population of KWH values that result from a given amount of AC use.

F Value, Prob > F

gives the test statistic and *p*-value associated with a test of hypothesis of whether variation in the *y*-variable is due to variation in the *x*-variables. The null hypothesis states that variation in *y* is unrelated to variation in *x*. For the KILOWATT data, the *p*-value of 0.0001 indicates highly significant evidence that the AC explains a portion of the variation in KWH.

R-square

equals *Model SS* divided by *Total SS*. Because *Total SS* is the sum of *Model SS* and *Error SS*, *R-square* is the fraction of *Total SS* made up of *Model SS*. In other words, *R-square* is the fraction of the total variation in *y* due to the *x*-variables in the model. *R-square* can range from 0 to 1. The closer it is to 1, the better your model is accounting for variation in the data. For the KILOWATT data, .5856 is the fraction of variation in KWH due to variation in AC. Expressed as a percent, approximately 59% of the KWH variation is due to variation in AC. *R-square* is related to the correlation coefficient from Output 9.3: *R-square* = r^2. In this case, $.5856 = .7653^2$.

Confidence Limits for the Parameter Estimates

The test in Output 9.5 tells you whether the parameter estimates are significantly different from 0. However, it is sometimes more useful to form a confidence interval for the estimates.

To find the confidence limits, multiply the standard error for the estimate by a *t*-value (to be explained later) with degrees of freedom equal to the *DF for Error*. For example, a 95% confidence interval about the slope estimate is

$$[5.34 - (2.09 \times 1.03), 5.34 + (2.09 \times 1.03)] = (3.19, 7.49)$$

The number 2.09 is the *t*-value associated with 19 degrees of freedom, and 95% confidence. It can be found in tables in statistical textbooks, or it can be obtained from the following SAS statements:

```
data;
   t=tinv(19,.975);
   put t;
run;
```

The value of *t* would appear in your SAS LOG.

The confidence limits tell you that you can be 95% confident that the true slope is between 3.19 and 7.49. For practical purposes, remember that the slope is the average number of kilowatt-hours consumed for each hour that the air conditioner is used.

Predicted Values and Prediction Limits

This section shows how to get prediction limits from the regression equation. Use *prediction limits* to find bounds for a single predicted value. Use *confidence limits* to find bounds around the mean.

Now that you know how to get the regression equation using PROC REG, you are ready to apply it. Suppose you had the AC turned on for eight hours yesterday and you may want to predict the kilowatt-hour consumption. Earlier you saw how to do this graphically. Read upward from AC=8 to the regression line and then read over to the vertical axis to predict KWH. Using the regression equation to predict KWH is more precise. Simply put the value of AC into the regression equation and do the arithmetic to get the predicted KWH. The predicted KWH for AC=8 is

$$\text{predicted KWH} = 27.85 + (5.34 \times 8) = 70.57$$

The actual number of kilowatt-hours consumed on this day with AC=8 is not going to be exactly 70.57. Remember, three days in the data set have AC=8 and KWH values of 65, 66, and 75. Also, the plot in Figure 9.2 shows that reasonable KWH values for AC=8 could range from 50 to 90, depending on what other factors might affect kilowatt-hour consumption on that day. You can put bounds around a single predicted value such as 70.57. These bounds give a probable range for the number of kilowatt-hours that will be consumed on a given day. Such bounds are called *prediction limits*. Prediction limits take into account the variation in the dependent variable for observations that have the same value as the independent variable. These limits also take into account prediction error in the fitted regression line.

The next section shows how to use PROC REG to compute the predicted KWH and prediction limits.

Using PROC REG to Get Predicted Values and Prediction Limits

Predicted KWH values and 95% prediction limits are given by the CLI option in the PRINT statement. To see the results, type

```
print cli;
title 'Model Relating KWH and AC';
run;
```

The results are shown in Output 9.6. If you only want predicted values, replace CLI with P in the PRINT statement.

Output 9.6   Prediction Limits for Model Relating KWH and AC

Model Relating KWH and AC

Obs	AC	Dep Var KWH	Predict Value	Std Err Predict	Lower95% Predict	Upper95% Predict	Residual
1	1.5	35.0000	35.8627	6.423	2.7597	68.9657	-0.8627
2	4.5	63.0000	51.8859	4.026	20.4834	83.2884	11.1141
3	5.0	66.0000	54.5565	3.728	23.3158	85.7971	11.4435
4	2.0	17.0000	38.5332	5.979	5.7963	71.2702	-21.5332
5	8.5	94.0000	73.2503	3.545	42.1028	104.4	20.7497
6	6.0	79.0000	59.8976	3.296	28.8704	90.9247	19.1024
7	13.5	93.0000	99.9557	7.471	65.9024	134.0	-6.9557
8	8.0	66.0000	70.5797	3.342	39.5312	101.6	-4.5797
9	12.5	94.0000	94.6146	6.551	61.4013	127.8	-0.6146
10	7.5	82.0000	67.9092	3.208	36.9223	98.8961	14.0908
11	6.5	78.0000	62.5681	3.185	31.5919	93.5443	15.4319
12	8.0	65.0000	70.5797	3.342	39.5312	101.6	-5.5797
13	7.5	77.0000	67.9092	3.208	36.9223	98.8961	9.0908
14	8.0	75.0000	70.5797	3.342	39.5312	101.6	4.4203
15	7.5	62.0000	67.9092	3.208	36.9223	98.8961	-5.9092
16	12.0	85.0000	91.9441	6.105	59.1057	124.8	-6.9441
17	6.0	43.0000	59.8976	3.296	28.8704	90.9247	-16.8976
18	2.5	57.0000	41.2038	5.548	8.8010	73.6065	15.7962
19	5.0	33.0000	54.5565	3.728	23.3158	85.7971	-21.5565
20	7.5	65.0000	67.9092	3.208	36.9223	98.8961	-2.9092
21	6.0	33.0000	59.8976	3.296	28.8704	90.9247	-26.8976

Sum of Residuals   0
Sum of Squared Residuals   3968.9088
Predicted Resid SS (Press)   4728.5664

The following list explains Output 9.6:

Obs

identifies the observations.

AC

identifies each observation by the value of AC. This column is printed because you used the ID statement with the PROC REG statement.

Dep Var KWH

gives the actual values of the response variable KWH.

Predict Value

gives the predicted values of the measurement variable. Notice that all observations with AC=8 (observations 8, 12, and 14) have the same predicted KWH value of 70.58. This differs slightly (because of round-off error) from the 70.57 that was computed above.

Std Err Predict

gives the standard error of prediction.

Lower95% Predict, Upper95% Predict

give the prediction limits. For observation 12 with AC=8, the 95% limits are 39.53 and 101.6. This means that you can be 95% confident that the kilowatt-hour consumption on a day with AC=8 will be somewhere between 39.53 and 101.6. This interval is even wider than the 50-to-90 range that you estimated from the plot in Output 9.4. The wide range is a result of variation in KWH values caused by factors other than AC.

Residual

gives the residuals, which are the differences between actual and predicted values. These are calculated as actual minus predicted. For observation 1, this is 35.0–35.86=–0.86. The residual is the amount by which the fitted regression line "missed" the actual data point.

In summary, to use the fitted regression equation to predict KWH from AC, insert the value of AC into the equation. Use the CLI option in PROC REG to get both predicted values and prediction limits.

Estimating the Mean and Confidence Limits for the Mean

Suppose you don't want to predict kilowatt-hour consumption for one given day when the air conditioner is used for 8 hours. Instead, you want to estimate the mean kilowatt-hour consumption for all days when the air conditioner is used for 8 hours. To get an estimate for each day, insert the value AC=8 into the fitted regression equation. Because AC is the same for all these days, you get the same predicted value for KWH. It makes sense to use this predicted value as an estimate of the mean KWH value for all the days. In other words, to predict either a single future value or to estimate the mean response for a given value of the independent variable, use the same value from the regression equation.

Suppose you also want a confidence interval for the estimate of the mean KWH value. This is where estimating a mean KWH value differs from predicting a single KWH value. Because the mean is a population parameter, the mean KWH value for all the days with a given value for AC doesn't change. Compare this with the actual KWH values for these same days, which do vary. Because the mean doesn't vary and the actual values do, it makes sense that a *confidence interval for the mean* would be smaller than the confidence interval for a single predicted value. With a single predicted value, you need to account for the variation between actual values as well as for any error in the line. With the mean, you only need to account for the error in the line. Confidence intervals around the mean are called confidence limits for the mean.

Using PROC REG to Get Confidence Limits for the Mean

To get 95% confidence limits for mean KWH values corresponding to given AC values, use CLM instead of CLI in the PRINT statement. For the KILOWATT data, type

```
print clm;
title 'Model Relating KWH and AC';
run;
```

The results from these statements as shown in Output 9.7 are very similar to the results shown in Output 9.6. There are only two differences, which are described in the section that follows Output 9.7.

Output 9.7   Confidence Limits for the Mean for Model Relating KWH and AC

```
                         Model Relating KWH and AC

                 Dep Var   Predict   Std Err   Lower95%  Upper95%
    Obs    AC     KWH       Value     Predict     Mean      Mean    Residual

      1   1.5   35.0000   35.8627     6.423    22.4197   49.3057   -0.8627
      2   4.5   63.0000   51.8859     4.026    43.4585   60.3134   11.1141
      3   5.0   66.0000   54.5565     3.728    46.7536   62.3593   11.4435
      4   2.0   17.0000   38.5332     5.979    26.0186   51.0478  -21.5332
      5   8.5   94.0000   73.2503     3.545    65.8295   80.6710   20.7497
      6   6.0   79.0000   59.8976     3.296    52.9991   66.7960   19.1024
      7  13.5   93.0000   99.9557     7.471    84.3181    115.6    -6.9557
      8   8.0   66.0000   70.5797     3.342    63.5856   77.5739   -4.5797
      9  12.5   94.0000   94.6146     6.551    80.9023    108.3    -0.6146
     10   7.5   82.0000   67.9092     3.208    61.1939   74.6245   14.0908
     11   6.5   78.0000   62.5681     3.185    55.9025   69.2337   15.4319
     12   8.0   65.0000   70.5797     3.342    63.5856   77.5739   -5.5797
     13   7.5   77.0000   67.9092     3.208    61.1939   74.6245    9.0908
     14   8.0   75.0000   70.5797     3.342    63.5856   77.5739    4.4203
     15   7.5   62.0000   67.9092     3.208    61.1939   74.6245   -5.9092
     16  12.0   85.0000   91.9441     6.105    79.1666    104.7    -6.9441
     17   6.0   43.0000   59.8976     3.296    52.9991   66.7960  -16.8976
     18   2.5   57.0000   41.2038     5.548    29.5916   52.8160   15.7962
     19   5.0   33.0000   54.5565     3.728    46.7536   62.3593  -21.5565
     20   7.5   65.0000   67.9092     3.208    61.1939   74.6245   -2.9092
     21   6.0   33.0000   59.8976     3.296    52.9991   66.7960  -26.8976

Sum of Residuals                     0
Sum of Squared Residuals        3968.9088
Predicted Resid SS (Press)      4728.5664
```

First, the values under the heading *Predict Value* now represent estimates of mean KWH values for all possible days with the given AC values. For example, for observation 12 that has AC=8, the value 70.58 now estimates the average kilowatt-hours that are consumed on all days that have AC=8.

Second, two headings are different. They are labeled *Lower95% Mean* and *Upper95% Mean* and are the confidence limits for the means. If you compare these limits with the prediction limits in Output 9.6, you see that the confidence limits for the means are much narrower than the prediction limits. The 95% confidence limits for the mean KWH for all days that have

AC=8 are 63.59 for the lower limit and 77.57 for the upper limit. Recall that the 95% prediction limits for a given day that has AC=8 are 39.53 and 101.6.

Producing Plots of the Regression Line and Confidence Limits

Just as it is useful to look at a plot of the data, it is also useful to look at a plot that contains the observed data that has the fitted regression line plotted through the points. Adding prediction limits or confidence limits gives you a better picture of how well the line describes the data. This kind of plot can be obtained easily with PROC REG. If you want to plot the data, fitted line, and 95% prediction limits (corresponding to Output 9.6), type the following PLOT statement after a MODEL statement:

```
plot kwh*ac pred.*ac l95.*ac u95.*ac / overlay;
title 'Model Relating KWH and AC';
run;
```

The results are shown in Output 9.8. The different characters for the line (dot), data values (×), and prediction limits (+) result from using SYMBOL statements as shown in the example SAS program at the end of this chapter. The SYMBOL statements are not needed if you are not using the high-resolution graphics capabilities of SAS. Another set of statements are included at the end of the chapter to illustrate plotting without graphics capabilities.

Output 9.8   **Plotting the Data, Regression Line, and Prediction Limits**

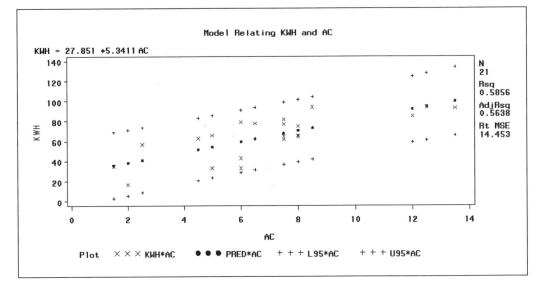

In Output 9.8, an observed data point is an ×, the fitted line is a series of dots, and the prediction limits are +'s. Notice how wide the prediction limits are. All the data points (×'s) are contained between them (+'s). Don't expect this to happen every time, though. With larger data sets, some of the data points would be outside the prediction limits.

If you wanted to show only the fitted regression line and the actual data points, you would type

```
plot kwh*ac pred.*ac / overlay;
run;
```

This statement produces a plot similar to the one in Output 9.4.

To obtain the same type of plot that contains confidence limits (corresponding to Output 9.7) instead of prediction limits, type

```
plot kwh*ac pred.*ac l95m.*ac u95m.*ac / overlay
     vaxis=0 to 140 by 20;
title 'Model Relating KWH and AC';
run;
```

The results are shown in Output 9.9. Compare these confidence limits with the prediction limits in Output 9.8. The confidence limits for the mean (the +'s in Output 9.9) are much narrower. Also, the +'s in Output 9.9 don't enclose all the data points as do the +'s in Output 9.8. The +'s are confidence limits for the mean KWH at a given value of AC, and are not intended to enclose individual KWH values at a given AC value. However, the confidence limits do enclose the regression line. Notice that none of the dots on the line in Output 9.9 are outside the +'s.

Output 9.9   Plotting the Data, Regression Line, and Confidence Limits

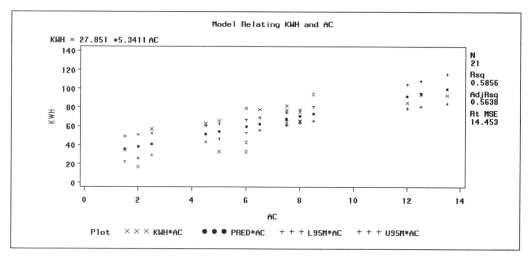

Summary of Straight-Line Regression

Straight-line regression uses least squares to fit a line through a set of data points. Predicted values for y for a given x are computed by inserting the value of x into the equation for the fitted regression line. Prediction limits take into account both the error in fitting the regression line and the variation between values at a given x. Confidence limits for the mean only need to take into account the error in fitting the regression line because the mean doesn't vary. Plots of the observed values, fitted line, and confidence limits or prediction limits are useful in summarizing the regression.

After fitting a regression equation, your next step is to perform regression diagnostics. These tools help you decide if the regression equation is adequate or if you need to add more terms to the model. Perhaps another variable needs to be added, or perhaps a curve fits the data better than a straight line. Chapter 10 covers a set of basic tools to use for this purpose.

The next section covers regression with more than one independent variable.

Regression with Two or More Independent Variables

So far, this chapter has discussed how to predict the dependent variable KWH by using the independent variable AC. But what if some other variables were measured that should also affect kilowatt-hour consumption? Can these variables be used in addition to AC to predict KWH? The answer is yes. Regression that has more than one independent variable is referred to as *multiple regression* because there are multiple independent variables.

Multiple regression is harder to picture in terms of a plot. For two independent variables, you can think of a three-dimensional picture, as shown in Figure 9.3. The two independent variables are on the axes labeled X_1 and X_2, and the dependent variable is on the axis labeled Y. You can think of multiple regression as the process of finding the best-fitting plane through the data points. Here, *best-fitting* means the plane that minimizes the squared distances between all the points and the plane.

Figure 9.3   Diagram Depicting Multiple Regression

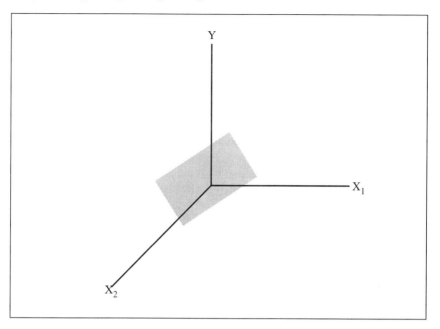

For this case of two independent variables, the estimated regression equation is

$$y = b_0 + b_1 x_1 + b_2 x_2$$

where b_0, b_1, and b_2 estimate the population parameters β_0, β_1, and β_2.

Recall that the homeowner who wanted to predict kilowatt-hour consumption also counted the number of times the electric clothes dryer was used. These values are recorded in the KILOWATT data set. A printout of the entire data set is shown in Output 9.10.

Output 9.10   **Listing of Entire KILOWATT Data Set**

```
              Listing of KILOWATT Data Set

              OBS    KWH     AC    DRYER

               1      35    1.5      1
               2      63    4.5      2
               3      66    5.0      2
               4      17    2.0      0
               5      94    8.5      3
               6      79    6.0      3
               7      93   13.5      1
               8      66    8.0      1
               9      94   12.5      1
              10      82    7.5      2
              11      78    6.5      3
              12      65    8.0      1
              13      77    7.5      2
              14      75    8.0      2
              15      62    7.5      1
              16      85   12.0      1
              17      43    6.0      0
              18      57    2.5      3
              19      33    5.0      0
              20      65    7.5      1
              21      33    6.0      0
```

Using PROC REG for Multiple Regression

To use PROC REG for multiple regression, use a different MODEL statement. You can use several MODEL statements within the same run of PROC REG. Alternatively, you can run PROC REG several times and use a different MODEL statement each time. To fit the multiple regression model with the KILOWATT data set and obtain revised parameter estimates, predicted values, and prediction limits, type the following statements after the ones that perform straight-line regression:

```
    model kwh=ac dryer;
    print cli;
    title 'Model Relating KWH to Both AC and DRYER';
run;
```

The results are shown in Output 9.11.

Output 9.11   PROC REG Output for Multiple Regression Model

```
                        Model Relating KWH to Both AC and DRYER

Model: MODEL1
Dependent Variable: KWH

                              Analysis of Variance

                           Sum of          Mean
     Source        DF      Squares        Square     F Value    Prob>F

     Model          2    9299.80154    4649.90077    300.241    0.0001
     Error         18     278.76989      15.48722
     C Total       20    9578.57143

            Root MSE        3.93538     R-square      0.9709
            Dep Mean       64.85714     Adj R-sq      0.9677
            C.V.            6.06777

                            Parameter Estimates

                    Parameter      Standard     T for H0:
     Variable  DF    Estimate        Error     Parameter=0    Prob > |T|

     INTERCEP   1    8.105385     2.48085116      3.267        0.0043
     AC         1    5.465903     0.28075519     19.469        0.0001
     DRYER      1   13.216600     0.85621937     15.436        0.0001

                    Model Relating KWH to Both AC and DRYER

             Dep Var    Predict    Std Err   Lower95%   Upper95%
      Obs      KWH       Value     Predict    Predict    Predict    Residual

        1    35.0000    29.5208     1.796     20.4322    38.6095     5.4792
        2    63.0000    59.1351     1.193     50.4958    67.7745     3.8649
        3    66.0000    61.8681     1.120     53.2718    70.4644     4.1319
        4    17.0000    19.0372     2.061      9.7045    28.3699    -2.0372
        5    94.0000    94.2154     1.666     85.2368    103.2      -0.2154
        6    79.0000    80.5506     1.611     71.6167    89.4845    -1.5506
        7    93.0000    95.1117     2.058     85.7811    104.4      -2.1117
        8    66.0000    65.0492     0.978     56.5299    73.5686     0.9508
        9    94.0000    89.6458     1.813     80.5429    98.7486     4.3542
       10    82.0000    75.5329     1.004     67.0003    84.0654     6.4671
       11    78.0000    83.2836     1.598     74.3602    92.2070    -5.2836
       12    65.0000    65.0492     0.978     56.5299    73.5686    -0.0492
       13    77.0000    75.5329     1.004     67.0003    84.0654     1.4671
       14    75.0000    78.2658     1.037     69.7155    86.8161    -3.2658
       15    62.0000    62.3163     0.946     53.8129    70.8196    -0.3163
       16    85.0000    86.9128     1.694     77.9115    95.9141    -1.9128
       17    43.0000    40.9008     1.523     32.0352    49.7664     2.0992
       18    57.0000    61.4199     1.999     52.1462    70.6937    -4.4199
       19    33.0000    35.4349     1.602     26.5085    44.3613    -2.4349
       20    65.0000    62.3163     0.946     53.8129    70.8196     2.6837
       21    33.0000    40.9008     1.523     32.0352    49.7664    -7.9008

Sum of Residuals                    0
Sum of Squared Residuals      278.7699
Predicted Resid SS (Press)    390.5237
```

The coefficients for the fitted regression equation are shown under the heading *Parameter Estimate.* The equation is

$$KWH = 8.11 + 5.47(AC) + 13.22(DRYER)$$

The numbers in the equation are interpreted as follows:

- b_0=8.11 is still called the intercept, and it estimates the number of kilowatt-hours consumed on days when neither the air conditioner nor the dryer was used. (Put AC=0 and DRYER=0 into the equation and you get KWH=8.11.)

- b_1=5.47 is the estimate of the kilowatt-hours consumed for each hour that the air conditioner is turned on.

- b_2=13.22 is the estimate of the kilowatt-hours consumed for each use of the dryer.

To the far right of the first page of output under the heading *Prob >|T|*, you find significance probabilities for the 3 estimates in the fitted regression equation. The significance probabilities for AC and DRYER are both 0.0001. This shows overwhelming evidence of the significant effect of these variables on the amount of kilowatt-hour consumption. The *p*-value for the intercept is 0.0043. This shows evidence that a significant (nonzero) number of kilowatt-hours are consumed even when neither the air conditioner nor the dryer is used.

Explaining "Significance"

With multiple regression, "significance" is not easy to understand in terms of the slope of a line. What does it mean for the variables AC and DRYER to have a significant effect on the value of KWH? It means that the amount of electricity consumed by these appliances is large enough to be measured above the random variation in the data. This is because these are major appliances. A small appliance, such as an electric razor, uses electricity, but the amount it uses is so small that its contribution would not be detected in the midst of all the other electrical devices in the house. If you put a variable RAZOR in the model, the *p*-value for its parameter estimate would be large, maybe 0.4 or 0.7, indicating that this source of variation is "not significant."

Differences between Straight-Line and Multiple Regression

If you compare Output 9.11 to Output 9.5, you see that the Error Sum of Squares is much smaller in Output 9.11. The value for the multiple regression is 278.77 compared to 3968.91 for the straight-line regression. Recall that 3968.91 is the variation in the KWH values that is not due to changes in AC. (AC was the only variable in the model.) The value 278.77 is the amount of variation in KWH that is not due to variation in AC or DRYER because AC and DRYER are the variables in the model. This additional accounting of variation due to including DRYER in the model along with AC also shows up in an increased R-square. The R-square is 0.97 in Output 9.11 and 0.59 in Output 9.4. In terms of percentages, 59% of the KWH variation is due to AC alone, and 95% is due to AC and DRYER combined.

Predicted values for the multiple regression model are shown in Output 9.11. They change from Output 9.6 because you included DRYER in the model. Notice also how much the residuals have changed. The largest residual (in absolute value) in Output 9.11 is 7.90 for observation 21, compared to 26.89 in Output 9.6. This reflects the improved prediction due to including DRYER in the model.

Summarizing Multiple Regression

Multiple regression involves the use of two or more independent variables to estimate the dependent variable. Individual predicted values, predicted values for the mean, prediction limits, and confidence limits can be obtained the same way as for the straight-line model.

After you fit a regression equation, the next step is to perform diagnostics to check the fit of your model. Chapter 10 discusses a basic set of diagnostic tools. Usually, the process of fitting a model is an iterative one. First you fit a model, and then you look at the fit, revise the fit according to what you've learned from the tools, look at the revised fit, and so on.

Fitting Curves

A straight line was used to represent the relationship between KWH and AC. In other cases, the relation between two variables is not well represented by a straight line. In such cases, another type of model, such as a polynomial curve, can relate the dependent variable to the independent variable. A quadratic polynomial has the equation

$$y = b_0 + b_1 x + b_2 x^2$$

Once again, with least squares regression, b_0, b_1, and b_2 are estimates of unknown population parameters. If you could measure all values in the entire population, you would know the exact relation between x and y. Because you can measure only values in a sample, you estimate the relation using regression. Least squares regression for curves minimizes the sum of squared differences between the points and the curve, as shown in Figure 9.4.

Figure 9.4   **Least Squares Regression for a Quadratic Model**

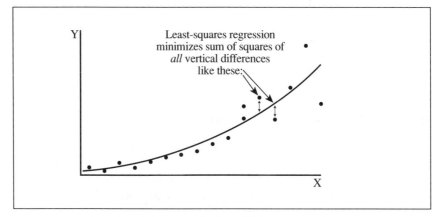

Using PROC REG to Fit Curves

The data used in this section is from an experiment that tested the performance of an industrial engine. The experiment used a mixture of diesel fuel and gas derived from distilling organic materials. The horse-power (POWER) produced from the engine was measured at several speeds (SPEED), where speed is measured in hundreds of revolutions per minute (rpm × 100). The following statements create a SAS data set named ENGINE

with variables SPEED and POWER, and produce the plot shown in
Output 9.12:

```
data engine;
    input speed power @@;
    datalines;
22.0 64.03 20.0 62.47 18.0 54.94 16.0 48.84 14.0 43.73
12.0 37.48 15.0 46.85 17.0 51.17 19.0 58.00 21.0 63.21
22.0 64.03 20.0 59.63 18.0 52.90 16.0 48.84 14.0 42.74
12.0 36.63 10.5 32.05 13.0 39.68 15.0 45.79 17.0 51.17
19.0 56.65 21.0 62.61 23.0 65.31 24.0 63.89
;

proc gplot data=engine;
    plot power*speed;
    title 'Plot of POWER vs. SPEED for ENGINE Data Set';
run;
```

Output 9.12   Curved Relationship between POWER and SPEED

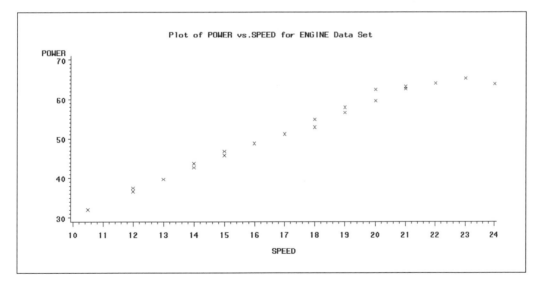

You probably can see that the relationship between POWER and SPEED
might not be represented very well with a straight line. POWER increases
with SPEED up to a point where it seems to level off or curve back down.
You need some other kind of model to relate POWER to SPEED. From the
plot, it looks like a quadratic curve would fit the data.

Before you can fit a curve to the data, you first must create a new variable with squared values of SPEED. Add a program statement to the DATA step to create the new variable (called SPEEDSQ).

```
data engine;
   input speed power @@;
   speedsq=speed*speed;
   datalines;
data lines
;
```

Then type the following statements to get a listing of the data:

```
proc print data=engine;
   title 'Listing of ENGINE Data Set';
run;
```

These statements produce Output 9.13. (Program statements are discussed in Chapter 7. See Table 7.2 for a step-by-step guide to creating new variables in a DATA step.)

Output 9.13   Listing of ENGINE Data Set with New Variable Added

```
                 Listing of ENGINE Data Set

       OBS    SPEED    POWER     SPEEDSQ

        1     22.0     64.03      484.00
        2     20.0     62.47      400.00
        3     18.0     54.94      324.00
        4     16.0     48.84      256.00
        5     14.0     43.73      196.00
        6     12.0     37.48      144.00
        7     15.0     46.85      225.00
        8     17.0     51.17      289.00
        9     19.0     58.00      361.00
       10     21.0     63.21      441.00
       11     22.0     64.03      484.00
       12     20.0     59.63      400.00
       13     18.0     52.90      324.00
       14     16.0     48.84      256.00
       15     14.0     42.74      196.00
       16     12.0     36.63      144.00
       17     10.5     32.05      110.25
       18     13.0     39.68      169.00
       19     15.0     45.79      225.00
       20     17.0     51.17      289.00
       21     19.0     56.65      361.00
       22     21.0     62.61      441.00
       23     23.0     65.31      529.00
       24     24.0     63.89      576.00
```

Now you are ready to fit a regression curve that relates POWER to SPEED. Type

```
proc reg data=engine graphics;
model power=speed speedsq;
title 'Quadratic Model Relating POWER to SPEED for ENGINE Data';
run;
```

These statements produce Output 9.14.

Output 9.14   Quadratic Model for ENGINE Data

```
                  Quadratic Model Relating POWER to SPEED for ENGINE Data

Model: MODEL1
Dependent Variable: POWER

                              Analysis of Variance

                              Sum of        Mean
        Source      DF        Squares      Square     F Value    Prob>F

        Model        2      2285.64535   1142.82268    749.837    0.0001
        Error       21        32.00598      1.52409
        C Total     23      2317.65133

            Root MSE        1.23454     R-square      0.9862
            Dep Mean       52.19333     Adj R-sq      0.9849
            C.V.            2.36533

                              Parameter Estimates

                       Parameter      Standard     T for H0:
        Variable   DF   Estimate         Error    Parameter=0    Prob > |T|

        INTERCEP    1   -17.663771    5.43597741      -3.249       0.0038
        SPEED       1     5.537760    0.64485316       8.588       0.0001
        SPEEDSQ     1    -0.084072    0.01852030      -4.539       0.0002
```

Coefficients for the fitted curve are found under the heading *Parameter Estimate*. The fitted equation is

$$POWER = -17.66 + 5.53(SPEED) - 0.08(SPEEDSQ)$$

In summary, the procedure for fitting the quadratic curve has two steps:

1. Create a new variable whose values are the squares of the values of the independent variable.

2. Fit a multiple regression model. The model should contain both the independent variable and the new variable of squared values.

Testing the Significance of Coefficients

How do you tell whether you really needed the quadratic regression model instead of the simpler regression model for the ENGINE data? You can look at the plot in Output 9.12 and see that a straight-line model wouldn't represent the relationship between POWER and SPEED very well. Also, you can test whether the coefficient for SPEEDSQ is significantly different from 0. The coefficient for SPEEDSQ is b_2=−0.08. This is not a very big number, but remember that it is multiplied by SPEEDSQ, which has large values. Also, the standard error of b_2 is very small, equal to 0.018. This gives the *t*-statistic for SPEEDSQ as shown below:

$$t = b_2/(\text{standard error of } b_2) = -0.08/0.018 = -4.539$$

The significance probability for this *t*-statistic is 0.0002. Thus, if the true relation is a straight line, then there are only about 2 chances out of 10,000 of getting a *t*-statistic as large as the one for SPEEDSQ in this data set. So, even though b_2=−0.08 isn't a very big number, the standard error is so small that b_2 is statistically different from 0. This tells you that the quadratic model really does represent the relation between POWER and SPEED better than the linear model.

In addition to testing to see if the coefficient for the squared term is significant, you can use other tools to decide if the term is needed. Chapter 10 discusses a basic set of regression diagnostics. Anytime you fit a regression equation, you should look at the fit of the model.

Predicted Values, Prediction Limits, and Confidence Limits

You can get predicted values, prediction limits, and confidence limits from the quadratic model just as you do for a straight-line model. To get predicted values and 95% prediction limits for the ENGINE data, add the statements below to your program:

```
print cli;
title 'Quadratic Model Relating POWER to SPEED for ENGINE Data'
run;
```

The results appear in Output 9.15.

Output 9.15 Predicted Values and Prediction Limits for ENGINE Data

```
              Quadratic Model Relating POWER to SPEED for ENGINE Data

            Dep Var   Predict   Std Err   Lower95%   Upper95%
      Obs    POWER     Value    Predict   Predict    Predict    Residual

        1   64.0300   63.4763    0.430    60.7580    66.1947     0.5537
        2   62.4700   59.4628    0.329    56.8059    62.1198     3.0072
        3   54.9400   54.7767    0.353    52.1067    57.4468     0.1633
        4   48.8400   49.4181    0.349    46.7501    52.0861    -0.5781
        5   43.7300   43.3869    0.348    40.7195    46.0542     0.3431
        6   37.4800   36.6831    0.524    33.8941    39.4720     0.7969
        7   46.8500   46.4865    0.339    43.8243    49.1488     0.3635
        8   51.1700   52.1815    0.357    49.5091    54.8538    -1.0115
        9   58.0000   57.2039    0.339    54.5416    59.8661     0.7961
       10   63.2100   61.5537    0.350    58.8849    64.2224     1.6563
       11   64.0300   63.4763    0.430    60.7580    66.1947     0.5537
       12   59.6300   59.4628    0.329    56.8059    62.1198     0.1672
       13   52.9000   54.7767    0.353    52.1067    57.4468    -1.8767
       14   48.8400   49.4181    0.349    46.7501    52.0861    -0.5781
       15   42.7400   43.3869    0.348    40.7195    46.0542    -0.6469
       16   36.6300   36.6831    0.524    33.8941    39.4720    -0.0531
       17   32.0500   31.2138    0.810    28.1430    34.2847     0.8362
       18   39.6800   40.1190    0.405    37.4172    42.8209    -0.4390
       19   45.7900   46.4865    0.339    43.8243    49.1488    -0.6965
       20   51.1700   52.1815    0.357    49.5091    54.8538    -1.0115
       21   56.6500   57.2039    0.339    54.5416    59.8661    -0.5539
       22   62.6100   61.5537    0.350    58.8849    64.2224     1.0563
       23   65.3100   65.2309    0.573    62.4005    68.0613     0.0791
       24   63.8900   66.8173    0.772    63.7890    69.8456    -2.9273

Sum of Residuals                    0
Sum of Squared Residuals      32.0060
Predicted Resid SS (Press)    52.2430
```

The columns in Output 9.15 have the same meaning as for the straight-line regression.

Plotting the Regression Equation

To plot the regression equation for the curved model, use the same statements as were used for the straight-line model. For a plot that shows the observed values, the predicted values, and the prediction limits, use the statements that follow (after first fitting the quadratic model):

```
plot power*speed pred.*speed u95.*speed l95.*speed /
    overlay;
    title 'ENGINE Data, Fitted Curve, and 95% Prediction'
            'Limits';
run;
```

These statements produce Output 9.16.

Output 9.16   Plotting Observed Values, Predicted Values, and Prediction Limits

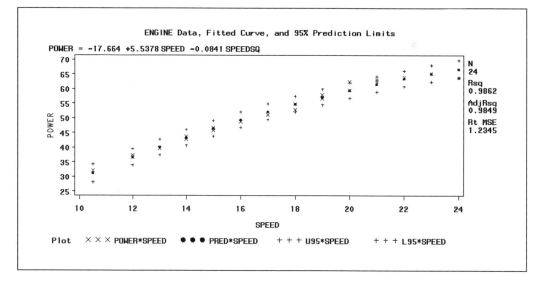

Correlation and Regression when Using PROC INSIGHT

PROC INSIGHT provides features for correlation and regression, which produce the same results as the procedures that are discussed earlier in this chapter.

Analyzing the KILOWATT Data

For the KILOWATT data, type

```
proc insight;
    open kilowatt / nodisplay;
    scatter kwh*ac;
    mult kwh ac;
    fit kwh = ac;
    fit kwh = ac dryer;
run;
```

These statements produce Outputs 9.17 through 9.23. The SCATTER statement produces a scatterplot of the two variables. The MULT statement produces the correlation coefficients. The first FIT statement fits the simple regression of KWH =AC, and the second FIT statement adds DRYER to the regression. The conclusions from the plots, correlations, and regressions are the same as those discussed earlier in the chapter for output from PROC GPLOT, PROC CORR, and PROC REG. The appearance of the output differs, as does the approach to produce confidence and prediction limits.

Output 9.17 shows a scatterplot of the data, and is similar to the plot that is shown earlier in Output 9.2. When a FIT statement with a straight-line regression is used in PROC INSIGHT, this scatterplot is automatically generated in the output for the regression. With multiple regression, the SCATTER statement is needed to produce the scatterplot.

Output 9.17   **Scatterplot from PROC INSIGHT**

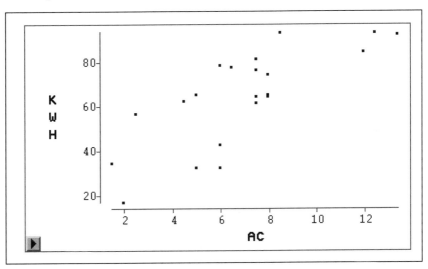

Output 9.18 shows the results of the MULT statement, which generates summary statistics and correlation coefficients. This output is similar to the PROC CORR output shown in Output 9.3.

Output 9.18   **Correlation Coefficients from PROC INSIGHT**

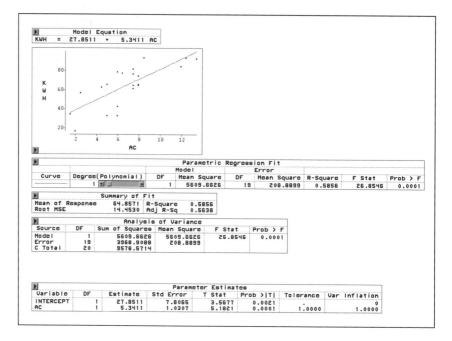

Output 9.19 shows the results of the straight-line regression.

Output 9.19   **Regression Line from PROC INSIGHT**

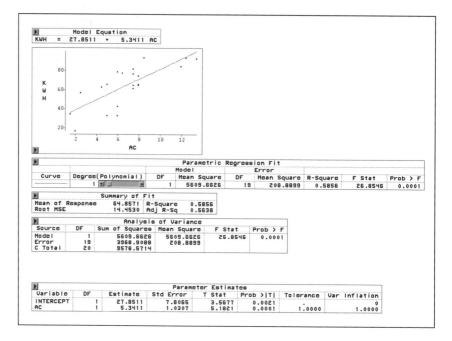

To obtain confidence intervals for the parameter estimates that are shown above, select `Tables` from the menu bar. Then select `C.I.(LR) for Parameters` and then `95%`. This generates Output 9.20.

Output 9.20　**Confidence Limits for Parameters from PROC INSIGHT**

| | 95% C.I. for Parameters | | |
Variable	Estimate	Lower	Upper
INTERCEPT	27.8511	11.5118	44.1903
AC	5.3411	3.1839	7.4983

Adding Confidence and Prediction Limits

Because the straight-line regression output includes the scatterplot and PROC INSIGHT has fit a regression line, you can interactively add the confidence limits for the mean and the prediction limits. From the menu bar, select `Curves`, then `Confidence Curves`, then `95%` to add confidence limits for the mean. Select `Curves`, then `Prediction`, then `95%` to add prediction limits for the mean. Output 9.21 shows the resulting plot. The output also includes text that summarizes the confidence and prediction limits. Because PROC INSIGHT is interactive, you can modify the appearance of the lines (straight, dotted, and the line thickness), and can also modify the confidence level; producing 90% confidence limits for example.

Output 9.21　**Confidence and Prediction Limits from PROC INSIGHT**

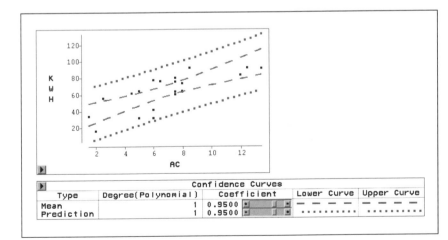

Performing Multiple Regression

The regression that involves both DRYER and AC is shown in Output 9.22 below.

Output 9.22   **Multiple Regression from PROC INSIGHT**

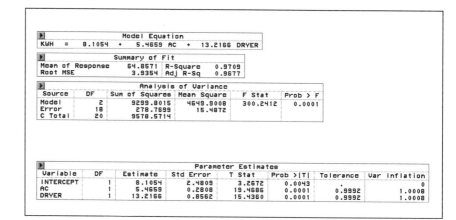

In each case, the residual-by-predicted plot is automatically produced. Output 9.23 shows the plot for the regression equation containing both AC and DRYER. Obtaining these kinds of plots using PROC REG is discussed in Chapter 10.

Output 9.23   **Residuals Plot from PROC INSIGHT**

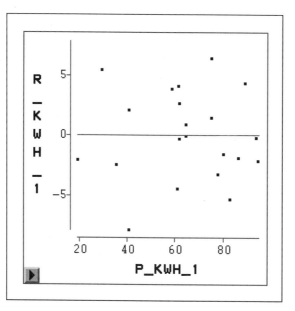

Analyzing the ENGINE Data

To analyze the ENGINE data using PROC INSIGHT, type

```
proc insight;
    open engine / nodisplay;
    scatter power*speed;
    mult power speed;
    fit power = speed;
    fit power = speed speedsq;
run;
```

The preceding statements generate Output 9.24 and 9.25 as well as additional output that is not shown. The MULT and straight-line regression statements produce output similar in form to that shown earlier for the KILOWATT data. The summary statistics match those shown in earlier outputs for the ENGINE data.

Output 9.24 shows the scatterplot produced by the SCATTER statement. Notice the similarity to the plot shown from PROC GPLOT in Output 9.12 earlier in the chapter.

Output 9.24   **Scatterplot for ENGINE Data from PROC INSIGHT**

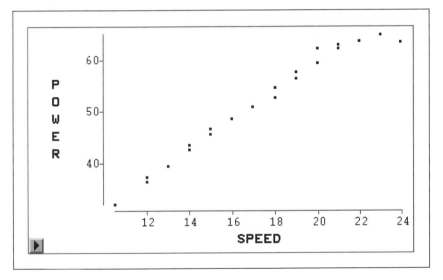

Output 9.25 shows the results of fitting the curve using SPEED and SPEEDSQ in the regression equation. These results are the same as those shown in Output 9.14.

Output 9.25   **Fitting a Curved Line for ENGINE Data from PROC INSIGHT**

```
                      Model Equation
 POWER   =  -   17.6638  +    5.5378  SPEED  -    0.0841  SPEEDSQ

                    Summary of Fit
 Mean of Response    52.1933  R-Square     0.9862
 Root MSE             1.2345  Adj R-Sq     0.9849

                 Analysis of Variance
 Source      DF   Sum of Squares   Mean Square   F Stat    Prob > F
 Model        2        2285.6454     1142.8227   749.8372    0.0001
 Error       21          32.0060        1.5241
 C Total     23        2317.6513
```

```
                        Parameter Estimates
 Variable    DF    Estimate   Std Error   T Stat   Prob >|T|  Tolerance  Var Inflation
 INTERCEPT    1    -17.6638      5.4360   -3.2494     0.0038                         0
 SPEED        1      5.5378      0.6449    8.5876     0.0001    0.0112          89.1253
 SPEEDSQ      1     -0.0841      0.0185   -4.5394     0.0002    0.0112          89.1253
```

Summaries

Key Ideas

- Use simple plots as an aid to understanding the relationship between two variables.

- The correlation coefficient, r, measures the strength of the relationship between two variables. However, it doesn't describe the form of the relationship nor does it show that one of the variables causes the other.

- Regression analysis describes relationships between variables. The simplest model fits a straight line that relates one dependent variable to one independent variable. Multiple regression relates one dependent variable to two or more independent variables. A special case of this is fitting a curve, which relates one dependent variable to an independent variable and the square of the independent variable.

- Once regression analysis has been performed, the fitted equation can be used to predict future values at a given value of the independent variable. Also, prediction limits put bounds around a future value. Finally, confidence limits for the mean put bounds around the mean value of the dependent variable at a given value of the independent variable.

- Plots of the actual data points, regression equation, and prediction or confidence limits are useful in seeing how the regression equation fits the data.

Syntax

- To produce a simple plot relating two variables,

  PROC GPLOT DATA = *data-set-name* ;
  PLOT *y-variable* * *x-variable* ;

  where *data-set-name* is the name of a SAS data set, *y-variable* is the variable for the vertical axis, and *x-variable* is the variable for the horizontal axis. If you don't have graphics capabilities, replace the GPLOT procedure with the PLOT procedure.

- To find the correlation coefficients relating variables,

  PROC CORR DATA = *data-set-name* ;
     VAR *variables* ;

  where *data-set-name* is the name of a SAS data set and *variables* are the names of the variables that you want to find correlations for.

- To fit regression equations; to find predicted values, prediction limits, and confidence limits; to identify observations in the output with values of a variable; and to plot the equation, data, and limits; use the following statements:

  PROC REG DATA = *data-set-name* **GRAPHICS** ;
     MODEL *dependent-variable* = *independent-variables* ;
     ID *id-variable* ;
     VAR *variables* ;
  RUN ;
     PRINT *options* ;
     PLOT *y-variable* * *x-variable* ... / **OVERLAY** ;
  RUN ;

  where items in italic are either as defined earlier or are described in the following list:

id-variables
  is a variable used to identify observations in the output.

variables
  listed in the VAR statement are variables that you may want to use in statements after the first RUN statement, such as a PLOT statement.

options
  are one or more of the following:

  CLI   to print predicted values and prediction limits.

  CLM   to print predicted values and confidence limits for the mean.

The GRAPHICS option in the PROC REG statement is needed to obtain high-resolution graphic plots.

The OVERLAY option in the PLOT statement superimposes plots on the same page.

Note the placement of the two RUN statements. You must specify a PROC REG statement and a MODEL statement before the first RUN statement. If you want to use an ID statement or a VAR statement, then they must also be specified before the first RUN statement.

Variables in the PLOT statement should be specified either in a VAR statement or in MODEL statements before the first RUN statement. Statistics that are produced by PROC REG can also be used in plots. To specify a statistic, use the SAS name for the statistic followed by a period. SAS names for various statistics in PROC REG are

P
  predicted values. (PREDICTED and PRED are also valid.)

R
  residual values. (RESIDUAL is also valid.)

U95, L95
  upper and lower 95% prediction limits, respectively.

U95M, L95M
  upper and lower 95% confidence limits for the mean, respectively.

- To end the REG procedure when you are using it as an interactive procedure, type

    QUIT;

PROC REG works as an interactive procedure starting with Release 6.03.

- To produce scatterplots of two variables, summary statistics, correlation coefficients, and regression using SAS/INSIGHT, type

PROC INSIGHT ;
  OPEN *data-set-name* / **NODISPLAY** ;
  SCATTER *variable*variable* ;
  MULT *variables* ;
  FIT *variable=variables* ;
RUN ;

Example

The program below produces all the output that is shown in this chapter. The statements that are shown are available for Release 6.12. Plots use graphics capabilities.

```
options ps=55 nodate;
data kilowatt;
    input kwh ac dryer @@;
    datalines;
35 1.5 1 63 4.5 2 66 5.0 2 17 2.0 0 94 8.5 3 79 6.0 3
93 13.5 1 66 8.0 1 94 12.5 1 82 7.5 2 78 6.5 3 65 8.0 1
77 7.5 2 75 8.0 2 62 7.5 1 85 12.0 1 43 6.0 0 57 2.5 3
33 5.0 0 65 7.5 1 33 6.0 0
;

proc print data=kilowatt;
    var kwh ac;
    title 'Kilowatt-Hours and Air Conditioner Hours';
run;

symbol1 v=x h=.6 c=black;

proc gplot data=kilowatt;
    plot kwh*ac;
    title 'Plot of KWH against AC: KILOWATT Data Set';
run;

proc corr data=kilowatt;
    var kwh ac;
    title 'Correlation between KWH and AC: KILOWATT Data Set';
run;

proc reg data=kilowatt graphics;
    model kwh=ac;
    plot kwh*ac / nostat nomodel;
    title 'Model Relating KWH and AC';
run;
```

```
proc reg data=kilowatt graphics;
   model kwh=ac;
   id ac;
   var dryer;
   title 'Model Relating KWH and AC';
run;

   print cli;
   title 'Model Relating KWH and AC';
run;

   print clm;
   title 'Model Relating KWH and AC';
run;

symbol1 v=x h=.6 c=black;
symbol2 v=dot h=.4 c=black;
symbol3 v=plus h=.5 c=black;
symbol4 v=plus h=.5 c=black;

   plot kwh*ac pred.*ac l95.*ac u95.*ac / overlay;
   title 'Model Relating KWH and AC';
run;

   plot kwh*ac pred.*ac l95m.*ac u95m.*ac / overlay
        vaxis=0 to 140 by 20;
   title 'Model Relating KWH and AC';
run;

proc print data=kilowatt;
   var kwh ac dryer;
   title 'Listing of KILOWATT Data Set';
run;

proc reg data=kilowatt;
   model kwh=ac dryer;
   print cli;
   title 'Model Relating KWH to Both AC and DRYER';
run;
```

```
option nodate;
data engine;
   input speed power @@;
   speedsq=speed*speed;
   datalines;
22.0 64.03 20.0 62.47 18.0 54.94 16.0 48.84 14.0 43.73
12.0 37.48 15.0 46.85 17.0 51.17 19.0 58.00 21.0 63.21
22.0 64.03 20.0 59.63 18.0 52.90 16.0 48.84 14.0 42.74
12.0 36.63 10.5 32.05 13.0 39.68 15.0 45.79 17.0 51.17
19.0 56.65 21.0 62.61 23.0 65.31 24.0 63.89
;

symbol1 v=x h=.6 c=black;
symbol2 v=dot h=.4 c=black;
symbol3 v=plus h=.5 c=black;
symbol4 v=plus h=.5 c=black;

proc gplot data=engine;
   plot power*speed;
   title 'Plot of POWER vs.SPEED for ENGINE Data Set';
run;

proc print data=engine;
   title 'Listing of ENGINE Data Set';
run;

proc reg data=engine graphics;
   model power=speed speedsq;
   title 'Quadratic Model Relating POWER to SPEED for'
         'ENGINE Data';
run;

   print cli;
   title 'Quadratic Model Relating POWER to SPEED for'
         'ENGINE Data';
run;

plot power*speed pred.*speed u95.*speed l95.*speed /
   overlay;
   title 'ENGINE Data, Fitted Curve, and 95% Prediction'
         'Limits';
run;
```

```
proc insight;
   open kilowatt / nodisplay;
   scatter kwh*ac;
   mult kwh ac;
   fit kwh = ac;
   fit kwh = ac dryer;
run;

proc insight;
   open engine / nodisplay;
   scatter power*speed;
   mult power speed;
   fit power = speed;
   fit power = speed speedsq;
run;
```

The program below produces all output shown in this chapter. Statements shown are available for Release 6.12. Graphics capabilities are *not* needed.

```
options ps=55 nodate;
data kilowatt;
   input kwh ac dryer @@;
   datalines;
35 1.5 1 63 4.5 2 66 5.0 2 17 2.0 0 94 8.5 3 79 6.0 3
93 13.5 1 66 8.0 1 94 12.5 1 82 7.5 2 78 6.5 3 65 8.0 1
77 7.5 2 75 8.0 2 62 7.5 1 85 12.0 1 43 6.0 0 57 2.5 3
33 5.0 0 65 7.5 1 33 6.0 0
;

proc print data=kilowatt;
   var kwh ac;
   title 'Kilowatt-Hours and Air Conditioner Hours';
run;

proc plot data=kilowatt;
   plot kwh*ac='*';
   title 'Model Plot of KWH against AC: KILOWATT Data Set';
run;

proc corr data=kilowatt;
   var kwh ac;
   title 'Correlation between KWH and AC: KILOWATT Data Set';
run;

proc reg data=kilowatt;
   model kwh=ac;
   plot kwh*ac='*' pred.*ac='-' / overlay;
   title 'Model Relating KWH and AC';
run;
```

```
proc reg data=kilowatt;
   model kwh=ac;
   id ac;
   var dryer;
   title 'Model Relating KWH and AC';
run;

   print cli;
   title 'Model Relating KWH and AC';
run;

   print clm;
   title 'Model Relating KWH and AC';
run;

   plot kwh*ac='*' pred.*ac='-' l95.*ac='+' u95.*ac='+'
      / overlay;
   title 'Model Relating KWH and AC';
run;

   plot kwh*ac='*' pred.*ac='-' l95m.*ac='+' u95m.*ac='+'
      / overlay;
        vaxis=0 to 140 by 20;
   title 'Model Relating KWH and AC';
run;

proc print data=kilowatt;
   var kwh ac dryer;
   title 'Listing of KILOWATT Data Set';
run;

proc reg data=kilowatt;
  model kwh=ac dryer;
  print cli;
  title 'Model Relating KWH to Both AC and DRYER';
run;

option nodate;
data engine;
   input speed power @@;
   speedsq=speed*speed;
   datalines;
22.0 64.03 20.0 62.47 18.0 54.94 16.0 48.84 14.0 43.73
12.0 37.48 15.0 46.85 17.0 51.17 19.0 58.00 21.0 63.21
22.0 64.03 20.0 59.63 18.0 52.90 16.0 48.84 14.0 42.74
12.0 36.63 10.5 32.05 13.0 39.68 15.0 45.79 17.0 51.17
19.0 56.65 21.0 62.61 23.0 65.31 24.0 63.89
;
```

```
proc plot data=engine;
   plot power*speed;
   title 'Plot of POWER vs.SPEED for ENGINE Data Set';
run;

proc print data=engine;
   title 'Listing of ENGINE Data Set';
run;

proc reg data=engine;
   model power=speed speedsq;
   title 'Quadratic Model Relating POWER to SPEED for'
         'ENGINE Data';
run;

   print cli;
   title 'Quadratic Model Relating POWER to SPEED for'
         'ENGINE Data';
run;

plot power*speed='*' pred.*speed='-' u95.*speed l95.*speed /
   overlay symbol='+';
   title 'ENGINE Data, Fitted Curve, and 95% Prediction'
         'Limits';
run;
```

Further Reading

For more information about correlation and regression, see

* Mendenhall, William and Sincich, Terry. (1996), *A Second Course in Statistics, Regression Analysis*, 5th Edition. Upper Saddle River, NJ: Prentice Hall.
* Draper, N.R. and Smith, H. (1981), *Applied Regression Analysis*, 2nd Edition. New York: John Wiley & Sons, Inc.

For more about PROC PLOT or PROC CORR, see the

* *SAS® Procedures Guide, Version 6, Third Edition.*

For complete details about PROC REG, see the

* *SAS/STAT® User's Guide, Version 6, Fourth Edition, Volumes 1 and 2.*
* *SAS/STAT® Software: Changes and Enhancements through Release 6.12.*

For more information about SAS applications for regression, see

* Freund, R. J. and Littell, R. C. (1991), *SAS® System for Regression*. 2nd Edition. Cary, N.C.: SAS Institute Inc.

Chapter 10   # Basic Regression Diagnostics

How do you determine whether your regression model adequately represents your data? How do you tell when more terms should be added to the model? How do you identify outliers, that is, observations that don't fit in with the rest of the data? These are questions that can be answered by using regression diagnostics. *Residual analysis* is an important part of regression diagnostics. Residuals are the differences between observed and predicted values. One of the most effective methods of residual analysis is plotting residuals.

This chapter discusses residual analysis for basic validation of models. Major topics include

- understanding characteristics of residuals
- using residual plots to determine whether more terms should be added to the model
- using residual plots and frequency distributions to identify outliers
- using residual plots to detect a time sequence in the data.

Basic regression diagnostics and fitting regression models are intertwined. First you fit a model, and then you examine the model using diagnostics. This may lead you to fit a second model, which you also examine with diagnostics. The process continues until you find a model that fits the data well. (Note that you may not always find a good model.) This chapter demonstrates this process using the KILOWATT and ENGINE data sets from Chapter 9. It uses PROC REG and summarizes how the procedure is used. Syntax presented in Chapter 9 is not repeated here.

Contents

Diagnostic Tools

You can use many diagnostic tools to decide if your regression model fits well or not. This chapter concentrates on using simple plots. However, more advanced tools exist, especially for multiple regression models. If you fit a multiple regression model, particularly one with many independent variables, you should consult a statistician to find out more about these advanced tools. Also, the "Further Reading" section at the end of this chapter gives some references.

Characteristics of Residuals

Recall that a regression model fits an equation to an observed set of points. From this model, you can get predicted values. The differences between the observed and predicted values are called *residuals* (residual=observed−predicted). Residuals can be used in various plots and analyses to show you if your model is a good one or not. This section gives some basic facts about residuals that are helpful for understanding regression diagnostics.

Plotting Residuals against Predicted Values

If your model has all the terms it needs, then a plot of residuals against independent variables or against predicted values should look like a random scattering of points (a horizontal band). If your model needs another term, then a plot of residuals has a pattern that suggests what type of term should be added to the model. Some possible patterns are shown in Figure 10.1.

Figure 10.1   Possible Patterns in Plots of Residuals

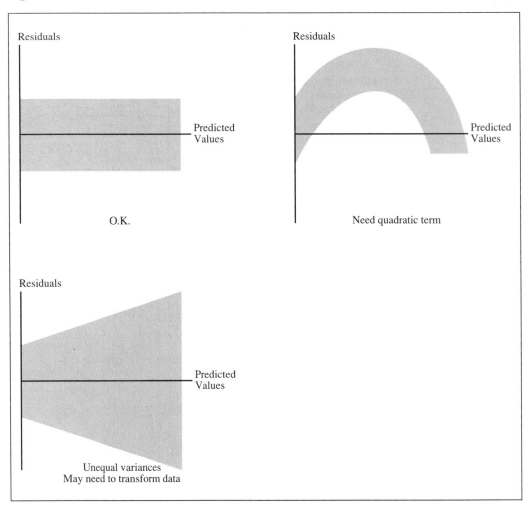

Figure 10.1 illustrates plots of residuals against predicted values. This basic plot is one tool for checking the fit of a regression model. Creating and interpreting these plots is discussed later in this chapter.

Residuals and Outliers

If your data is well represented by your model, then a plot of the residuals against the predicted values should look like a random scattering of points. However, if an observation is not represented by the model, then the residual for that observation is usually large because the predicted value tends to differ substantially from the observed value. "Large" refers to the absolute value of the residual, so a large residual can be either positive or negative. Observations that have large residuals might be *outliers*; they might not fit in with the rest of the data. Figure 10.2 is a plot of residuals against predicted values and contains a single outlier. If your data looks like this, you need to check the outlier carefully. It may simply be due to chance or to some special cause.

Figure 10.2   Example of an Outlier

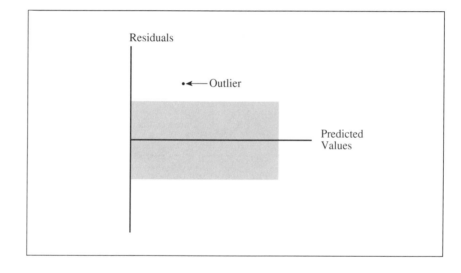

This type of plot is very useful in multiple regression where the model contains more than one dependent variable.

Sequence Trend

When data is collected over time, there is often a trend in the data caused by conditions that change with time. To help detect this trend, you can plot residuals against time (as shown in Figure 10.3). Note that *time* means the sequence in which the data is collected. In regression, your main interest is the relationship between a dependent variable and one or more independent variables. However. you can't always collect all the data at the same time, so a time sequence is often present in the data. Contrast this situation with one where you are interested in changes over time, for example, changes in the stock market. This second situation, where time is an independent variable in your model, is analyzed by using methods other than simple regression. These other methods are not discussed here.

Figure 10.3   Example of Plot Showing a Sequence Trend

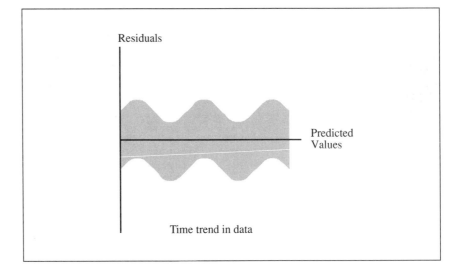

In summary, residuals can show you if

• you need to add more terms to a model

• your data contains outliers

• there is an important effect caused by the sequence in which you collected data.

The next five sections show how to use PROC REG to answer these questions for the ENGINE and KILOWATT data. These sections focus on the diagnostic tools and show how the tools are useful for different models for the ENGINE and KILOWATT data. The final section of this chapter focuses on the data sets and summarizes what the various tools tell you about the data sets and models.

Using Plots of Residuals against Predicted Values

The last section described a plot of residuals against predicted values as a basic tool for checking the fit of the model. Before plotting predicted values or residuals, you need to calculate them. To calculate and print the predicted values and residuals for the multiple regression model for the KILOWATT data set, use the P option in the MODEL statement. This option prints a subset of the items printed by the CLI or CLM options, which are discussed in Chapter 9. To produce the plot shown in Output 10.1 and the regression output shown in Chapter 9, type

```
proc reg data=kilowatt graphics;
    model kwh=ac dryer / p;
    plot residual.*predicted.;
    title 'KILOWATT Data with Both AC and DRYER in Model';
run;
```

This plot seems to be a random scatter of points.

Output 10.1   Plot of Residuals against Predicted Values: KILOWATT Data

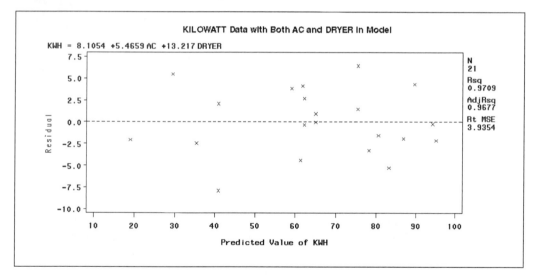

To use statistics produced by PROC REG in plots, type the SAS name for the statistics followed by a period(.). The "Syntax" summary at the end of the chapter gives details.

To calculate and print the predicted values for the quadratic model for the ENGINE data set, type

```
proc reg data=engine graphics;
    model power=speed speedsq / p;
    plot residual.*predicted.;
    title 'Regression for Quadratic Model: ENGINE Data';
run;
```

The preceding program produces Output 10.2. (Output from fitting the regression model is shown in Chapter 9.) This plot appears to be mostly a random scatter of points with possibly two or three outliers.

Output 10.2   Residuals against Predicted Values: ENGINE Data, Quadratic Model

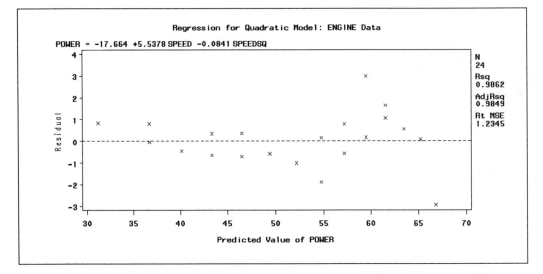

In general, use a plot of residuals against predicted variables as one of your first diagnostic tools to check a regression model. If this plot indicates that problems exist, use the tools discussed in the rest of this chapter. This chapter doesn't repeat plots of residuals against predicted values for all the models discussed in later sections. You may want to look at plots for other models to get a better understanding of how these plots can help you.

Finding Out if More Terms Are Needed in a Model

In Chapter 9, you used *t*-tests to find out if variables in a model were needed. A quadratic model was used to relate POWER to SPEED for the ENGINE data set, and a *t*-test was used to check whether the quadratic term was needed in the model. Also, *t*-tests were used in the KILOWATT data set to find out if AC and DRYER were important in accounting for the amount of electricity consumed. In both cases, the *t*-tests were performed on variables already in the model. If you have fitted a model that contains certain variables and you want to find out if other terms are needed in the model, two tools you can use are to plot observed and predicted values and to examine the values of residuals. To see how these methods work, consider a straight-line model for the ENGINE data set. Type the following statements:

```
proc sort data=engine;
   by speed;
run;

proc reg data=engine graphics;
   id speed;
   model power=speed / p;
   plot power*speed;
   title 'Regression for Straight-Line Model: ENGINE Data';
run;
```

Some of the results of the MODEL statement are shown in Output 10.3, and the plot is shown in Output 10.4. The next two sections examine this output and show how the plot and the printed residuals help you decide if the model fits well.

Output 10.3   **Residual Values for ENGINE Data: Straight-Line Model**

```
              Regression for Straight-Line Model: ENGINE Data

                              Dep Var     Predict
            Obs    SPEED        POWER       Value    Residual

              1     10.5       32.0500     33.9688    -1.9188
              2     12         37.4800     37.9092    -0.4292
              3     12         36.6300     37.9092    -1.2792
              4     13         39.6800     40.5362    -0.8562
              5     14         43.7300     43.1631     0.5669
              6     14         42.7400     43.1631    -0.4231
              7     15         46.8500     45.7901     1.0599
              8     15         45.7900     45.7901    -0.0001
              9     16         48.8400     48.4171     0.4229
             10     16         48.8400     48.4171     0.4229
             11     17         51.1700     51.0440     0.1260
             12     17         51.1700     51.0440     0.1260
             13     18         54.9400     53.6710     1.2690
             14     18         52.9000     53.6710    -0.7710
             15     19         58.0000     56.2980     1.7020
             16     19         56.6500     56.2980     0.3520
             17     20         62.4700     58.9249     3.5451
             18     20         59.6300     58.9249     0.7051
             19     21         63.2100     61.5519     1.6581
             20     21         62.6100     61.5519     1.0581
             21     22         64.0300     64.1789    -0.1489
             22     22         64.0300     64.1789    -0.1489
             23     23         65.3100     66.8058    -1.4958
             24     24         63.8900     69.4328    -5.5428

Sum of Residuals                     0
Sum of Squared Residuals       63.4120
Predicted Resid SS (Press)     84.4082
```

Output 10.4   **Plotting Data and Predicted Values for ENGINE Data:**
Straight-Line Model

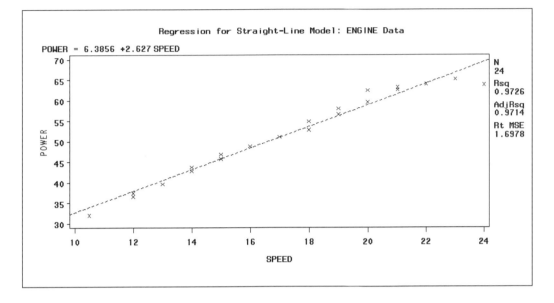

Plotting Observed and Predicted Values

Look first at the plot in Output 10.4. Each data point is represented by an x. At first glance, it may appear that the line passes through the data points pretty well. What's more, $R^2 = .97$ is large. However, you see that near the ends of the line the data points are mostly below the line, and near the middle part of the line the data points tend to be above the line. This is because of the curvature in the data, and it is a signal that a quadratic model is needed to represent the relationship between POWER and SPEED.

Because the amount of curvature in the data is small, the need for the quadratic model is not obvious from the plot. Other types of plots discussed in later sections more clearly show the need for a quadratic model. However, with a more dramatic curvature, this kind of plot would clearly show the need to add the quadratic term to the model.

In general, an overlaid plot of observed and predicted values shows you an obvious need for more variables in the model. When the need is subtle, other plots discussed in later sections are more helpful.

Using the Printed Residuals

Residuals from the linear model fitted to the ENGINE data set are shown in Output 10.3 under the heading *Residual*. Notice that the observations are ordered according to the value of SPEED; this is a result of using PROC SORT before PROC REG in the program.

Observation 1 has an observed value of POWER equal to 32.05, a predicted value equal to 33.97, and a residual of –1.92 (=32.05-33.97). The column that is labeled *Residual* contains mostly negative numbers for small and large values of SPEED (<16 or >21). These values correspond to the ends of the regression line in Output 10.4. However, the residuals for the middle part of the regression line (with values of SPEED between 16 and 21) are almost all positive. Once again, this trend is a result of the curvature in the data, and it reveals the need for a quadratic term in the model.

In general, look at the printed residuals and see if you can find a systematic pattern in the distribution of positive and negative values. Like the overlaid plot discussed above, this method is most useful when there is an obvious need to add variables to the model.

Using Plots of Residuals against Independent Variables

Plotting residuals against independent variables is an effective method for graphically checking whether another term or variable is needed in a model. If the model is adequate as is, the plot shows a random scattering of points. Obvious patterns in the data indicate a need to add more terms to the model. Like most plots that show residuals on the vertical axis, these are often called *residual plots*.

Example: Showing the Need for a Quadratic Term

To plot the residuals against the independent variable from the straight-line model fitted to the ENGINE data set, type

```
plot residual.*speed;
title 'Regression for Straight-Line Model: ENGINE Data';
run;
```

The plot is shown in Output 10.5. (Output 10.3 shows the output produced from fitting the model.) You can clearly see the up-and-down trend. It starts on the left with negative values, changes to positive values, and reverts back to negative values. The trend is more dramatic in the residual plot of Output 10.5 than in the data plot of Output 10.4 because of the change in scale of the vertical axis. This obvious pattern indicates that you need to add a quadratic term to the model.

Output 10.5   ENGINE Data, Straight-Line Model: Plot of Residuals against SPEED

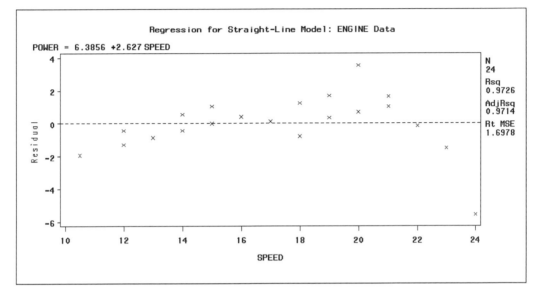

Now look at a plot of the residuals from the quadratic model. Type

```
plot residual.*speed;
title 'Regression for Quadratic Model: ENGINE Data';
run;
```

The output that is produced from fitting the regression is shown in Output 9.14. The plot appears in Output 10.6. Except for two or three points, the pattern looks like a horizontal band. Recall that this is the pattern you should obtain if your model represents the data reasonably well.

Output 10.6   ENGINE Data, Quadratic Model: Plot of Residuals against SPEED

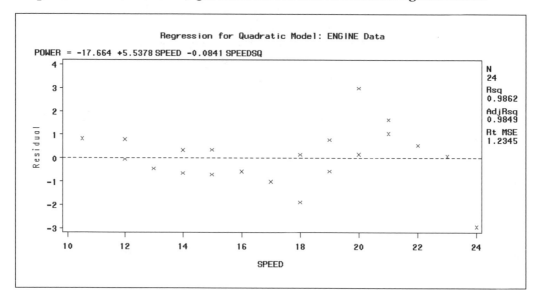

Notice that two points in Output 10.6 do not lie in the same general pattern as the other points. The point above SPEED=24 is below the others, and one of the points above SPEED=20 is above the others. Perhaps something is peculiar about these observations, or perhaps they occur simply by chance. The section "Looking for Outliers in the Data" shows how to use other plots to decide if these points are unusual or not.

Example: Showing the Need for Another Term

You can apply what you've learned about residual plots to the KILOWATT data set to see if you need to add terms to the model that contains AC and DRYER. To find out if the residual plots have definite patterns or if they appear to be a random scatter of points, type

```
proc reg data=kilowatt graphics;
   model kwh=ac dryer / p;
   plot residual.*ac residual.*dryer;
   title 'KILOWATT Data with Both AC and DRYER in Model';
run;
```

The output produced from fitting the model is shown in Output 9.11. The plots are shown in Output 10.7 and Output 10.8. First look at Output 10.7, which shows a plot of residuals against AC. There is no apparent trend in the plot, so there is no need to include a quadratic AC term in the model. Now look at Output 10.8, which shows a plot of residuals against DRYER. The curvature in the plot indicates a need for a quadratic term for DRYER.

Output 10.7   **KILOWATT Data: Plot of Residuals against AC for Model with AC and DRYER**

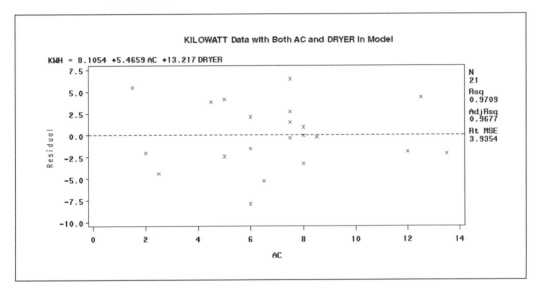

Output 10.8   KILOWATT Data: Plot of Residuals against DRYER for Model with AC and DRYER

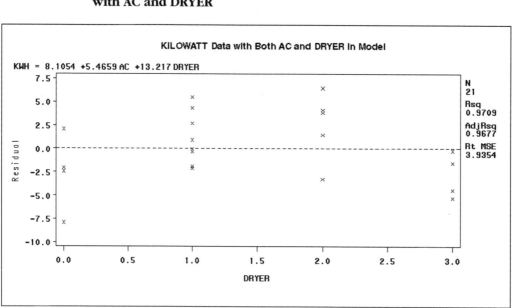

These results may seem unexpected: if each use of the dryer consumes the same amount of electricity, then the response to DRYER should be linear, and no quadratic term should be needed for DRYER. Perhaps smaller loads of clothes were dried on days with several loads, requiring less electricity per load on these days. This is a case where the subjective nature of residual plots comes into play and more advanced tools might be helpful.

In Chapter 9 you first saw a regression of KWH with only AC in the model. Later, DRYER was added to the model. To look at the model that contains only AC and examine residual plots for this model, type

```
proc reg data=kilowatt graphics;
   var dryer;
   model kwh=ac / p;
   plot residual.*ac residual.*dryer;
   title 'KILOWATT Data with Only AC in Model';
run;
```

The regression output is shown in Chapter 9, and the plots are shown in Output 10.9 and Output 10.10. Output 10.9 shows a random scatter of points, which indicates that a quadratic term for AC isn't needed. Output 10.10 is a plot of residuals from the model against the variable DRYER. It shows a definite increase in residuals with an increase in DRYER. This indicates that DRYER should be added to the model.

Output 10.9   **KILOWATT Data: Plot of Residuals against AC for Model with Only AC**

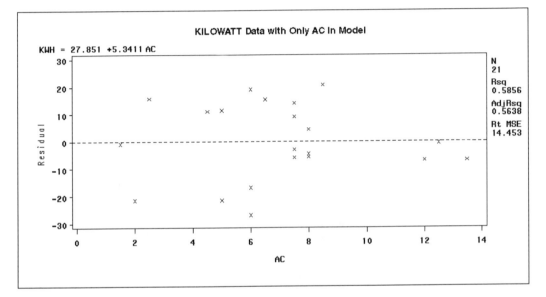

Output 10.10   KILOWATT Data: Plot of Residuals against DRYER for Model with Only AC

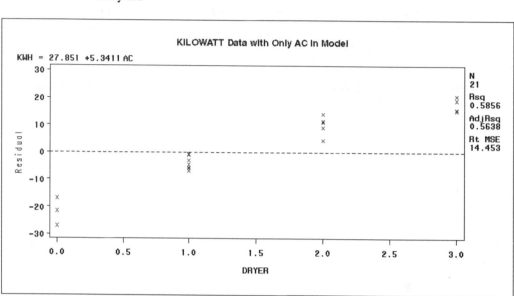

Technical Details

The plot in Output 10.10 is related to partial regression residual plots, which can also be produced with PROC REG. The partial regression residual plots can be more informative than a residual plot like the one in Output 10.10.

In summary, use plots of residuals against independent variables to check the need for more terms in the model. A curved plot indicates that you need to add a quadratic term to the model. A plot with a definite increasing or decreasing trend indicates that you need to add that variable to the model. For a multiple regression, plot the residuals against independent variables in the model and against independent variables that haven't been added to the model.

Looking for Outliers in the Data

Output 10.6 shows a plot of residuals from the quadratic model for the ENGINE data. As noted earlier, the residuals fall mostly in a horizontal band, except for two or three points that seem to lie away from the other points. The most notable points are above SPEED=20 and SPEED=24. To find out if these residuals are too large to have occurred reasonably by chance alone, you can use *studentized residuals*. These are obtained by dividing residuals by their standard errors. They are also called standardized residuals. PROC REG produces both a list and a simple plot of studentized residuals.

For a model that fits the data well and has no outliers, most of the studentized residuals should be close to 0. In general, studentized residuals that are less than or equal to 2.0 in absolute value ($-2.0 \leq$ studentized residual ≤ 2.0) can easily occur by chance. Values between 2.0 and 3.0 in absolute value occur infrequently, and values larger than 3.0 in absolute value occur very rarely by chance alone. If the studentized residual is between 2.0 and 3.0 in absolute value, then it might be considered suspicious. If it is 3.0 or larger in absolute value, then you can consider the observation a probable outlier. (Some statisticians use different cutoff values to decide if an observation is an outlier.)

Example: Data with Outliers

The residual plots in Output 10.2 and Output 10.6 for the quadratic model for the ENGINE data appeared to be a random scatter of points with a couple of exceptions. The studentized residuals can show if these points are more likely to be a result of chance or if they point out special situations. To get the studentized residuals, use the R (for residual) option in the MODEL statement:

```
proc reg data=engine;
   model power=speed speedsq / r;
   title 'Regression for Quadratic Model: ENGINE Data';
run;
```

These statements produce output from fitting the model, which isn't shown. The printout produced as a result of requesting the R option is shown in Output 10.11.

Output 10.11   Studentized Residuals: Example of Data with Outliers

```
                   Regression for Quadratic Model: ENGINE Data

       Dep Var  Predict  Std Err         Std Err   Student                    Cook's
Obs    POWER    Value    Predict Residual Residual Residual  -2-1-0 1 2          D

  1    64.0300  63.4763   0.430   0.5537   1.157    0.478   |       |      |    0.011
  2    62.4700  59.4628   0.329   3.0072   1.190    2.527   |       |***** |    0.163
  3    54.9400  54.7767   0.353   0.1633   1.183    0.138   |       |      |    0.001
  4    48.8400  49.4181   0.349  -0.5781   1.184   -0.488   |       |      |    0.007
  5    43.7300  43.3869   0.348   0.3431   1.184    0.290   |       |      |    0.002
  6    37.4800  36.6831   0.524   0.7969   1.118    0.713   |       |*     |    0.037
  7    46.8500  46.4865   0.339   0.3635   1.187    0.306   |       |      |    0.003
  8    51.1700  52.1815   0.357  -1.0115   1.182   -0.856   |     *|      |    0.022
  9    58.0000  57.2039   0.339   0.7961   1.187    0.671   |       |*     |    0.012
 10    63.2100  61.5537   0.350   1.6563   1.184    1.399   |       |**    |    0.057
 11    64.0300  63.4763   0.430   0.5537   1.157    0.478   |       |      |    0.011
 12    59.6300  59.4628   0.329   0.1672   1.190    0.140   |       |      |    0.001
 13    52.9000  54.7767   0.353  -1.8767   1.183   -1.586   |   ***|      |    0.074
 14    48.8400  49.4181   0.349  -0.5781   1.184   -0.488   |       |      |    0.007
 15    42.7400  43.3869   0.348  -0.6469   1.184   -0.546   |     *|      |    0.009
 16    36.6300  36.6831   0.524  -0.0531   1.118   -0.047   |       |      |    0.000
 17    32.0500  31.2138   0.810   0.8362   0.932    0.898   |       |*     |    0.203
 18    39.6800  40.1190   0.405  -0.4390   1.166   -0.376   |       |      |    0.006
 19    45.7900  46.4865   0.339  -0.6965   1.187   -0.587   |     *|      |    0.009
 20    51.1700  52.1815   0.357  -1.0115   1.182   -0.856   |     *|      |    0.022
 21    56.6500  57.2039   0.339  -0.5539   1.187   -0.467   |       |      |    0.006
 22    62.6100  61.5537   0.350   1.0563   1.184    0.892   |       |*     |    0.023
 23    65.3100  65.2309   0.573   0.0791   1.094    0.072   |       |      |    0.000
 24    63.8900  66.8173   0.772  -2.9273   0.963   -3.039   |******|      |    1.980

Sum of Residuals                        0
Sum of Squared Residuals          32.0060
Predicted Resid SS (Press)        52.2430
```

The column labeled *Student Residual* lists the values for the studentized residuals. These are calculated by dividing the items in the *Residual* column by those in the *Std Err Residual* column. For example, the studentized residual for Observation 1 is 0.478 (=0.554/1.157).

You can look at the column of studentized residuals in Output 10.11 and pick out observations that are either suspicious (between 2 and 3 in absolute value) or probable (greater than 3 in absolute value) outliers. However, the plot at the right of the output makes this easier. This plot, labeled -2 -1 -0 1 2, is a simple plot of studentized residuals. Each asterisk (*) corresponds to one half of a unit. Observations with four or five asterisks have studentized residuals between 2.0 and 3.0 and are in the suspicious range. Observations with six or more asterisks are probable outliers. This plot makes it easy for you to identify observation 2 as suspicious and observation 24 as a probable outlier.

The large positive residual above SPEED=20 in Output 10.6 corresponds to observation 2 in Output 10.11, and the large negative residual above SPEED=24 corresponds to observation 24. The studentized residual for observation 2 is 2.527, which is in the suspicious range. The studentized residual for observation 24 is -3.039, which puts it in the probable outlier range.

Now you've identified one observation that corresponds to SPEED=20 as suspicious and one observation that corresponds to SPEED=24 as a probable outlier. As the next step, you should go back to the source of the data and see if you can identify some reason for the outlying observations to be peculiar. Also, look for a sequence effect, as is shown later in this chapter.

Technical Details

If you run the program that contains a PROC SORT for the ENGINE data (see "Finding Out if More Terms Are Needed in a Model") and then run the program in this section in the same SAS job, your output looks different. Once you sort the data set, it remains sorted for subsequent PROC steps in the same program. In this case, the studentized residual for Observation 1 is 0.898 (=0.836/0.932). Also, the large positive residual corresponds to observation 17, and the large negative residual corresponds to observation 24.

Example: Data without Outliers

Residual plots for the KILOWATT data set did not show any obvious outliers. To check the KILOWATT data using studentized residuals, type

```
proc reg data=kilowatt;
   model kwh=ac dryer / r;
      title 'KILOWATT Data with Both AC and DRYER in Model';
run;
```

Results from the R option appear in Output 10.12.

Output 10.12   Studentized Residuals for KILOWATT Data

KILOWATT Data with Both AC and DRYER in Model

Obs	Dep Var KWH	Predict Value	Std Err Predict	Residual	Std Err Residual	Student Residual	-2-1-0 1 2	Cook's D
1	35.0000	29.5208	1.796	5.4792	3.501	1.565	| |*** |	0.215
2	63.0000	59.1351	1.193	3.8649	3.750	1.031	| |** |	0.036
3	66.0000	61.8681	1.120	4.1319	3.773	1.095	| |** |	0.035
4	17.0000	19.0372	2.061	-2.0372	3.353	-0.608	| *| |	0.046
5	94.0000	94.2154	1.666	-0.2154	3.565	-0.060	| | |	0.000
6	79.0000	80.5506	1.611	-1.5506	3.590	-0.432	| | |	0.013
7	93.0000	95.1117	2.058	-2.1117	3.354	-0.630	| *| |	0.050
8	66.0000	65.0492	0.978	0.9508	3.812	0.249	| | |	0.001
9	94.0000	89.6458	1.813	4.3542	3.493	1.247	| |** |	0.139
10	82.0000	75.5329	1.004	6.4671	3.805	1.700	| |*** |	0.067
11	78.0000	83.2836	1.598	-5.2836	3.596	-1.469	| **| |	0.142
12	65.0000	65.0492	0.978	-0.0492	3.812	-0.013	| | |	0.000
13	77.0000	75.5329	1.004	1.4671	3.805	0.386	| | |	0.003
14	75.0000	78.2658	1.037	-3.2658	3.796	-0.860	| *| |	0.018
15	62.0000	62.3163	0.946	-0.3163	3.820	-0.083	| | |	0.000
16	85.0000	86.9128	1.694	-1.9128	3.552	-0.538	| *| |	0.022
17	43.0000	40.9008	1.523	2.0992	3.629	0.579	| |* |	0.020
18	57.0000	61.4199	1.999	-4.4199	3.390	-1.304	| **| |	0.197
19	33.0000	35.4349	1.602	-2.4349	3.595	-0.677	| *| |	0.030
20	65.0000	62.3163	0.946	2.6837	3.820	0.703	| |* |	0.010
21	33.0000	40.9008	1.523	-7.9008	3.629	-2.177	| ****| |	0.278

Sum of Residuals   0
Sum of Squared Residuals   278.7699
Predicted Resid SS (Press)   390.5237

An examination of the plot indicates that no observation has more than four asterisks. Observation 21 has a studentized residual of -2.177 and is only mildly suspicious. In a data set with 21 observations, you are likely to find one or two residuals in the suspicious range due to chance alone. This is likely to occur even if there are no real outliers.

Residual Plots in Time Sequence

If data is collected over time, then there is a possibility that changing conditions will affect the measurement variable. This can be verified by plotting residuals against the sequence in which the data was collected. A random scatter of points indicates an unimportant (or unmeasurable) sequence effect; an obvious pattern indicates a possible problem.

Looking for a Sequence Effect for the KILOWATT Data

To plot the residuals against time, you need a variable that identifies the day on which an observation was collected. The observations in the KILOWATT data set were entered in chronological order. An easy way to create the variable DAY is to add a program statement to your DATA step as follows:

```
data kilowatt;
    input kwh ac dryer @@;
    day=_n_;
    datalines;
```

The program statement that creates the new variable DAY uses _N_, one of the *automatic variables* that is available in SAS software. For very simple DATA steps like the one above, _N_ can be used to identify the order of the observations because it increases by one for each new observation. For more complex DATA steps this may not be the case.

After using the DATA step outlined above, use the following statements to plot the KILOWATT residuals against time:

```
proc reg data=kilowatt graphics;
    var day;
    model kwh=ac dryer / p;
    plot residual.*day;
    title 'KILOWATT Data with Both AC and DRYER in Model';
run;
```

The plot, which is shown in Output 10.13, shows a modest decreasing trend. This indicates that the use of electricity may have decreased slightly with time. Perhaps the homeowner's overall use of electricity was affected by the knowledge that he was collecting data about the use of electricity. Or perhaps the days near the end of the experiment were cooler, and the air conditioner was used less. Just as with your own data, the true answer to this question may be unknown (as it is here), or careful sleuthing may turn up a cause for the sequence effect.

Output 10.13   Sequence Plot for KILOWATT Data

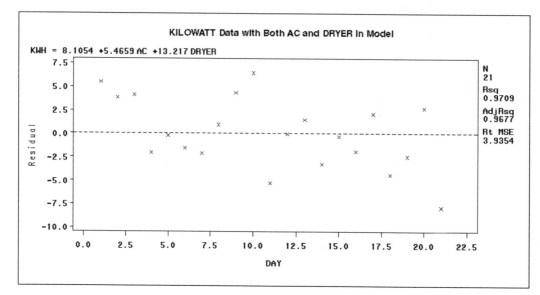

Looking for a Sequence Effect for the ENGINE Data

To look for a sequence effect in the ENGINE data set, you again need to create a new variable that identifies the sequence of observations. Use a program statement in the DATA step (just as you did for the KILOWATT data). The "Example" summary gives a sample program. After creating the data set with this new variable, type

```
proc reg data=engine graphics;
    var sequence;
    model power=speed speedsq / p;
    plot residual.*sequence;
    title 'Regression for Quadratic Model: ENGINE Data';
run;
```

These statements produce Output 10.14. Notice that the plot shows essentially a random scatter of points with two exceptions. The large positive residual occurred very early in time, and the large negative residual occurred late in time. At the beginning and end of an investigation, there is a chance that things will operate differently than during the middle part. For example, the process of measuring may be a little rough at the beginning; at the end, the researcher may be tired and fail to concentrate as closely as needed. This could be the reason for the exceptionally large and small values of POWER that are not explained by SPEED.

Output 10.14   Sequence Plot for ENGINE Data

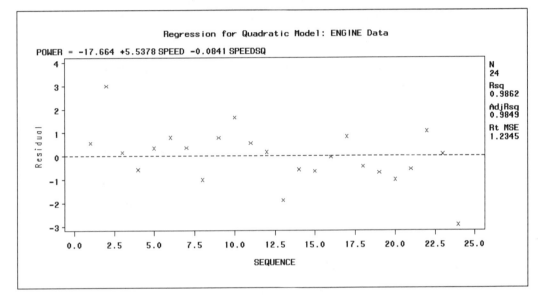

Summary of Diagnostics for **KILOWATT** and **ENGINE** Data

This chapter has focused on the diagnostic tools, and it used the KILOWATT and ENGINE data sets to show how to use the tools. Now, this section focuses on the two data sets and summarizes what the tools show you about the data sets and the models that are used to fit the data.

Using Diagnostics on the KILOWATT Data

As in Chapter 9, this chapter looked at both a straight-line model and a multiple regression model for the KILOWATT data. The straight-line model uses AC as the independent variable. The multiple regression model uses both AC and DRYER. For both models, the dependent variable is KWH.

For the straight-line model, residuals plotted against AC show you that you don't need a quadratic term for AC in the model. Plotting residuals against DRYER gives you a definite increasing pattern, which indicates that you should add DRYER to the model.

For the multiple regression model, a plot of residuals against predicted values shows a random horizontal band, which indicates that the model fits well and no obvious outliers exist. Further, a second plot of residuals (for the multiple regression model) against AC shows a random horizontal band, which indicates that you don't need a quadratic term for AC. A plot of residuals against DRYER seems to indicate a need for a quadratic term for DRYER, but this is a case where more advanced tools might be more helpful. To do another check for outliers (in addition to using the plot of residuals against predicted values), you look at the values of the studentized residuals and at the simple plot of the values of studentized residuals. There don't seem to be any obvious outliers. Finally, a plot of residuals against DAY shows a slight sequence effect in the data. This may be due either to a cooling trend during the time the data was collected or to some other cause, such as the homeowner's knowledge that the use of electricity was being monitored.

Using Diagnostics on the ENGINE Data

As in Chapter 9, this chapter looked at both a straight-line model and a quadratic model for the ENGINE data. For both models, the dependent variable is POWER. The straight-line model uses SPEED as an independent variable, and the quadratic model uses both SPEED and SPEEDSQ.

For the straight-line model, a simple listing of the residuals reveals a subtle pattern. The residuals associated with small and large values of SPEED are negative, and those residuals associated with values in the middle part of the regression line are positive. This indicates a need for a quadratic term in the model. A plot of the data overlaid with the fitted regression line shows a similar pattern. Near the ends of the line the data points are mostly below the line, and near the middle of the line the data points are mostly above the line. Again, this pattern is subtle and indicates that you need a quadratic term. Both these patterns would be more obvious for a data set with a dramatic need for a quadratic term.

A plot of residuals against predicted values for the straight-line model shows a definite curved pattern. This indicates that you need to add a quadratic term to the model.

Once you add the quadratic term SPEEDSQ, a second plot of residuals against predicted values shows a mostly random horizontal band. Two points are separated from the main group and may be outliers. Plotting the residuals against SPEED gives a random horizontal band of points, which indicates that the quadratic model is adequate. Again, however, two points appear to be outliers. Looking at the listing and a plot of the studentized residuals pinpoints these outliers but doesn't show why they are outliers. Plotting the residuals against the sequence in which the data was collected shows no overall sequence effect but does show that one of the outliers occurred near the beginning of the experiment and one occurred near the end of the experiment. Sometimes conditions differ at the beginning and at the end of an experiment, and this may be what has happened here.

Summaries

Key Ideas

- Regression analysis is an iterative process of fitting a model and performing diagnostics. Several simple plots show inadequacies in models. In addition, more complex tools may be needed for multiple regression.

- In general, in plots of residuals, you want to find a random scatter of points. Definite patterns indicate different situations, depending on the plot.

- Plot the actual and predicted values against an independent variable to find out if more terms are needed in a model. Also, look at a listing of the residuals for definite patterns. These two tools are most helpful in cases where there is a very obvious need for another variable.

- Plots of residuals against independent variables can show the need for a quadratic term or the need for another term in the model. If you need a quadratic term, this plot will be curved. If you need another term, the plot will follow a definite linear pattern. For multiple regression, plot residuals against independent variables in the model and against those not yet included in the model.

- Use studentized residuals to search for outliers. For a model that fits the data well, most of the studentized residuals should be close to 0.

- In multiple regression, check for outliers using a plot of residuals against predicted values.

- Residuals plotted against the time sequence in which the data was collected can show a possible time effect in the data.

Syntax

This chapter uses PROC REG. All of the statement syntax presented here has already been discussed in Chapter 9, with two exceptions. To obtain a listing of predicted and residual values or to use these values in plots, use the P option in the MODEL statement. The P option provides a subset of the items that are printed as a result of the CLI, CLM, or R options. To obtain predicted values, residuals, studentized residuals, and a simple plot of studentized residuals, use the R option. Use these options in the PRINT or the MODEL statement.

Specify variables in the PLOT statement either in a VAR statement or in MODEL statements before the first RUN statement. To specify a statistic in a PLOT statement, use the SAS name followed by a period(.). SAS names for statistics in PROC REG are

P
  predicted values. (PREDICTED and PRED are also valid.)

R
  residual values. (RESIDUAL is also valid.)

U95, L95
  upper and lower 95% prediction limits, respectively.

U95M, L95M
  upper and lower 95% confidence limits for the mean, respectively.

Example

The following statements produce all the output that is shown in this chapter.

```
options ps=55 nodate;
data kilowatt;
   input kwh ac dryer @@;
   day=_n_;
   datalines;
35 1.5 1 63 4.5 2 66 5.0 2 17 2.0 0 94 8.5 3 79 6.0 3
93 13.5 1 66 8.0 1 94 12.5 1 82 7.5 2 78 6.5 3 65 8.0 1
77 7.5 2 75 8.0 2 62 7.5 1 85 12.0 1 43 6.0 0 57 2.5 3
33 5.0 0 65 7.5 1 33 6.0 0
;
```

```
symbol1 v=x h=.6 c=black;

proc reg data=kilowatt graphics;
   model kwh=ac dryer / p;
   plot residual.*predicted.;
   title 'Kilowatt Data with Both AC and DRYER';
run;


   plot residual.*ac;
   title 'KILOWATT Data with Both AC and DRYER in Model';
run;
   plot residual.*dryer;
   title 'KILOWATT Data with Both AC and DRYER in Model';
run;

proc reg data=kilowatt graphics;
   var dryer;
   model kwh=ac / p;
   plot residual.*ac;
   title 'KILOWATT Data with Only AC in Model';
run;
   plot residual.*dryer;
   title 'KILOWATT Data with Only AC in Model';
run;

proc reg data=kilowatt;
   model kwh=ac dryer / r;
   title 'KILOWATT Data with Both AC and DRYER in Model';
run;

proc reg data=kilowatt graphics;
   var day;
   model kwh=ac dryer / p;
   plot residual.*day;
   title 'KILOWATT Data with Both AC and DRYER in Model';
run;
```

```
options ps=55 nodate;
data engine;
   input speed power @@;
   speedsq=speed*speed;
   sequence=_n_;
   datalines;
22.0 64.03 20.0 62.47 18.0 54.94 16.0 48.84 14.0 43.73
12.0 37.48 15.0 46.85 17.0 51.17 19.0 58.00 21.0 63.21
22.0 64.03 20.0 59.63 18.0 52.90 16.0 48.84 14.0 42.74
12.0 36.63 10.5 32.05 13.0 39.68 15.0 45.79 17.0 51.17
19.0 56.65 21.0 62.61 23.0 65.31 24.0 63.89
;

symbol1 v=x h=.6 color=black;
proc reg data=engine graphics;
   model power=speed speedsq / p;
   plot residual.*predicted.;
   title 'Regression for Quadratic Model: ENGINE Data';
run;

proc sort data=engine;
   by speed;
run;

proc reg data=engine graphics;
   id speed;
   model power=speed / p;
   title 'Regression for Straight-Line Model: ENGINE Data';
run;
   plot power*speed;
   title 'Regression for Straight-Line Model: ENGINE Data';
run;
   plot residual.*speed;
   title 'Regression for Straight-Line Model: ENGINE Data';
run;

proc sort data=engine;
   by sequence;
run;
```

```
proc reg data=engine graphics;
   var sequence;
   model power=speed speedsq / r;
   title 'Regression for Quadratic Model: ENGINE Data';
run;
   plot residual.*speed;
   title 'Regression for Quadratic Model: ENGINE Data';
run;
   plot residual.*sequence;
   title 'Regression for Quadratic Model: ENGINE Data';
run;
```

Further Reading

For more information about basic diagnostic plots in regression analysis, see

- Draper, N.R. and Smith, H. (1981), *Applied Regression Analysis*, 2nd Edition. New York: John Wiley & Sons, Inc.

For an advanced discussion of more diagnostic tools, see

- Belsley, D.A., Kuh, E., and Welsch, R.E. (1980), *Regression Diagnostics*, New York: John Wiley & Sons, Inc.

For more information about using the tools available in PROC REG, see the chapter about the REG procedure in

- *SAS/STAT® User's Guide, Version 6, Fourth Edition, Volumes 1 and 2*
- *SAS/STAT® Software: Changes and Enhancements through Release 6.12.*

Part 5 **Data in Tables**

---

11 **Creating and Analyzing Crosstabulations**

Chapter 11   **Creating and Analyzing Crosstabulations**

In many studies, particularly surveys, you collect information that classifies members of the sample but doesn't measure a quantitative variable. For example, a survey may classify people into groups according to religious beliefs, political party membership, and opinions about welfare. A government survey may classify companies into groups according to the type of products they make, the area of the country where they are located, and whether or not they sell their products internationally. A market research study to investigate the appeal of a new product may classify consumers into groups according to whether or not they have seen advertising for the new product and whether or not they have bought the product. These types of data are conveniently summarized in tables that show the number of observations in each group. This chapter discusses

- creating tables and using PROC FREQ to summarize classification data
- testing for independence between the classification variables
- using measures of association between classification variables.

The methods in this chapter are appropriate for nominal, ordinal, and interval variables.

Contents

Creating Tables

This chapter covers the situation where you have several variables that classify the data (*classification variables*) and you want to use a table to summarize the data. To make discussing tables easier, this section first introduces some basic notation.

Tables that summarize two or more classification variables are called *crosstabulations*. Tables that summarize two variables are commonly called *two-way tables*, tables that summarize three variables are called *three-way tables*, and so on. A special case of the two-way table occurs when both variables have only two levels. This special case is called a *2×2 table*. Although this chapter shows how to create crosstabulations involving several variables, the analyses that are discussed are appropriate only for two-way tables. The basic parts of a crosstabulation are shown in Figure 11.1.

Figure 11.1   **Parts of a Crosstabulation**

As you might expect, the table is composed of rows and columns. The generic table shown in Figure 11.1 contains r rows and c columns, and it is called an $r \times c$ table. The rows and columns form *cells*. Each cell of a table can be uniquely indexed according to its row and column. For example, the cell in the second row and first column is indexed as $cell_{21}$. A crosstabulation often shows the number of observations for each combination of the row and column variables. The total number of observations in the table is represented by n. The number of observations in each cell is indexed the same way as the cells in Figure 11.1 are indexed. For example, the number of observations in $cell_{21}$ is represented by n_{21}. The number of observations in a cell is sometimes called the *cell frequency*.

The crosstabulation in Figure 11.1 is a two-way table because it summarizes two variables. **The phrase "two-way" doesn't refer to the number of rows or columns but to the number of variables that are included in the table.**

Often, you will only need to find out how many observations are in each combination of levels of the classification variables. Other times, the data will be collected in tabular form and you will already have a table, but you will want to create a data set and analyze the table. The next two sections show how to create a data set and how to use PROC FREQ to create a table for these two cases.

Creating a Table from Raw Data

In some cases, you collect data and want to find out how many observations are in each cell of a crosstabulation. To illustrate this process, data from an introductory statistics class is used. The gender (F or M) and major (S for statistics or NS for other) of each student in the class are recorded. The following statements create the data set and use a TABLES statement in PROC FREQ. They produce Output 11.1.

```
proc format;
    value $gentxt 'M' = 'Male'
                  'F' = 'Female';
    value $majtxt 'S' = 'Stat'
                  'NS' = 'Non-stat';
run;

data statclas;
    input student gender $ major $ @@;
    format gender $gentxt.;
    format major $majtxt.;
    datalines;
1 M S 2 M NS 3 F S 4 M NS 5 F S 6 F S 7 M NS 8 M NS 9 M S
10 F S 11 M NS 12 F S 13 M S 14 M S 15 M NS 16 F S
17 M S 18 M NS 19 F NS 20 M S
;

proc freq data=statclas;
    tables gender*major;
    title 'Major and Gender for Students in Statistics Class';
run;
```

Output 11.1   Table of Gender By Major Created from Raw Data

```
    Major and Gender for Students in Statistics Class            1

                        TABLE OF GENDER BY MAJOR

            GENDER      MAJOR

            Frequency|
            Percent  |
            Row Pct  |
            Col Pct  |Non-stat|Stat     | Total
            ---------+--------+--------+
            Female   |      1 |      6 |      7
                     |   5.00 |  30.00 |  35.00
                     |  14.29 |  85.71 |
                     |  12.50 |  50.00 |
            ---------+--------+--------+
            Male     |      7 |      6 |     13
                     |  35.00 |  30.00 |  65.00
                     |  53.85 |  46.15 |
                     |  87.50 |  50.00 |
            ---------+--------+--------+
            Total           8       12       20
                        40.00    60.00   100.00
```

Each cell in Output 11.1 contains four numbers. The top left-hand corner of the table identifies each number. *Frequency* is the cell frequency, and *Percent* is the percent of the total observations represented by the cell frequency. The table shows that the statistics class has 1 female student who isn't majoring in statistics. She represents 5% of the total number of people in the class.

Row Pct gives the percent of observations in the row that are represented by the cell frequency. For example, the 1 female nonstatistics major represents 14.29% of the total number of females in the class. Notice that the row percents for a specific row sum to 100%.

Col Pct gives the percent of observations in the column that are represented by the cell frequency. For example, the 1 female nonstatistics major represents 12.5% of the nonstatistics majors in the class. The other 87.5% of the nonstatistics majors are males. Notice that the column percents for a specific column sum to 100%.

Around the edges of the table are the *Totals* for the rows and columns. These numbers show the total frequency for the observations in a specific row or column. This frequency is also shown as a percent of the total observations. For example, 7 students (or 35% of the total) are female, and 13 students (65%) are males. Eight students (40%) are not statistics majors, and 12 students (60%) are statistics majors.

Finally, the total number of students in the class is 20. Because there aren't any missing observations, this matches the number of observations in the data set. However, if you only knew the gender and did not know the major for 1 of the students, the table would contain only 19 observations.

The general form of the statements for creating a crosstabulation from raw data is:

DATA statement
    INPUT *row-variable column-variable* ;
    DATALINES statement
data lines
;
PROC FREQ DATA= *data-set-name* ;
    TABLES *row-variable * column-variable* ;

where *row-variable* is the variable that defines rows, *column-variable* is the variable that defines columns, and *data-set-name* is the name of the data set.

Your data lines must list *row-variable* and *column-variable* in the same order specified in your INPUT statement. However, you aren't required to use the INPUT statement shown above; you can enter the *column-variable* first and then enter the *row-variable*.

Creating a Table from an Existing Table

Sometimes you already know how many observations fit in each cell of the table. You may have collected the information by first creating the table and then marking the observations in each cell as you collected the data. Or, you may be using data that is already published in a table. In these cases, you don't need an observation for each member of the sample. To create a table for this type of data, you first create a data set where each observation in the data set represents a cell frequency (the number of observations in the cell), and then use PROC FREQ with a WEIGHT statement. This process is illustrated using data that investigates the effect of a defendant's race on whether or not the death penalty is imposed after the defendant has been convicted for homicide.[1] The statements below create a data set and produce Output 11.2:

```
data penalty;
    input decision $ defrace $ count @@;
    datalines;
Yes White 19 Yes Black 17
No White 141 No Black 149
;

proc freq data=penalty;
    tables decision*defrace;
    weight count;
    title 'Table for Death Penalty Data';
run;
```

Output 11.2   Table Produced Using WEIGHT Statement

```
                   Table for Death Penalty Data                     1

                   TABLE OF DECISION BY DEFRACE

          DECISION       DEFRACE

          Frequency|
          Percent  |
          Row Pct  |
          Col Pct  |Black   |White   |  Total
          ---------+--------+--------+
          No       |    149 |    141 |    290
                   |  45.71 |  43.25 |  88.96
                   |  51.38 |  48.62 |
                   |  89.76 |  88.13 |
          ---------+--------+--------+
          Yes      |     17 |     19 |     36
                   |   5.21 |   5.83 |  11.04
                   |  47.22 |  52.78 |
                   |  10.24 |  11.88 |
          ---------+--------+--------+
          Total         166      160      326
                        50.92    49.08   100.00
```

---

[1] Data is from Table 2.1 in Agresti, A. (1984), *Analysis of Ordinal Categorical Data*, New York: John Wiley & Sons, Inc. Used with permission. Copyright © 1984.

The numbers in each cell have the same meaning here as they do when you create a table from raw data. For example, the number of white defendants who were given the death penalty is 19.

Notice that with this second case, you enter the names of the rows and columns in the DATA step as you do in the case where you enter each observation. However, in this case when you know the number of observations in each cell, you add a variable (NUMCELL in this case). This new variable identifies the number of observations in each cell. Since this table has only 4 cells, the data set contains only 4 observations.

The WEIGHT statement names the variable that identifies how many observations are in each cell. If you use the TABLES statement without the WEIGHT statement, you will get a table with 1 observation in each cell. The general form of the statements for creating a table from an existing table is:

> DATA statement
>   **INPUT** *row-variable column-variable weight-variable* ;
>   DATALINES statement
> data lines
>
> ;
> **PROC FREQ DATA=** *data-set-name* ;
>   **TABLES** *row-variable * column-variable* ;
>   **WEIGHT** *weight-variable*;
>
> where *row-variable* is the variable that defines rows, *column-variable* is the variable that defines columns, *weight-variable* is the variable that gives the number of observations in each cell, and *data-set-name* is the name of the data set.
>
> You need to enter the *row-variable, column-variable,* and *weight-variable* in the same order in which they are listed in your INPUT statement. You can use different INPUT statements than the one above. For example, you can list the *column-variable,* then *row-variable,* and then *weight-variable.*

Creating Crosstabulations for Several Variables

To create crosstabulations for several variables, use the DATA step and PROC FREQ as used in the previous two sections. Create the data set and use PROC FREQ with a TABLES statement and with a WEIGHT statement, if needed. In the TABLES statement, use asterisks (*) to join all the variables that form the table. The final two variables in the list define the rows and columns of a two-way table that is produced for each combination of levels of the other variables in the list.

For example, suppose you conducted an opinion survey about welfare reform in 7 cities. In addition to asking the opinion question and recording the city for each person, you also asked their political affiliation (Democrat, Republican, or Independent) and employment status (Employed, Unemployed, Student, or Retired). The following statements produce a two-way table of political affiliation by opinion for each of the 28 (=7×4) combinations of city and employment status.

```
proc freq data=welfare;
   tables city*employ*politic*opinion;
```

You should use caution before you enter a long list of variables joined by asterisks and, as a result, create an enormous number of tables. Notice that for the example above, 28 tables are created. If CITY and EMPLOY each had ten levels, 100 tables would have been created!

Printing Only One Table Per Page

PROC FREQ automatically fits as many tables as possible on each page of output. This uses less paper, which is important at many sites where the cost of a computer job is based in part on the number of pages printed.

You can override this default and print only one table on each page. To do so, use the PAGE option in the PROC FREQ statement. For example, return to the welfare reform survey discussed in the previous section. The statements

```
proc freq data=welfare page;
   tables city*employ*politic*opinion;
```

produce 28 tables, each on its own page.

The PAGE option does not affect tables that can't fit on one page. If you have two variables with many levels for each variable, PROC FREQ may not be able to fit the entire table on one page. Before trying the PAGE

option, you may want to first try increasing your linesize option with
LINESIZE= in the OPTIONS statement.

The general form for using the PAGE option is simply to add PAGE to the
PROC FREQ statement.

Suppressing Some Cell Information

In Outputs 11.1 and 11.2, there are four statistics in each cell. In many
cases, you only want the number of observations and not the percent,
the row percent, or the column percent. There are four options in the
TABLES statement that let you suppress the four statistics. To use three of
these options for the death penalty data, type

```
proc freq data=penalty;
   tables decision*defrace / norow nocol nopercent;
   weight count;
   title 'Death Penalty Data: Cell Frequencies Only';
run;
```

In the preceding program, notice that you still need the WEIGHT statement; adding options doesn't change the basic statements needed to create
a table. The following statements produce Output 11.3. Notice that only the
number of observations is printed in each cell.

Output 11.3   Using Options to Suppress Statistics in Table Cells

```
            Death Penalty Data:  Cell Frequencies Only      1

                    TABLE OF DECISION BY DEFRACE

            DECISION      DEFRACE

            Frequency|Black   |White   |  Total
            ---------+--------+--------+
            No       |   149  |   141  |   290
            ---------+--------+--------+
            Yes      |    17  |    19  |    36
            ---------+--------+--------+
            Total        166      160      326
```

The four options to suppress statistics for cells in a crosstabulation are shown below:

NOCOL   suppresses printing of the column percentages.

NOFREQ   suppresses printing of the number of observations in the cell. (Recall these are also called cell frequencies.)

NOPERCENT   suppresses printing of cell percentages.

NOROW   suppresses printing of row percentages.

The general form of the statements for using these options is:

> **PROC FREQ DATA=** *data-set-name* ;
>   **TABLES** *row-variable * column-variable / options* ;
>
> where *options* can be **NOCOL, NOFREQ, NOPERCENT,** or **NOROW**, and other items in italic are as defined previously. If an option is used, the slash is required.
>
> These options are also available when you use a WEIGHT statement.

Testing for Independence between Classification Variables

When you collect classification data, you usually want to know more than how many observations appear in each cell. For instance, you may want to know if the variables that form the rows and columns of the table are related in some way or not. For the death penalty data, is the defendant's race related to the verdict or not? In other words, does knowing the defendant's race tell you anything about the likelihood that the defendant will receive the death penalty?

In statistical terms, the null hypothesis is that the row and column variables are independent. The alternative hypothesis is that the row and column variables are not independent. To test for independence, you compare the observed cell frequencies to the cell frequencies that would be seen in the situation where the null hypothesis is true. One commonly used test is a *chi-square test*, which tests the hypothesis of independence. A test statistic is calculated and compared to a critical value from a *chi-square distribution*. Suppose you want to test the hypothesis of independence at the 10% significance level for the death penalty data. The next section shows how to use PROC FREQ to perform this test.

Performing a Chi-Square Test

To test for independence with a chi-square test, add the CHISQ option to the TABLES statement in PROC FREQ. To help you understand the test, you may want to add the EXPECTED option. To make the output simpler to read, you may want to also add the NOCOL, NOROW, and NOPERCENT options. For the death penalty data, type

```
proc freq data=penalty;
    tables decision*defrace / expected chisq nocol norow
                              nopercent;
    weight count;
    title 'Death Penalty Data: Statistical Tests';
run;
```

These statements produce Output 11.4. Notice that you need to use the WEIGHT statement with this data because each observation in the data set represents a cell frequency.

Output 11.4   Chi-Square Test for Death Penalty Data

```
              Death Penalty Data:  Statistical Tests              1

                   TABLE OF DECISION BY DEFRACE

              DECISION      DEFRACE

              Frequency
              Expected |Black    |White    |  Total
              ---------+---------+--------+
              No       |     149 |     141 |    290
                       |  147.67 |  142.33 |
              ---------+---------+--------+
              Yes      |      17 |      19 |     36
                       |  18.331 |  17.669 |
              ---------+---------+--------+
              Total          166       160      326


            STATISTICS FOR TABLE OF DECISION BY DEFRACE

      Statistic                     DF     Value        Prob
      ------------------------------------------------------------
      Chi-Square                     1     0.221        0.638
      Likelihood Ratio Chi-Square    1     0.221        0.638
      Continuity Adj. Chi-Square     1     0.086        0.769
      Mantel-Haenszel Chi-Square     1     0.221        0.638
      Fisher's Exact Test (Left)                        0.741
                          (Right)                       0.384
                          (2-Tail)                      0.725
      Phi Coefficient                      0.026
      Contingency Coefficient              0.026
      Cramer's V                           0.026

      Sample Size = 326
```

The second number in each cell gives the cell frequency expected
under the null hypothesis. This number is printed as a result of using
the EXPECTED option. Notice how close the expected cell frequencies
are to the actual cell frequencies. This leads you to the intuitive conclusion that the defendant's race and the verdict (death penalty or not) are
independent. This intuitive conclusion is supported by the results of the
statistical test. Look at the line of output labeled *Chi-Square* under the
heading *Statistic*. This line gives the results of the Pearson chi-square test
for independence. The *p*-value (labeled *Prob*) is 0.638, which clearly sup-

ports the null hypothesis. You conclude that there isn't enough evidence to reject the hypothesis of independence between the defendant's race and the death penalty verdict. (Refer to Agresti (1984) for an additional analysis of this data that considers the race of the victim. This more complete analysis for a three-way table isn't discussed in this book.)

On the same line as the chi-square test results, you see a column labeled *DF* and one labeled *Value*. *Value* refers to the value of the test statistic, which is compared to a critical value to obtain *Prob* (the *p*-value). The critical value depends on *DF*, or degrees of freedom, for the table. These are a function of the number of rows and columns in the table. If you have a table with r rows and c columns, the degrees of freedom for the chi-square test are $(r-1) \times (c-1)$. For the death penalty data, the table has 2 rows and 2 columns, so the degrees of freedom are $(2-1) \times (2-1) = 1$.

Technical Details

Under the null hypothesis, the expected cell frequencies can be found by multiplying the percents for row and column totals, and then multiplying by the total number of observations. For example, the expected cell frequency for the "Black-No" cell is 147.67. To get this result, use this formula:

$$(\text{Row \% for No}/100) \times (\text{Column \% for Black}/100)$$
$$\times (\text{Total } N \text{ for table})$$
$$= 0.8896 \times 0.5092 \times 326$$
$$= 147.67$$

The percents are expressed in decimals in the formula above. Because row and column percents are only approximates, you can use a more exact formula. Multiply the row and column totals and then divide by the total number of observations. For the "Black-No" cell, the formula is:

$$\frac{(\text{Row total for No}) \times (\text{Column total for Black})}{(\text{Total } N \text{ for table})}$$
$$= (290 \times 166) / 326$$
$$= 147.67$$

In this example, both formulas give the same result. If you don't get the same results with both formulas, use the second (more precise) formula.

Note the values of the expected cell frequencies. The chi-square test is always valid if there are no empty cells (no cells with a cell frequency of 0) and if the expected cell frequency for all cells is 5 or more. Because this is true for the death penalty data, the chi-square test is a valid test. If these two conditions are not met, PROC FREQ prints a warning message to tell you that the chi-square test may not be valid. There is some disagreement among statisticians about exactly when the test should not be used and what to do when the test is not valid.

Output 11.4 shows several other statistics. *Sample Size* is the total sample size for the table. The section labeled *Fisher's Exact Test* provides one alternative to the Pearson chi-square test and is discussed in the next section. Other parts of the output correspond to other tests (most of which are not discussed here). However, if your data do not meet the conditions for a chi-square test, you should either use Fisher's exact test or you should consult a statistician because some of these other tests may be appropriate.

Performing Fisher's Exact Test

Fisher's exact test was originally developed for the special case of a 2×2 table. This test is often very useful when the conditions for a chi-square test are not met. Fisher's exact test is based on another type of theoretical distribution, the hypergeometric distribution. It is especially appropriate for tables with small cell frequencies.

Look at the line labeled *Fisher's Exact Test* in Output 11.4. Find the line labeled *2-Tail*. This line gives the *p*-value for the null and alternative hypotheses described earlier. For the death penalty data, the *p*-value is 0.725, so you fail to reject the null hypothesis of independence. (Recall that you also failed to reject the null hypothesis for the chi-square test.)

Fisher's exact test is performed automatically for 2×2 tables when you request a chi-square test with the CHISQ option. For larger two-way tables, the EXACT option performs Fisher's exact test. The test is not performed automatically for larger two-way tables because it can take longer to run.

Summarizing Tests for Independence

Two tests for independence are the chi-square test and Fisher's exact test. Both are performed using PROC FREQ. The general form of the statements is

> **PROC FREQ DATA=***data-set-name* ;
>   **TABLES** *row-variable*column-variable* / **CHISQ EXPECTED**
>   **EXACT** ;
>
> where items in italic are as defined previously. The slash and the **CHISQ** option are required for the chi-square test and also automatically give Fisher's exact test for 2×2 tables. The **EXPECTED** option is not required, but it can be useful in helping you to understand where the observed and expected cell frequencies differ. The **EXACT** option is required for Fisher's exact test for tables that are larger than 2×2.
>
> These options are also available when you use a WEIGHT statement.

Measures of Association with Ordinal Variables

The methods that are discussed in the previous section test whether or not the variables are independent, but they don't provide any information about how the variables are related if they aren't independent. In addition, the tests for independence require only that the classification variables are nominal. However, if your classification variables are ordinal, you can take advantage of this fact in your analysis. With ordinal variables, you can answer more specific questions than you can answer with nominal variables. This type of information is given by various *measures of association*.

One measure of association is Kendall's *tau-b*. Another measure of association is the *Spearman correlation coefficient*. Both measures range from −1.0 to 1.0. Values close to 1.0 indicate a positive association and values close to −1.0 indicate a negative association. (If you have read Chapter 9, you'll notice that this is similar to a correlation coefficient. In fact, the Spearman correlation coefficient is essentially the Pearson correlation that is discussed in Chapter 9, but applied to the ranks of the values instead of to the actual values.) The next section shows how to use PROC FREQ to calculate these coefficients.

Using PROC FREQ to Find Measures of Association

An animal epidemiologist tested dairy cows for the presence of a bacterial disease. The disease is detected by analyzing blood samples, and the disease severity for each animal was classified as none (0), low (1), or high (2). The size of the herd that each cow belonged to was classified as large, medium, or small. The number of animals in each of the 9 categories of disease severity and herd size was recorded. Because the categories for herd size and for disease severity are ordered, both variables are ordinal. The disease is transmitted from cow to cow by bacteria, so the epidemiologist wanted to know if disease severity is affected by herd size. In other words, as the herd size gets larger, is there either an increasing or a decreasing trend in disease severity?

With this data, you could use the chi-square test of independence to check for an association between herd size and disease severity. However, this test wouldn't answer the question of whether there is a trend in disease severity related to an increase in herd size. Kendall's *tau-b* statistic or Spearman's correlation coefficient can answer this question. The following statements create and analyze the COWS data set, which contains the epidemiologist's data:

```
data cows;
    input herdsize $ disease numcows @@;
    datalines;
large 0 11 large 1 88 large 2 136
medium 0 18 medium 1 4 medium 2 19
small 0 9 small 1 5 small 2 9
;

proc freq data=cows;
    tables herdsize*disease / measures expected cl
           nopercent norow nocol;
    weight numcows;
    title 'Dairy Cow Disease Data';
run;
```

These statements produce Output 11.5. Notice the WEIGHT statement is needed for this data because you already know the cell frequency for each cell. The MEASURES option in the TABLES statement requests several measures of association, including Kendall's *tau-b* and Spearman's correlation coefficient. The CL option requests confidence limits for the measures of association. The other options are discussed earlier in this chapter.

Output 11.5   Measures of Association for COWS Data

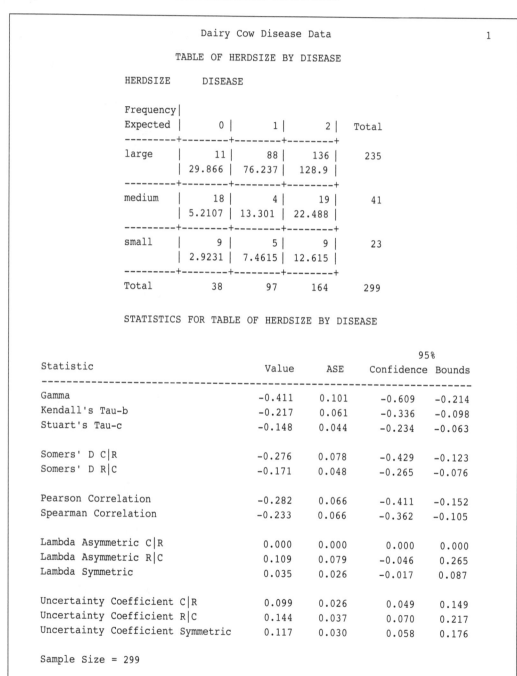

```
                         Dairy Cow Disease Data                              1

                    TABLE OF HERDSIZE BY DISEASE

           HERDSIZE      DISEASE

           Frequency|
           Expected |     0 |     1 |     2 |  Total
           ---------+--------+--------+--------+
           large    |    11 |    88 |   136 |   235
                    | 29.866 | 76.237 | 128.9 |
           ---------+--------+--------+--------+
           medium   |    18 |     4 |    19 |    41
                    | 5.2107 | 13.301 | 22.488 |
           ---------+--------+--------+--------+
           small    |     9 |     5 |     9 |    23
                    | 2.9231 | 7.4615 | 12.615 |
           ---------+--------+--------+--------+
           Total         38      97     164      299


              STATISTICS FOR TABLE OF HERDSIZE BY DISEASE


                                                       95%
      Statistic                   Value    ASE    Confidence Bounds
      ---------------------------------------------------------------
      Gamma                       -0.411   0.101    -0.609   -0.214
      Kendall's Tau-b             -0.217   0.061    -0.336   -0.098
      Stuart's Tau-c              -0.148   0.044    -0.234   -0.063

      Somers' D C|R               -0.276   0.078    -0.429   -0.123
      Somers' D R|C               -0.171   0.048    -0.265   -0.076

      Pearson Correlation         -0.282   0.066    -0.411   -0.152
      Spearman Correlation        -0.233   0.066    -0.362   -0.105

      Lambda Asymmetric C|R        0.000   0.000     0.000    0.000
      Lambda Asymmetric R|C        0.109   0.079    -0.046    0.265
      Lambda Symmetric             0.035   0.026    -0.017    0.087

      Uncertainty Coefficient C|R       0.099   0.026     0.049    0.149
      Uncertainty Coefficient R|C       0.144   0.037     0.070    0.217
      Uncertainty Coefficient Symmetric 0.117   0.030     0.058    0.176

      Sample Size = 299
```

In Output 11.5, you first see the crosstabulation of HERDSIZE and DISEASE. Each cell contains two numbers: the cell frequency and the expected cell frequency. The expected cell frequency is produced by the EXPECTED option, and it gives the number of cows that would be expected in each cell if the herd size and disease severity were independent. Look in the first row of the crosstabulation, which corresponds to HERDSIZE=large. You see that the cell frequency is less than expected for DISEASE=0, but it is more than expected for DISEASE=2. Now look in the bottom row of the crosstabulation, which corresponds to HERDSIZE=small. You see the opposite trend than for large herds: the cell frequency is larger than expected for DISEASE=0, but it is smaller than expected for DISEASE=2. Your overall intuitive conclusion is that large herds have worse disease patterns than small herds; in other words, disease severity increases with herd size.

To check this intuitive conclusion, use Kendall's *tau-b*. Look at the section of Output 11.5 labeled *STATISTICS FOR TABLE OF HERDSIZE BY DISEASE*, and find *Kendall's Tau-b*. The value of –0.217 is a measure of the association between disease severity and herd size. A negative value means that as one variable decreases, the other variable increases, which seems counter to your intuitive conclusion. However, PROC FREQ uses the alphabetic ordering of the values of character variables such as HERDSIZE, so that the "order" is large-medium-small. The negative Kendall's *tau-b* means that the disease severity increases as herd size changes from small to medium to large. This is exactly what you concluded from looking at the cell frequencies and the expected cell frequencies.

Similarly, you can verify this intuitive conclusion by using Spearman's correlation coefficient. In the section of Output 11.5 labeled *STATISTICS FOR TABLE OF HERDSIZE BY DISEASE*, find *Spearman Correlation*. The value –0.233 is another measure of the association between disease severity and herd size. The same issue of alphabetic ordering discussed above for Kendall's *tau-b* also applies here. The negative Spearman correlation means that the disease severity increases as herd size changes from small to medium to large. Again, this is what you concluded from looking at the cell frequencies and the expected cell frequencies.

One additional caution about the "order" of your variables is needed here. In the example above, the "order" of HERDSIZE is large-medium-small. You could use large=1, medium=2, and small=3, and you would obtain the same results. However, you would receive incorrect results if the "order" of values didn't match an increasing or decreasing trend. For example, if you use large=2, medium=1, and small=3, Kendall's *tau-b* is meaningless. In general, you need to look at the values of your variables (both character and numeric) when using Kendall's *tau-b*, and be sure that the "order" of the values makes sense.

The column labeled *ASE* (for asymptotic standard error) shows an estimate of the standard error for the measures of association. This estimate should be used only for large sample sizes.

The columns labeled 95% *Confidence Bounds* show the lower and upper confidence limits for the measures of association. Because the confidence interval for Spearman's correlation coefficient doesn't include 0, you can be fairly sure that the association between disease severity and herd size is an increasing one. Interpret the confidence interval to mean that there is a 95% chance that Spearman's correlation coefficient is between –0.362 and –0.105. Refer to Chapter 6, "Estimating the Mean," for a discussion of the confidence interval for the mean. The general principles introduced in Chapter 6 apply to all confidence intervals.

Releases before 6.12

The CL option is available in SAS/STAT software beginning with Release 6.12. For previous releases, you can use the ASE to form an approximate 95% confidence interval for Spearman's. Multiply the ASE by two and then add and subtract it from Spearman's. For the COWS data, the 95% confidence interval for Spearman's correlation coefficient calculated by using this formula is:

$$-0.233 \pm (2 \times 0.066) = (-0.365, -0.101)$$

To find Kendall's *tau-b* or the Spearman correlation coefficient, add the MEASURES option to the TABLES statement. The general form of the statements is:

> **PROC FREQ DATA=***data-set-name* ;
>   **TABLES** *row-variable*column-variable* / **MEASURES CL**;

where items in italic are as defined previously. You can use the **MEASURES** option in combination with other options discussed in this chapter. The **CL** option generates 95% confidence limits and is available beginning with Release 6.12 of SAS/STAT software.

These options are also available when you use a WEIGHT statement.

PROC FREQ also provides several other measures of association, which are not discussed in this book. For more detail about these measures of association, see the references in "Further Reading."

PROC INSIGHT and Crosstabulations

PROC INSIGHT can summarize data from crosstabulations, just as it can summarize other data. In addition, you can use PROC INSIGHT to perform analyses for categorical data. However, those analyses are outside the scope of this book.

Summaries

Key Ideas

- Crosstabulations are tables that summarize two or more classification variables. The rows and columns of a table form cells, and the number of observations in a cell is the cell frequency for that cell.

- Various ways of using PROC FREQ allow you to create a table from raw data, create a table when you already know the cell frequencies, print only one table per page, and suppress some of the statistics that are usually printed.

- Both the chi-square test and Fisher's exact test are used to test for independence between two classification variables. Generally, the chi-square test shouldn't be used when some cells are empty or when cells have expected cell frequencies of less than 5.

- Kendall's *tau-b* is a measure of association that provides information about how strongly ordinal variables are related. For large samples, you can use this statistic to decide if there is an increasing or a decreasing trend in the two variables or if there is no trend at all.

- Spearman's correlation coefficient is another measure of association that provides information about how strongly variables are related. In addition, you may want to form confidence intervals for this statistic.

Syntax

To create a crosstabulation from raw data, test for independence, and find Kendall's *tau-b* and Spearman's correlation coefficient,

> DATA statement
> **INPUT** *row-variable column-variable* ;
> DATALINES statement
> data lines
> ;
> **PROC FREQ DATA=** *data-set-name* **PAGE**;
>   **TABLES** *row-variable* * *column-variable* / *options* ;

where *row-variable* is the variable that defines rows, *column-variable* is the variable that defines columns, and *data-set-name* is the name of the data set. Options can be one or more of the following:

CHISQ	requests the chi-square test and Fisher's exact test for 2×2 tables. Several other tests are also printed.
CL	requests 95% confidence limits on the measures of association.
EXACT	requests Fisher's exact test for tables larger than 2×2.
EXPECTED	requests expected cell frequencies.
MEASURES	requests Kendall's *tau-b*, Spearman's correlation coefficient and other measures of association.
NOCOL	suppresses printing of the column percents.
NOFREQ	suppresses printing of the cell frequencies.
NOPERCENT	suppresses printing of the cell percents.
NOROW	suppresses printing of the row percents.

The **PAGE** option in the PROC FREQ statement prints only one table on each page.

- To create a crosstabulation and perform analyses when you already know the cell frequencies,

  > DATA statement
  >   **INPUT** *row-variable column-variable weight-variable* ;
  >   DATALINES statement
  > data lines
  > ;
  > **PROC FREQ DATA=** *data-set-name*;
  >   **TABLES** *row-variable * column-variable* ;
  >   **WEIGHT** *weight-variable*;

where *weight-variable* is the variable that gives the number of observations in each cell and other items in italic are as defined previously. All of the options described earlier are available when you use the WEIGHT statement.

Example

The following program produces all the output shown in this chapter:

```
proc format;
    value $gentxt 'M' = 'Male'
                  'F' = 'Female';
    value $majtxt 'S' = 'Stat'
                  'NS' = 'Non-stat';
run;

data statclas;
    input student gender $ major $ @@;
    format gender $gentxt.;
    format major $majtxt.;
    datalines;
1 M S 2 M NS 3 F S 4 M NS 5 F S 6 F S 7 M NS 8 M NS 9 M S
10 F S 11 M NS 12 F S 13 M S 14 M S 15 M NS 16 F S
17 M S 18 M NS 19 F NS 20 M S
;

proc freq data=statclas;
    tables gender*major;
    title 'Major and Gender for Students in Statistics Class';
run;
```

```
data penalty;
   input decision $ defrace $ count @@;
   datalines;
Yes White 19 Yes Black 17
No White 141 No Black 149
;

proc freq data=penalty;
   tables decision*defrace;
   weight count;
   title 'Table for Death Penalty Data';
run;

proc freq data=penalty;
   tables decision*defrace / norow nocol nopercent;
   weight count;
   title 'Death Penalty Data: Cell Frequencies Only';
run;

proc freq data=penalty;
   tables decision*defrace / expected chisq
         norow nocol nopercent;
   weight count;
   title 'Death Penalty Data: Statistical Tests';
run;

data cows;
   input herdsize $ disease numcows @@;
   datalines;
large 0 11 large 1 88 large 2 136
medium 0 18 medium 1 4 medium 2 19
small 0 9 small 1 5 small 2 9
;

proc freq data=cows;
   tables herdsize*disease / measures expected cl
         nopercent norow nocol;
   weight numcows;
   title 'Dairy Cow Disease Data';
run;
```

Further Reading

For more information about tests and measures of association for cross-tabulations, see the following:

- Agresti, A. (1984), *Analysis of Ordinal Categorical Data*, New York: John Wiley & Sons, Inc.

- Agresti, A. (1990), *Categorical Data Analysis*, New York: John Wiley & Sons, Inc.

- Agresti, A. (1996), *An Introduction to Categorical Data Analysis*, New York: John Wiley & Sons, Inc.

- Fleiss, J.L. (1981), *Statistical Methods for Rates and Proportions*, 2nd Edition, New York: John Wiley & Sons, Inc.

- Freeman, D.H., Jr. (1987), *Applied Categorical Data Analysis*, New York: Marcel Dekker, Inc.

- Stokes, M.E., Davis, C.S., and Koch, G.G. (1995), *Categorical Data Analysis Using the SAS® System*, Cary, NC: SAS Institute Inc.

For more information about creating crosstabulations and about tests and measures of association that are produced with PROC FREQ, see the chapter about the FREQ procedure in the following:

- *SAS® Procedures Guide, Version 6, Third Edition*

- *SAS/STAT® User's Guide, Version 6, Fourth Edition, Volumes 1 and 2*

- *SAS/STAT® Software: Syntax, Version 6, First Edition*

Although there may also be technical reports with updated information for various releases, the best source of the most recent information is the online help and online documentation. These are most appropriate in display manager mode.

Appendices

Appendix 1 # Display Manager Basics

This appendix is designed to get you started with the SAS Display Manager System. It discusses basic features that include how to enter SAS statements, copy, cut and paste, and how to submit SAS statements to run after you have finished editing them. It also discusses the basic windows that appear in display manager mode and explains how to include programs you have written when using a text editor.

Display manager is updated often and has subtle changes with almost every release of SAS software. These typically include additions or revisions in the choices available from the items on the menu bar (File, Edit, and so on). As a result, the information in this appendix is appropriate for Release 6.12. If you are using a different release, the appearance of display manager may differ. In that case, your best source of information is the online help or online documentation for SAS.

For easier reading, this appendix abbreviates the "Display Manager System" as "DMS."

Contents

Windows in DMS

After starting SAS in display manager mode, the software appears as shown in Output A.1 below.

Output A.1   **Basic DMS windows**

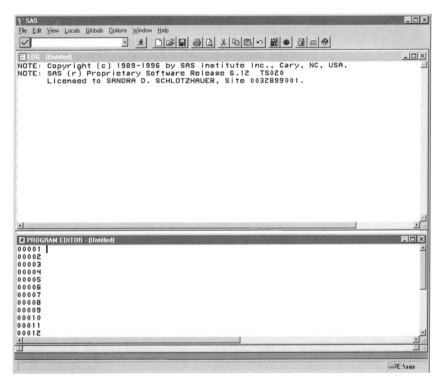

In the *PROGRAM EDITOR window*, you enter SAS statements to create data sets and run procedures. The *LOG window* shows the SAS log, which includes notes, warnings, and error messages. Behind these two windows, you see the border of the *OUTPUT window*, which contains the output from your programs. These are the three basic DMS windows and you can use DMS just by using these windows. As you learn more about DMS, there are many more windows that can be useful.

An important concept is that one DMS window is active at a time. The active window displays the window title in a different color from the other windows. The color depends on your operating system and possibly on the color scheme selected for a PC. In Output A.1, the PROGRAM EDITOR window is active.

Above the LOG window is a command field, which is the blank area to the right of the check box. We won't discuss the command field here; as you become experienced with using SAS, you may learn commands that can be typed in the command field. Until then, you may want to hide this area. In the command field, type

```
command close
```

and press ENTER. The field area disappears and the basic DMS windows now appear as shown in Output A.2.

Output A.2   Basic DMS Windows without Command Field

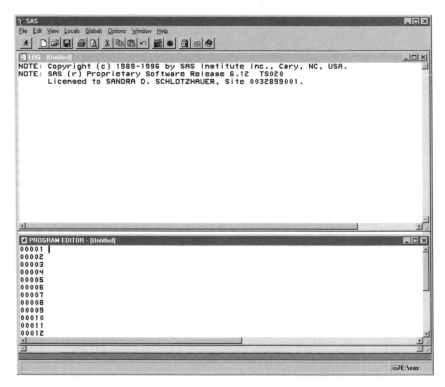

The *toolbar* now appears just above the LOG window, and the *menu bar* appears above the toolbar. All the choices on the toolbar are also available from the menu bar. Some of these choices are explained later in this appendix. The last toolbar choice (the book with a ?) displays the SAS HELP window.

Typing in and Running a SAS Program

You submit SAS programs in the PROGRAM EDITOR window. The simplest approach is to start by typing text in the window. Place the cursor in the window and type; use the ENTER key to move to the next line.

When ready to run the program, select the first icon on the toolbar (the running person), or, select `Locals` on menu bar and then select `Submit`. You should see your statements begin to appear in the LOG window. When the program finishes, the OUTPUT window displays. If it doesn't, first check the LOG for errors. The program may not have generated any output. Anytime you want to go to the OUTPUT window, select `Globals` on menu bar and then select `Output`.

For the rest of this appendix, menu bar selections (File, Edit, and so on) and the choices from that selection use two right angle brackets (>>) to separate them. For example, submitting a program is indicated as follows: `Locals>>Submit`.

Copying, Cutting, and Pasting

After entering a program, you may want to re-arrange the text before you submit the program; for example, you may need to put the DATALINES statement after the INPUT statement. To copy, select the text and then select `Edit>>Copy`. To cut, select the text and then select `Edit>>Cut`. To paste after copying or cutting, place the cursor where you want the text to appear and select `Edit>>Paste`. On a PC, the usual keyboard accelerators can be used. Select the text and use CTRL-C to copy, CTRL-X to cut, and CTRL-V to paste. Finally, the toolbar has choices for copy, cut, and paste. The simplest way to find these choices on your system is to place the cursor on the toolbar items and wait a couple of seconds. A pop-up field displays and tells you what the item does.

Inserting Lines

If you want to add a LABEL statement to the program before you submit it, place the cursor at the end of the line before the line where you want to insert another statement and press ENTER. A new blank line appears, and you can add the LABEL statement.

If a line doesn't appear, try pressing the INSERT key on your keyboard. The Program Editor is similar to many word-processing packages in that it has both an insert and a type-over mode. The INSERT key toggles between these two modes.

Undoing Changes

To reverse the last change in your program, select Edit>>Undo. Or select the undo arrow on the toolbar. If you haven't made changes, these choices cannot be selected.

Recalling a Submitted Program

Suppose you type in a program, submit it, and decide to make changes. To recall the previously submitted statements, select Locals>>Recall text. If you have submitted several programs, you can use this repeatedly to recall previous programs.

Saving a Program

To save a program, select File>>Save, or select the Save toolbar icon (the diskette). This displays a Save-As window as shown in Output A.3 below. The window that you see may differ by operating system. Output A.3 shows the appearance under Windows 95. The output also shows how to select the location for saving the program.

Output A.3   Saving a Program

SAS automatically saves programs with the extension SAS. It's a good idea to follow this convention as it will make it easier for the software to recognize saved programs.

Including a Saved Program

Suppose you have entered the SAS program in a text editor or word-processor. In a word-processor, be sure to save the file as an ASCII text file (not as a word-processor file). Of course, you want to copy the program to the PROGRAM EDITOR instead of re-typing it.

If the text editor or word-processor is active, you may be able to copy the text in the text editor and then paste the text into the PROGRAM EDITOR. This is usually straightforward on stand-alone PCs, but it may not work in a client/server environment. You may need to ask your SAS Software Consultant if you can do this on your system.

Another approach is to include the file that contains the SAS program. Select File>>Open or the Open toolbar icon (the opening folder). This displays an Open window; the appearance differs under various operating systems. Output A.4 shows the Open window under Windows 95.

Output A.4   Including a Saved Program

The program CH3.SAS is selected; to include it, select the Open button. Notice the Submit choice in the upper right corner of the Open window. Selecting this will include and submit the saved program.

After you include a saved program, the title of the PROGRAM EDITOR window changes to include the name of the saved file. This is helpful when saving the file with changes. You may want to replace the old file or you may want to use File>>Save As to save the revised file with a new name.

Printing a Program

To print a program, select File>>Print. The Print window displays; again, this may differ under various operating systems. Output A.5 shows the Print window under Windows 95.

Output A.5   Printing a Program to a File

In addition to printing a program to a printer, you can use the Print window to print a program to a file on some systems. Output A.5 shows printing the contents of the PROGRAM EDITOR window to the TICKETS.SAS file.

Line-based Editing

In some cases, your site may not support full-screen editing features. Or, you may see other SAS programmers who use a PROGRAM EDITOR window that displays line numbers to the left of the SAS statements. The line-number fields accept commands for copying lines, moving lines, deleting lines, and more. The best source for details about the line-based commands are the SAS reference manuals.

Printing and Saving Output

After generating output, you may want to print it or to save it to a file.

To print the output, first be sure that the OUTPUT window is the active DMS window (its border should be a different color than the other windows). Then select `File>>Print`. The Print window appears; its appearance varies by the operating system. Output A.6 shows the appearance under Windows 95.

Output A.6   **Printing Output**

Notice the difference between Output A.5 and Output A.6. Both are Print windows, but Output A.5 prints the contents of the PROGRAM EDITOR and Output A.6 prints the contents of the OUTPUT window. Output A.6 also is printing a hard copy of the output, and Output A.5 is printing to a file.

To save output, first be sure that the OUTPUT window is the active DMS window. Then select `File>>Save` and the Save window appears. Output A.7 shows the appearance of this window under Windows 95; your window may differ under another operating system.

Output A.7   Saving Output to a File

The Save window displays files of type LST, which is the automatic SAS extension for output. It's a good idea to use this extension for your output files as well.

Appendix 2 # **Troubleshooting**

This appendix contains a set of common problems and suggests possible solutions. The first section gives a list of quick checks to make whenever your program doesn't run. All other sections are organized around a particular problem, and they give possible solutions to the problem. If none of these solve your problem, call your SAS Software Consultant for help.

Contents

Solving Common Program Problems

The following list contains common errors to look for whenever your program doesn't run:

1. Be sure that all statements end with a semicolon.

2. Be sure that all SAS keywords are spelled correctly.

3. Be sure that all variable names and data set names are spelled correctly.

4. Be sure that all titles and footnotes are completely enclosed in quotes. Remember that the ending quote must be placed before the semicolon.

5. If you use interactive line mode or display manager mode, be sure that the last line in your program is a RUN statement.

Can't Get SAS Software to Run

Problem: You can't get anything to work. You've tried typing in the first line of a SAS program, and the system responds with something like

```
DATA COMMAND NOT FOUND
```

Alternatively, your batch job abends due to an operating system error (for example, a JCL error).

Solution: The most common cause of this problem is that you have forgotten to start SAS. If you use SAS software interactively, you may have forgotten to enter SAS before starting your SAS program. For a batch job, you may have forgotten to include a statement that begins execution of SAS software.

Received Message about Syntax Error

Problem: You received a message about a syntax error, but the statement you received the message about is right.

Solution: The problem is often in the statement before the one where you received the error message. The most common cause is forgetting a semicolon at the end of a statement. SAS software doesn't know that the previous statement is finished, and it is trying to use the second statement as part of the first statement.

Received Error Message about Invalid Data

Problem: In a DATA step, you received at least one error message that looks something like this

```
Invalid data for variable X in columns 1-3.
```

Solution: The most common cause of this message is forgetting to use a dollar sign ($) to specify character variables. If you forget the dollar sign ($), the software reads all variables as numeric variables and prints an error message when it finds character values. Review your INPUT statement, and add a $ where needed.

A second possible cause for this problem is typing a variable value in the wrong column. If you specify column locations for variables, look to see that values for all data points are in the correct columns.

A third possible cause is forgetting to specify a period for missing numeric values. If you omit column locations, you must indicate each missing value by entering a period (.). For example, the following statements produce an error message:

```
data failure;
    input name $ age;
    datalines;
Carl 45 Janet 30 Mike Jane 58
;
```

To correct these statements, add a period to indicate the missing value of AGE for Mike:

```
data success;
    input name $ age;
    datalines;
Carl 45 Janet 30 Mike . Jane 58
;
```

Formatted Values Incomplete

Problem: You formatted the values of a variable, but the printed values don't show the complete format.

Solution: This shouldn't occur with PROC PRINT, but it may occur with other procedures. Some procedures allow only a certain number of spaces for the values of a variable. If your values exceed this number, the procedure prints as many values as it can in the allotted space. For example,

PROC UNIVARIATE can print values of a variable in the *Extremes* section, but it doesn't allow the entire 200 spaces available for formats.

If this problem occurs with PROC PRINT, call your SAS Software Consultant. With another procedure, you can shorten the length of the format by revising PROC FORMAT and re-creating the data set. Or you can delete the FORMAT statement from your DATA step and not use formats.

Received "Wrong" Summaries and an Error Message

Problem: You wanted several summaries, one for each of several groups, but the summaries you received don't look right and you received an error message that looks something like

```
Data set WORK.X is not sorted in ascending sequence.
```

Solution: You didn't sort the data set before you used the procedure to summarize it. Use PROC SORT with a BY statement, then use the summary procedure with the same BY statement. The statements below produce this problem and an error message:

```
data apples;
    input type $ numsold @@;
    datalines;
reddel 15 yeldel 10 granny 8 mac 2 misc 4
reddel 29 yeldel 17 granny 10 mac 5 misc 9
reddel 35 yeldel 14 granny 5 mac 0 misc 0
;

proc means data=apples;
    by type;
    var numsold;
run;
```

The statements below give the correct analysis:

```
proc sort data=apples;
    by type;
proc means data=apples;
    by type;
    var numsold;
run;
```

Received One Summary Instead of Several

Problem: You wanted several summaries, one for each of several groups, but you received one summary for the entire data set.

Solution: Add a BY statement to your procedure. Not only do you need to first sort the data, you need to use the same BY statement in the subsequent procedure. The following statements give just one summary for the entire data set:

```
proc sort data=zoos;
   by species;
proc univariate data=zoos;
   var sex;
run;
```

These statements give a summary for each level of SPECIES in the data set:

```
proc sort data=zoos;
   by species;
proc univariate data=zoos;
   by species;
   var sex;
run;
```

"Wrong" Chart Produced

Problem: You tried to customize a chart by using options, and you didn't get what you expected.

Solution: You probably used more than one option in a situation where you can use only one option. Remember that the LEVELS=, MIDPOINTS=, and DISCRETE options cannot be used in combination with one another. The table below shows what happens when you combine these options; see if one of these fits your situation.

If you use these two options . . .	then you see the effect of . . .
MIDPOINTS= and LEVELS=	MIDPOINTS=
MIDPOINTS= and DISCRETE	MIDPOINTS=
DISCRETE and LEVELS=	DISCRETE

Didn't Get an Analysis of Variance

Problem: You submit PROC ANOVA with a MODEL statement, and you receive an error message like this:

```
Variable X should be numeric or in CLASS list.
```

In addition, your analysis of variance isn't performed.

Solution: You need to use a CLASS statement with PROC ANOVA. Add a CLASS statement that has a variable that classifies your data into groups.

Didn't Get Multiple Comparison Procedures

Problem: You perform an analysis of variance by using PROC ANOVA, and you request multiple comparison procedures by using a MEANS statement. Instead of getting output for the multiple comparison procedures, you receive an error message that looks something like this:

```
Effects used in the MEANS statement must have appeared
previously in the MODEL statement.
```

Solution: Look to see if the MEANS statement was specified after the MODEL statement. If it wasn't, PROC ANOVA doesn't know what effects are in the MODEL statement, and it can't perform a multiple comparison procedure.

Also, be sure that you spelled the variable name the same way in both the MODEL and MEANS statements.

Couldn't Add Variable to Regression

Problem: You tried to add a variable to a regression model and couldn't. You received an error message that looks something like this:

```
Only independent variables in the MODEL or the
VAR statement can be used.
```

Solution: The variable that you want to add must be specified in a VAR statement or in a MODEL statement that occurs before the first RUN statement. The statements below produce this problem and an error message:

```
proc reg data=kilowatt;
   model kwh=ac;
run;
   model kwh=ac dryer;
run;
```

These statements give the correct analysis:

```
proc reg data=kilowatt;
    var dryer;
    model kwh=ac;
run;
    model kwh=ac dryer;
run;
```

Different Regression Results for Same MODEL Statements

Problem: You get different results when you use different MODEL statements within the same PROC REG and when you put the different MODEL statements in separate PROC steps.

Solution: Your data set contains missing values for at least one variable that is being used in one model and not used in another. For the first MODEL statement, PROC REG uses only observations that don't have missing values for the variables in the model, and then it uses those observations to fit models that are given in subsequent MODEL statements.

When you put the different MODEL statements in one PROC REG, all models use the same set of observations—those that were used in the first model. When you put the different MODEL statements in separate PROC steps, each model uses all the observations possible. The differences you see in regression results are caused by the regression being performed on different numbers of observations. If your data has missing observations for variables in MODEL statements, you may want to fit the models in separate PROC steps.

Table Doesn't Show All Levels of a Variable

Problem: You created a frequency table or crosstabulation by using PROC FREQ, and some of the levels of your variable(s) seem to be missing.

Solution: PROC FREQ groups variables by using their formatted values. Before Release 6.12, PROC FREQ used only the first 16 characters of a variable to define groups. If either the formatted or unformatted values of your variable are the same for the first 16 characters, PROC FREQ grouped these values together. To get a table that shows all levels of your variable, the values need to differ before the 16th character. To check the release of SAS software that you are using, look at the message in the log. See Table 2.2 for details about how to check this message for the different modes of using SAS.

Appendix 3 **Additional Information**

This appendix describes how you can get additional information about SAS software. You can write, call, or fax all requests for more information to the Institute at:

SAS Institute Inc.
SAS Campus Drive
Cary, NC 27513
Telephone: 919 677-8000
        800-727-3228 (book orders only)
        800-833-7660 (register for training or request consulting
            services only)
Fax: 919-677-4444
E-mail: sasbook@sas.com

Or access the Institute online via the World Wide Web.

URL: www.sas.com

Contents

Publications Catalog

The *SAS® Publications Catalog* is printed twice a year, and it describes all documentation available from SAS Institute. This includes basic software documentation, manuals for specific operating systems, manuals for additional software products, special applications guides that give extensive detail on parts of the software, and Books by Users.

For a free copy of the current catalog, contact SAS Institute using the information shown at the beginning of this appendix.

Consulting Services and Training

SAS Institute provides a complete training program that includes online training software, trainer's kits, video-based training, and instructor-based training for novice computer users, statisticians, programmers, and SAS Software Consultants at many training facilities. Contact the Professional Services Division at SAS Institute to receive a free copy of *SAS Professional Services*. This magazine, published twice a year, describes all training products and consulting service options that are currently offered by the Institute. See the beginning of this Appendix for contact information.

News Magazine

SAS Communications is a quarterly news magazine published by SAS Institute. Each issue describes software development underway, lists the current training schedule, announces new books and manuals, and contains ideas for more effective use of SAS software. For a free subscription, send your name and complete address to the SAS Institute Mailing List. See the beginning of this Appendix for contact information.

Technical Journal

Observations is an online technical journal published by SAS Institute. Articles are typically written by SAS users and reflect their experience and expertise in using the software. To access *Observations* via the World Wide Web, use this URL: www.sas.com/obs.

Technical Support

SAS Institute supports users through the Technical Support Department. If you have a problem running a SAS job, you should first contact your site's SAS Software Consultant. If the problem can't be resolved, your Software Consultant can call the Technical Support Department or, for some statistical problems, your consultant may ask you to call directly. This free support is available on weekdays between 9:00 a.m. and 8:00 p.m. Eastern time.

In addition, if you have access to the Internet, the SAS Institute website describes additional technical support features. The address is www.sas.com.

SAS Users Group International (SUGI)

SUGI is a nonprofit association of professionals who are interested in how others are using SAS software. Although SAS Institute provides administrative support, SUGI is independent from the Institute. Membership is open to all users at all SAS sites and is free.

SUGI holds annual conferences with invited and contributed papers, tutorials, demonstrations, and discussion sessions. These conferences are open to all users, who can also submit papers to be presented. Papers approved for presentation at the conference are published in the *SUGI Proceedings*, which are distributed free to attendees. Extra copies can be purchased from SAS Institute.

SUGI also produces the SASware Ballot, which allows users to provide input to future SAS software development by ranking their priorities on the ballot. The top vote-getters are announced at the SUGI conference and complete results of the SASware Ballot are printed in the *SUGI Proceedings*.

Licensing SAS Software

SAS software is licensed to customers in the Western Hemisphere from the Institute's headquarters in Cary, North Carolina. For international customers, SAS Institute has several subsidiaries and licensed distributors in many countries. For a complete list of offices and information about licensing SAS software, contact the Institute using the information that is shown at the beginning of this appendix.

Appendix 4 **Syntax Summary**

This task-oriented syntax summary combines and condenses the "Syntax" summaries from the end of each chapter. Note that it doesn't summarize all the capabilities of the SAS procedures that are shown; it summarizes only the topics discussed in this book.

General Statements

- For titles and footnotes,

    TITLE*n* *'title text'* ;
    FOOTNOTE*n* *'footnote text'* ;

- To execute statements,

    RUN;

- To set options as shown in output in this book,

    OPTIONS PAGESIZE=60 LINESIZE=80 NODATE;

- To exit from SAS software,

    ENDSAS;

DATA Step Statements

1. **DATA** *data-set-name* ;
2.   **INPUT** *variable* $ *location* . . . ;

    or

        INPUT *variable* $ . . . ;

    or

        INPUT variable $ . . . @@;
3.   **DATALINES**;
4.   *data lines*
5.   **Null** statement (;), to end the lines of data.

Printing, Sorting, Labeling, and Formatting Data

- To print a data set,

    PROC PRINT DATA=*data-set-name***;**
       VAR *variables*;

- To sort a data set,

    PROC SORT DATA=*data-set-name***;**
       BY *sorting-variables*;

- To label variables and format values and print them,

    PROC FORMAT;
       VALUE *format-name value=format*

                   .
                   .
                   .

                   value=format;

DATA statement
  INPUT statement
  FORMAT *variable format-name*. **;**
  LABEL *variable*='*label*' . . . **;**
  DATALINES statement
data lines
;
PROC PRINT DATA=*data-set-name* **LABEL;**
  FORMAT *variable format-name*. **;**

Summarizing Variables and Paired Groups

For variables, simply use the variable. For paired groups, use the difference variable.

- For a few descriptive statistics,

    PROC MEANS DATA=*data-set-name***;**
       VAR *measurement-variables*;

- For many descriptive statistics, a frequency table, and EDA plots,

    PROC UNIVARIATE DATA=*data-set-name* **FREQ PLOT;**
       VAR *measurement-variables*;
       ID *id-variables*;

- For a frequency table,

    PROC FREQ DATA=*data-set-name***;**
       TABLES *variables*;

- For vertical bar charts,

  > **PROC GCHART DATA=***data-set-name*;
  >   **VBAR** *variables* / *option*;

  where *option* is either omitted or is one of the following:
  MIDPOINTS=*list-of-numbers*, **LEVELS=***number*, or **DISCRETE.**

- For horizontal bar charts, specify **HBAR** instead of VBAR. *option* is either omitted or can be one or more of the following: **NOSTAT**, one of the three options shown for a vertical bar chart, **DESCENDING,** and **SUMVAR=***sum-variable*.

- To create side-by-side charts, add this option to the VBAR or HBAR statement (after the slash):

  > **GROUP=***grouping-variable*;

- To get a bar chart and summary statistics using SAS/INSIGHT,

  > **PROC INSIGHT;**
  >   **OPEN** *data-set-name* / **NODISPLAY**;
  >   **DIST** *variables*;

Summarizing Two or More Independent Groups

> **PROC SORT DATA=***data-set-name*;
>   **BY** *grouping-variable*;
> **PROC MEANS DATA=***data-set-name*;
>   **BY** *grouping-variable*;
>   **VAR** *measurement-variables*;

You can also use the UNIVARIATE, FREQ, and GCHART procedures instead of the MEANS procedure in the pattern above. To summarize two or more independent groups with PROC INSIGHT, use PROC SORT, then

> **PROC INSIGHT ;**
>   **OPEN** *data-set-name* / **NODISPLAY** ;
>   **BY** *grouping-variable* ;
>   **DIST** *measurement-variable* ;

Testing for Normality and Producing Normality Plots

> **PROC UNIVARIATE DATA=***data-set-name* **NORMAL PLOT;**
>   **VAR** *variables*;

Confidence Intervals for the Mean

- To calculate a confidence interval,

  PROC MEANS DATA=*data-set-name* **N MEAN STD CLM**
  ALPHA=*value* **MAXDEC=***number***;**
  VAR *measurement-variables* **;**

Comparing Two Independent Groups

- For a two-sample *t*-test,

  PROC TTEST DATA=*data-set-name***;**
  CLASS *class-variable***;**
  VAR *measurement-variables***;**

- For a Wilcoxon Rank Sum test,

  PROC NPAR1WAY DATA=*data-set-name* **WILCOXON;**
  CLASS *class-variable***;**
  VAR *measurement-variables***;**

Comparing Paired Groups

- For a paired-difference *t*-test or a Wilcoxon Signed Rank test,

  PROC UNIVARIATE DATA=*data-set-name***;**
  VAR *measurement-variables***;**

Comparing Several Groups

- To perform an analysis of variance and multiple comparison procedures,

  PROC ANOVA DATA=*data-set-name***;**
  CLASS *class-variable***;**
  MODEL *measurement-variable=class-variable***;**
  MEANS *class-variable* / *options***;**

  where options are either omitted or are one or more of the following:
  HOVEST, T, BON, CLDIFF, LINES, and **ALPHA=***level*.

- To perform a Kruskal-Wallis test,

  PROC NPAR1WAY DATA=*data-set-name* **WILCOXON;**
  CLASS *class-variable***;**
  VAR *measurement-variable***;**

- To perform an analysis of variance using PROC INSIGHT,

    PROC INSIGHT;
        OPEN *data-set-name* **/ NODISPLAY;**
        FIT *measurement-variable=class-variable*;

Simple Plots

    PROC GPLOT DATA=*data-set-name*;
        PLOT *y-variable*x-variable*;

Correlation Coefficients

    PROC CORR DATA=*data-set-name* ;
        VAR *variables* ;

Regression

To fit regression equations; find predicted values, prediction limits, and confidence limits; to identify observations on the output with values of a variable; and to plot the equation data, and limits

    PROC REG DATA=*data-set-name* **GRAPHICS;**
        MODEL *dependent-variable=independent-variables* **/ CLI CLM;**
        ID *id-variable*;
        VAR *variables*;
    RUN;
        PRINT *options*;
        PLOT *y-variable*x-variable* . . . **/ OVERLAY;**
    RUN;

where *options* are **CLI** and **CLM**. Plot variable can also be names of statistics when they are followed by a period: **P., R., U95., L95., U95M.,** and **L95M**.

- To end the REG procedure when you are using it as an interactive procedure,

    QUIT;

PROC REG works as an interactive procedure starting with Release 6.03.

- To find correlation coefficients, perform regressions, and produce scatter-plots using PROC INSIGHT,

    PROC INSIGHT;
    >**OPEN** *data-set-name* ;
    >**SCATTER** *y-variable*x-variable* ;
    >**MULT** *variables* ;
    >**FIT** *dependent-variable=independent-variable* ;

Creating and Analyzing Crosstabulations

- To create a crosstabulation from raw data, test for independence, and find Kendall's *tau-b* and Spearman's correlation coefficient,

    DATA statement
    >**INPUT** *row-variable column-variable*;
    >DATALINES statement
    data lines
    >;
    >**PROC FREQ DATA=**data-set-name **PAGE;**
    >>**TABLES** *row-variable*column-variable / options*;

    PAGE is optional and asks for only one table per page. *options* are one or more of the following: **CHISQ** gives tests for independence, **CL** requests 95% confidence limits on measures of association, **EXACT** requests Fisher's exact test for tables that are larger than 2×2, **EXPECTED** requests expected cell frequencies, and **MEASURES** requests Kendall's *tau-b* and Spearman's correlation coefficient. **NOCOL**, **NOFREQ**, **NOROW**, and **NOPERCENT** suppress column percents, cell frequencies, row percents, and cell percents, respectively.

- To create a crosstabulation, test for independence, and find Kendall's *tau-b* when cell frequencies are known,

    DATA statement
    >**INPUT** *row-variable column-variable weight-variable*;
    >DATALINES statement
    data lines
    >;
    >**PROC FREQ DATA=**data-set-name;
    >>**TABLES** *row-variable*column-variable / options*;
    >>**WEIGHT** *weight-variable*;

Glossary of SAS® Terms

ANOVA

SAS procedure that compares several independent groups. In this book, *ANOVA* (in italic) refers to an analysis of variance.

batch mode

one of the four ways to use SAS software. In batch mode, you submit a complete program to the computer and it is executed.

CHART

SAS procedure that produces vertical and horizontal bar charts (as well as other types of charts that are not discussed in this book).

CORR

SAS procedure that gives correlation coefficients and simple statistics.

DATA step

part of a SAS job that creates a SAS data set. Also, the DATA step can create new variables, modify old variables, and attach labels to variable names and to individual values of variables.

DF

degrees of freedom. Output from several SAS procedures uses this abbreviation.

display manager mode

one of the four ways to use SAS software. Display manager mode uses a full-screen windowing system where statements are executed as you submit them.

FORMAT

SAS procedure that defines labels for values of variables. The labels for the individual values are called formats. FORMAT is also the name of a statement that can be used in the DATA step and with many procedures.

FREQ

SAS procedure that creates and analyzes simple frequency tables and crosstabulations. FREQ is also an option in PROC UNIVARIATE.

interactive line mode

> one of the four ways to use SAS software. In interactive line mode, statements are executed as you enter them.

interactive procedure

> a procedure that accepts new statements after the first RUN statement. The ANOVA and REG procedures are interactive (as are several other SAS procedures not discussed in this book).

keywords

> parts of a SAS statement that must be spelled exactly as shown. "Spelling" in this case includes equal signs, as in DATA=.

log

> type of output produced by SAS software. The log contains the program statements, summarizes actions taken, and gives error messages and other information.

MEANS

> SAS procedure that produces descriptive statistics. MEANS is also a statement in the ANOVA procedure.

MS

> Mean Square. Output from several SAS procedures uses this abbreviation.

MSE

> Mean Square for Error. Output from several SAS procedures uses this abbreviation.

noninteractive mode

> one of the four ways to use SAS software. In noninteractive mode, you prepare a file that contains a SAS program. Then, you execute SAS software with an option that identifies the file that contains your program. This program is then submitted and run.

null statement

> in a SAS program, a semicolon alone. The null statement is used to end the lines of data in a DATA step. (It has other uses in more advanced SAS programs.)

OBS

> identifies the observations on the printout in several procedures, including the PRINT, REG, and UNIVARIATE procedures. The column that is labeled Obs appears automatically in SAS output.

observation number
> identifies the position of the observation in the data set. In some output, this is abbreviated as Obs.

observations
> in a SAS data set, the items about which information is collected. In a PROC PRINT listing of a SAS data set, the observations appear as rows in the printout. See also variables.

option
> in a SAS statement, a keyword (or a combination of keywords and information that you supply) that isn't required in the statement.

PLOT
> SAS procedure that produces plots. Also, a statement in PROC PLOT, an option in PROC UNIVARIATE, and a statement in PROC REG.

PRINT
> SAS procedure that prints a SAS data set.

procedure output
> type of output produced by SAS software. The procedure output contains the results that are produced by the SAS program.

PROC step
> part of a SAS job that includes a set of statements for a SAS procedure.

program statements
> statements used in the DATA step. These appear between the INPUT and DATALINES statements and have many uses. One of the most common uses is to create new variables.

REG
> SAS procedure that performs linear regression.

SAS data set
> a data set created by and used in SAS software.

SAS statement
> starts with one or more keywords, possibly followed by information that you supply, and ends with a semicolon.

SORT
> SAS procedure that sorts a SAS data set.

specification

keywords or combinations of keywords and information that you supply, that can appear in a SAS statement. Some specifications are required; others are optional. As an example, DATA=*data-set-name* is a specification in the PROC statement.

SS

Sum of Squares. Output from several SAS procedures uses this abbreviation.

TTEST

SAS procedure that performs exact and approximate *t*-tests to compare two independent groups.

UNIVARIATE

SAS procedure that produces extensive descriptive statistics, a frequency table, exploratory plots, a test for normality, and tests to compare paired groups.

variables

in a SAS data set, the specific pieces of information that are collected. In a PROC PRINT listing of the data set, variables are shown in columns. See also observations.

Index

Call your local SAS® office to order these books available through Books by Users℠ Press

JMP® Books

Basic Business Statistics: A Casebook
by **Dean P. Foster, Robert A. Stine,**
and **Richard P. Waterman** . . . . .Order No. A56813

Business Analysis Using Regression: A Casebook
by **Dean P. Foster, Robert A. Stine,**
and **Richard P. Waterman** . . . . .Order No. A56818

JMP® Start Statistics, Version 3
by **John Sall** *and* **Ann Lehman** . . . . .Order No. A55626

JMP® Start Statistics, Second Edition
by **John Sall, Ann Lehman,**
and **Leigh Creighton** . . . . .Order No. A58166